STUDIES IN SPIRITUALITY
A WEEKLY READING OF THE JEWISH BIBLE

OUPRESS MAGGID

Other works by the author

Faith in the Future

The Politics of Hope

Celebrating Life

A Letter in the Scroll / Radical Then, Radical Now

The Dignity of Difference

The Jonathan Sacks Haggada

From Optimism to Hope

To Heal a Fractured World

The Home We Build Together

Covenant & Conversation Series

Future Tense

The Koren Sacks Siddur

The Koren Sacks Maḥzorim

Not in God's Name

Ceremony and Celebration

Morality: Restoring the Common Good in Divided Times

Judaism's Life-Changing Ideas

Rabbi Jonathan Sacks

STUDIES IN SPIRITUALITY

A Weekly Reading of the Jewish Bible

Maggid Books & OU Press

Studies in Spirituality
A Weekly Reading of the Jewish Bible
First Edition, 2021

Maggid Books
An imprint of Koren Publishers Jerusalem Ltd.

POB 8531, New Milford, CT 06776-8531, USA
& POB 4044, Jerusalem 9104001, Israel
www.maggidbooks.com

The publication of this book was made possible
through the generous support of *The Jewish Book Trust*.

ISBN 978-1-59264-576-3, *hardcover*

Printed and bound in the United States

In memory of

Irving and Toni Rosen

Our parents, grandparents and great-grandparents

The Rosen Family

Contents

Foreword

Writing Our Own Chapter

Sivan Rahav Meir*

Do not read this book. If this book has made its way into your hands, Rabbi Jonathan Sacks' first to be published in English since his passing, I beg of you: Do not read it. What should be done with it? Two things.

First, learn it. It's a good idea to do this together with someone else, and best if it is someone from the next generation, one of your children or grandchildren, or other young people in your community. Rabbi Sacks did not just write "another book" to be read between a thriller, a cookbook, and political non-fiction. He wanted us to read his words actively, not passively. This is the only way that we can pass on

---

* Sivan Rahav Meir is one of the most popular media personalities in Israel today. She is a primetime anchor on Channel 2 News; has a column in Israel's largest newspaper, *Yediot Aharonot*; and has a weekly radio show on Galei Tzahal (Army Radio). She is one of the very few public intellectuals who is well respected across the religious-secular spectrum, and has attracted a large following on social media for her Torah-infused, family-centered insights into Jewish life and tradition. Her lectures on *parashat hashavua* attract thousands of viewers every week.

our heritage to the next generation: with passion, through discussions, questions and answers, with curiosity, with a spark in our eyes (and who can forget the spark in Rabbi Sacks' eyes when he learned and taught?). Judaism is not something to be learned by rote, and its students are not meant to be robots, he would constantly remind us. This is history's most captivating story, and we are called upon to write our own chapter in it.

Rabbi Sacks' legacy is not reading material. It is life-changing, reality-altering content. So take this book and try to internalize its message. Agree or disagree with it. Try to ensure that your objective is not reading but application. Ask yourself: How are these nice ideas relevant to my life? Read it to others and discuss it, or at least stop every few paragraphs to consider your own opinions.

Second, don't think that by buying this book, you have done something to ensure Rabbi Sacks' legacy. We all loved him very much. We were all deeply pained when he was suddenly taken from us. Although he was not a victim of COVID-19, his passing occurred at the height of the pandemic, meaning that only a small group of people could escort him to his resting place, with thousands joining online. So perhaps we feel that if we have his new book on our bookshelf, we have done something to honor his memory. But the great vacuum that has been created in the Jewish world by his parting will not be filled if we love Rabbi Sacks. It will only be filled if we strive to *be* Rabbi Sacks. The task that he left us is not to purchase his books, but to adopt his path. Exactly as he said about the Lubavitcher Rebbe: "This man did not want to create followers, he wanted to create leaders." Rabbi Sacks did not want people only to know how to quote his ideas by copying and pasting. He desired that people take responsibility, that they transcend themselves in order to change the Jewish world and bring the Torah to every Jew. After all, he too could have remained a student who was satisfied to buy nice Jewish books. But he understood that the most pressing problem of our times is the Jewish people's ignorance and their disappearance, and therefore he changed his life course to dedicate himself to this cause. Although he was a Lord, a professor, a scholar, and a commentator, he was first and foremost a Rabbi. Above his studies of the works of Shakespeare, Goethe, and Nietzsche, he placed Jewish continuity.

That is why it moved me so deeply to hear the way in which his wife, Lady Elaine, began the memorial ceremony marking one month since his passing. Participating in the worldwide virtual ceremony were Tony Blair and Gordon Brown, Prince Charles and the Archbishop of Canterbury, and yet, Lady Elaine's opening words were these: "We received so many letters and stories this past month. People told us that they sent their children to get a Jewish education because of my husband." This was her message, before all of the eulogies delivered by honored guests, because this truly was Rabbi Sacks' core idea. Not to sit in lavish mansions with kings and princes, but to make sure that one more Jewish child will continue on the path of his or her ancestors.

* * *

After having shared those two preliminary "warnings," you are invited to enjoy this wonderful book, which follows our eternal Jewish heartbeat, the weekly Torah reading. And, lo and behold, when I studied two readings that were significant to me, I discovered precisely the two messages that I presented above.

Rabbi Sacks passed away on Shabbat morning, just as, throughout the Jewish world, the portion of *Vayera* was being read. What did Rabbi Sacks teach us about this portion? That the most fundamental principle is education. "Who was Abraham, and why was he chosen?" he asks, and answers: Abraham is not described as a righteous man, as Noah is, or as one who protests injustice, like Moses, or as a warrior, like David, or a prophet, like Isaiah. There is only one place, in *Parashat Vayera*, where the Torah mentions why God chose Abraham: "For I have chosen him, so that he will direct his children and his household after him, to keep the way of the Lord by doing what is right and just." To translate this into our vernacular, it is as if God is saying: I know this guy. I know what he's all about. And do you know what he is? He is a good teacher. A good parent. A good educator. And I know that I can trust him in the area that is most important to Me. Not the army, not money, not territory, not charisma – but education. He will know how best to pass the flame on to the next generation, and to ignite the same spark in their eyes. The point is not to amass knowledge. Abraham is not meant to compel his children to read many books, but to live their lives in accordance with these books. Abraham succeeds in his task, and for this reason, to this day, we all call him "our father." Rabbi Sacks passed away on the Shabbat that reminds us all to continue the path of our father Abraham, to direct our sons and daughters to safeguard God's path.

I then skimmed to the end of the book, toward the portion *Vezot Haberakha*. On the way, I passed the foundational portions of the book of Genesis, the redemption story of the book of Exodus, the topics of sanctity and the Temple in the book of Leviticus, and the stories of the Jewish people's wanderings in the desert in the book of Numbers. Rabbi Sacks shines an original and inspiring light on all these stories. When I reached the final portion of the final book of the Torah, I discovered that it was missing. Rabbi Sacks did not finish formulating his insights on the portion before he passed away. Let us try, humbly, to look at it for a moment through his lenses. Undoubtedly, he would have focused on one of the first verses: *Torah tziva lanu Moshe, morasha kehillat Yaakov*, "Moses charged us with the Torah, heritage of the community of Jacob." This was his life's motto. The best inheritance that we pass on to subsequent generations is the Torah, our identity, our heritage.

But at the very end of the portion, after Moses blesses all of the tribes, his passing from the world is described. According to some of the commentators, Moses, who wrote all of the Torah, did not write the description of his own death. Rather, his student Joshua wrote the end of the Torah after his teacher passed away. This, perhaps, is the most powerful message that Rabbi Sacks could have left us. The fact that this book lacks a commentary on the final portion says to us: Do not be followers. Be leaders. Do not be fans or spectators, be players. The Torah awaits our commentary as well.

Introduction

A Sense of Eternity in the Midst of Time

Τhis volume on the weekly *parashot* is about spirituality, about the search for God and His place in our lives. Where and how do we find God? What difference does it make? How does Judaism help us become better, more sensitive and generous as individuals? How does it affect our emotional life? Does it help us order our priorities so that we care for the things that are important, not just urgent? Does it give us the strength to survive hard times, to keep going despite the falls, the failures, and the losses? Does it help us to endure without loss of hope, and persist without loss of energy? Does it teach us to love and forgive? Does it bring us joy?

Spirituality is not the same as "religion," though the two are related. In essence spirituality is what happens when we open ourselves to something greater than ourselves. Some find it in the beauty of nature, or art, or music. Others find it in prayer, or performing a mitzva, or learning a sacred text. Yet others find it in helping other people, or in friendship, or love.

Spirituality is what tells us that "man does not live by bread alone but by everything that comes from the mouth of God" (Deut. 8:3). We are not just physical beings with biological drives. We have hopes, dreams, fears, loves. We strive for connection. We make sacrifices for the sake of others. We search for meaning. We experience transcendence.

I, like many others, have found God in the depths of despair and the heights of joy. I found Him in a Jerusalem sunset, standing on Mount Scopus looking out toward the Judean hills, as the whole landscape turned red-gold and the world seemed ablaze with a divine radiance. I felt Him lifting me in some of the most difficult moments of my life, helping me to stand up and carry on. I sensed Him when our children and grandchildren were born, as the love that brings new life into being. I feel Him each Friday evening as He surrounds our Shabbat table with clouds of glory. I turn to Him for strength whenever I begin a new stage of life's journey. I try to express my thanks to Him every time I feel I have done something He would have wanted me to do.

I decided to write about spirituality because so many people I meet are searching for it, and because they say they do not always find it in Judaism today. Those who are engaged in a spiritual search are not always religious in the conventional sense. Some describe themselves as secular, or cultural, or ethnic Jews. I find this very beautiful because it confirms what the Sages said, describing the moment when Moses said to God about the Israelites, "They won't believe in me" (Ex. 4:1). God, according to the Talmud (Shabbat 97a), replied, "They are believers, the children of believers, but in the end, you will not believe." Sometimes ordinary people who don't see themselves as religious can have more faith than religious leaders. Not everyone is a master of Jewish law, but spirituality is engraved in all our souls. God enters, said the Rebbe of Kotzk, wherever we let Him in.

There is, undeniably, something of a crisis in Jewish spirituality today. This is sad, because for many centuries Jews were the God-intoxicated people. If there is a single sentence that sums up Jewish history, it is surely the statement of the prophet Zechariah: "Not by power and not by might but by My spirit, says the Lord of hosts" (Zech. 4:6). Jews never had much power despite what the *Protocols of the Elders of Zion* might say. That always was a fantasy. Nor did they have might. Christianity and Islam built massive, monumental empires. Jews never did.

What our ancestors had in full measure was God's spirit. They felt God close. There is something moving about the word Jews used to describe this. They called it the *Shekhina*, usually translated as the Divine Presence, but which actually means something more striking. A *shakhen* is a neighbour, the person who lives next door. That is how close Jews felt God to be. Yes, He is more distant than the furthest galaxy, but He is also closer to us than we are to ourselves. The God of Abraham is not a distant God. He is enthroned in majesty in heaven. But He is also parent, partner, neighbour, mentor, friend.

So it was for many centuries. Then something changed, something too complex to be analysed here. But at a certain point in the modern age, many Jews became ultra-rationalists. They pioneered in physics, medicine, sociology, anthropology, mathematics, and philosophy. They became shapers of the modern mind. But in the process, many lost that sense of intimacy with God that resonated so powerfully with our ancestors, giving them their sense of hope and courage and singularity.

No faith ever held God so close. Yes, we wrestled with Him, and He with us. Jews questioned, argued, challenged. We were not passive accepters of our fate. It was always a tempestuous relationship. But it was never less than a relationship. For us, as Martin Buber said, God was always a Thou, not an It, a person not a concept, a source of love not a metaphysical abstraction.

In these essays, I will be a little more personal than usual. The reason is that in Judaism there is no one form of spirituality. There are many. The Torah signals this in a subtle way. Three times in the book of Exodus we read of how the Israelites agreed to the covenant with God at Mount Sinai, but there is a subtle difference between the first two and the third:

> The people all *responded together*, "We will do [*naaseh*] everything the Lord has said." (Ex. 19:8)

> When Moses went and told the people all the Lord's words and laws, they *responded with one voice*, "Everything the Lord has said we will do [*naaseh*]." (24:3)

Then he took the Book of the Covenant and read it to the people. They *responded*, "We will do and hear [*naaseh venishma*] everything the Lord has said." (24:7)

Note how, in the first two verses, which refer only to action (*naaseh*), there is unanimity. The people respond "together." They do so "with one voice." In the third case, which refers not only to doing but also to hearing (*nishma*), there is no unanimity. "Hearing" here means many things: listening, paying attention, understanding, and responding. It means, in other words, the spiritual dimension of Judaism. Hence the special and distinctive feature of Judaism, that we are a community of doing rather than of thinking, understanding, and feeling. There is an authoritative code of Jewish law. When it comes to halakha, the way of Jewish doing, we seek consensus. However, as Maimonides writes several times in his *Commentary to the Mishna*,[1] there is no *psak*, no authoritative ruling, when it comes to non-halakhic aspects of Judaism. We each have our own way of understanding Judaism, our own path to God.

So there is the way of the priest and the way of the prophet. Judaism has its poets, its philosophers, its rationalists, and its mystics. Hasidim found God in joy. Others found God in study. Some found Him in visions, others in prayer, yet others in a sensed presence that had and needed no words. For many the supreme book of spirituality is the book of Psalms – the lexicon of the Jewish soul.

We all need times when we silence the clamorous demands of the self and open ourselves to the majestic beauty of the created world, the inner voice of the divine command, and God's call to mend some of the fractures of our deeply injured world. What is beautiful about the Torah is that it shows the heroes and heroines of our people's past not as epitomes of perfection but as human beings – great, to be sure, but always human – wrestling with God and finding Him wrestling with us.

We are spiritual beings. We are not just random mutations of genes, blindly replicating themselves into the future. Nor are we merely profit-maximisers or pleasure-seekers. We seek meaning in our lives, and we are lifted when we are able to endow ordinary acts with the

---

1. See, e.g., *Commentary to Mishna*, Sanhedrin 10:3.

charisma of holiness. In this, we have the precedent of the great lives of those who came before us, whose stories, recorded in our sacred texts, still speak to us, showing how ordinary people can be raised to extraordinary heights when they open their minds and moods to the One who is beyond us yet within us.

"Not by power and not by might but by My spirit, says the Lord of hosts." That was the voice of faith twenty-five centuries ago, and it still holds true. We will need spiritual strength even more than military, economic, or technological strength in the years ahead. For it is spirituality that teaches us that life is sacred, that there is more to happiness than the pursuit of wealth, power, success, or fame, and that though life is short we can, at blessed moments, experience the transformative power of joy giving us a sense of eternity in the midst of time.

I hope the very personal nature of these essays helps you to find your own way to the Divine Presence, which is always there: the music beneath the noise, the call beneath the clamour, the voice of God within the human soul.

Genesis
בראשית

The Art of Listening

What exactly was the first sin? What was the Tree of Knowledge of good and evil? Is this kind of knowledge a bad thing such that it had to be forbidden, and was only acquired through sin? Isn't knowing the difference between good and evil essential to being human? Isn't it one of the highest forms of knowledge? Surely God would want humans to have it? Why then did He forbid the fruit that produced it?

In any case, did not Adam and Eve already have this knowledge before eating the fruit, precisely in virtue of being "in the image and likeness of God"? Surely this was implied in the very fact that they were commanded by God: Be fruitful and multiply. Have dominion over nature. Do not eat from the tree. For someone to understand a command, they must know it is good to obey and bad to disobey. So they already had, at least potentially, the knowledge of good and evil. What then changed when they ate the fruit? These questions go so deep that they threaten to make the entire narrative incomprehensible.

Maimonides understood this. That is why he turned to this episode at almost the very beginning of *Guide for the Perplexed*. His answer, though, is perplexing. Before eating the fruit, he says, the first humans knew the difference between truth and falsehood. What they acquired by eating the fruit was knowledge of "things generally accepted."[1] But what does Maimonides mean by "things generally accepted"? It is generally accepted that murder is evil, and honesty good. Does Maimonides mean that morality is mere convention? Surely not. What he means is that after eating the fruit, the man and woman were embarrassed that they were naked, and that is a mere matter of social convention because not everyone is embarrassed by nudity. But how can we equate being embarrassed that you are naked with "knowledge of good and evil"? It does not seem to be that sort of thing at all. Conventions of dress have more to do with aesthetics than ethics.

It is all very unclear, or at least it was to me until I came across one of the more fascinating moments in the history of the Second World War.

After the attack on Pearl Harbor in December 1941, Americans knew they were about to enter a war against a nation, Japan, whose culture they did not understand. So they commissioned one of the great anthropologists of the twentieth century, Ruth Benedict, to explain the Japanese to them, which she did. After the war, she published her ideas in a book, *The Chrysanthemum and the Sword*.[2] One of her central insights was the difference between shame cultures and guilt cultures. In shame cultures the highest value is honour. In guilt cultures it is righteousness. Shame is feeling bad that we have failed to live up to the expectations others have of us. Guilt is what we feel when we fail to live up to what our own conscience demands of us. Shame is other-directed. Guilt is inner-directed.

Philosophers, among them Bernard Williams, have pointed out that shame cultures are usually visual. Shame itself has to do with how you appear (or imagine you appear) in other people's eyes. The instinctive reaction to shame is to wish you were invisible, or somewhere else. Guilt, by contrast, is much more internal. You cannot escape it by becoming invisible or being elsewhere. Your conscience accompanies you wherever you go, regardless of whether you are seen by others. Guilt cultures are cultures of the ear, not the eye.

---

1. Maimonides, *Guide for the Perplexed*, I:2.
2. Ruth Benedict, *The Chrysanthemum and the Sword* (Boston: Houghton Mifflin Harcourt, 1946).

With this contrast in mind, we can now understand the story of the first sin. It is all about appearances, shame, vision, and the eye. The serpent says to the woman, "God knows that on the day you eat from it, your eyes will be opened, and you will be like God, knowing good and evil" (Gen. 3:5). That is, in fact, what happens: "The eyes of both of them were opened, and they realised that they were naked" (v. 7). It was the appearance of the tree that the Torah emphasises: "The woman saw that the tree was good to eat and desirable to the eyes, and that the tree was attractive as a means to gain intelligence" (v. 6). The key emotion in the story is shame. Before eating the fruit, the couple were "naked… but unashamed" (2:25). After eating it they feel shame and seek to hide. Every element of the story – the fruit, the tree, the nakedness, the shame – has the visual element typical of a shame culture.

But in Judaism we believe that God is heard not seen. The first humans "heard God's voice moving about in the garden with the wind of the day" (3:8). Replying to God, the man says, "I heard Your voice in the garden and I was afraid because I was naked, so I hid" (v. 10). Note the deliberate, even humorous irony of what the couple did. They heard God's voice in the garden, and they "hid themselves from God among the trees of the garden" (v. 8). But you can't hide from a voice. Hiding means trying not to be seen. It is an immediate, intuitive response to shame. But the Torah is the supreme example of a culture of guilt, not shame, and you cannot escape guilt by hiding. Guilt has nothing to do with appearances and everything to do with conscience, the voice of God in the human heart.

The sin of the first humans in the Garden of Eden was that they followed their eyes, not their ears. Their actions were determined by what they saw, the beauty of the tree, not by what they heard, namely the word of God commanding them not to eat from it. The result was that they did indeed acquire a knowledge of good and evil, but it was the wrong kind. They acquired an ethic of shame, not guilt; of appearances not conscience. That, I believe, is what Maimonides meant by his distinction between true and false and "things generally accepted." A guilt ethic is about the inner voice that tells you, "This is right, that is wrong," as clearly as "This is true, that is false." But a shame ethic is about social convention. It is a matter of meeting or not meeting the expectations others have of you.

Shame cultures are essentially codes of social conformity. They belong to groups where socialisation takes the form of internalising the values of the group such that you feel shame – an acute form of embarrassment – when you break them, knowing that if people discover what you have done you will lose honour and face.

Judaism is precisely not that kind of morality, because Jews do not conform to what everyone else does. Abraham was willing, say the Sages, to be on one side while all the rest of the world was on the other. Haman says about Jews, "Their customs are different from those of all other people" (Est. 3:8). Jews have often been iconoclasts, challenging the idols of the age, the received wisdom, the "spirit of the age," the politically correct.

If Jews had followed the majority, they would have disappeared long ago. In the biblical age they were the only monotheists in a pagan world. For most of the post-biblical age they lived in societies in which they and their faith were shared by only a tiny minority of the population. Judaism is a living protest against the herd instinct. Ours is the dissenting voice in the conversation of humankind. Hence the ethic of Judaism is not a matter of appearances, of honour and shame. It is a matter of hearing and heeding the voice of God in the depths of the soul.

The drama of Adam and Eve is not about apples, or sex, or original sin, or "the Fall" – interpretations the non-Jewish West has given it. It is about something deeper. It is about the kind of morality we are called on to live. Are we to be governed by what everyone else does, as if morality were like politics: the will of the majority? Will our emotional horizon be bounded by honour and shame, two profoundly social feelings? Is our key value appearance? How we seem to others? Or is it something else altogether, a willingness to heed the word and will of God? Adam and Eve in Eden faced the archetypal human choice between what their eyes saw (the tree and its fruit) and what their ears heard (God's command). Because they chose the first, they felt shame, not guilt. That is one form of "knowledge of good and evil," but from a Jewish perspective, it is the wrong form.

Judaism is a religion of listening, not seeing. That is not to say there are no visual elements in Judaism. There are, but they are not primary. Listening is the sacred task. The most famous command in Judaism is *Shema Yisrael,* "Listen, Israel." What made Abraham, Moses, and the prophets different from their contemporaries was that they heard the voice that to others was inaudible. In one of the great dramatic scenes of the Bible God teaches Elijah that He is not in the whirlwind, the earthquake, or the fire, but in the "still, small voice" (I Kings 19:12).

It takes training, focus, and the ability to create silence in the soul to learn how to listen, whether to God or to a fellow human being. Seeing shows us the beauty of the created world, but listening connects us to the soul of another, and sometimes to the soul of the Other, God as He speaks to us, calls to us, summoning us to our task in the world.

If I were asked how to find God, I would say: Learn to listen. Listen to the song of the universe in the call of birds, the rustle of trees, the crash and heave of the waves. Listen to the poetry of prayer, the music of the Psalms. Listen deeply to those you love and who love you. Listen to the words of God in the Torah and hear them speak to you. Listen to the debates of the sages through the centuries as they tried to hear the texts' intimations and inflections.

Don't worry about how you or others look. The world of appearances is a false world of masks, disguises, and concealments. Listening is not easy. I confess I find it formidably hard. But listening alone bridges the abyss between soul and soul, self and other, I and the Divine.

Jewish spirituality is the art of listening.[3]

---

3. For more on the theme of listening in Judaism, see *Parashat Bemidbar,* "The Sound of Silence," and *Parashat Ekev,* "The Spirituality of Listening."

Noah

The Courage to Live with Uncertainty

For each of us there are milestones on our spiritual journey that change the direction of our life and set us on a new path. For me one such moment came when I was a rabbinical student at Jews' College and thus had the privilege of studying with one of the great rabbinic scholars of our time, Rabbi Dr. Nachum Rabinovitch, *zt"l*.

He was a giant: one the most profound Maimonidean scholars of the modern age, equally at home with virtually every secular discipline as with the entire rabbinic literature, and one of the boldest and most independent of *posekim*, as his several published volumes of responsa show. He also showed what it was to have spiritual and intellectual courage, and that in our time has proved, sadly, all too rare.

The occasion was not special. He was merely giving us one of his regular *divrei Torah*. The week was *Parashat Noaḥ*. But the midrash he quoted to us was extraordinary. In fact, it is quite hard to find. It appears in the book known as *Buber's Tanḥuma*, published in 1885 by Martin Buber's grandfather Shlomo from ancient manuscripts. It is a very early text – some say as early as the fifth century – and it has some overlap with an ancient Midrash of which we no longer have the full text known as *Midrash Yelamdenu*.

The text is in two parts, and it is a commentary on God's words to Noah: "Come out of the ark" (Gen. 8:16). On this the midrash says:

> Noah said to himself, "Since I only entered the ark with permission [from God], shall I leave without permission?" The Holy One blessed be He said to him: "Are you looking for permission? In that case I give you permission: 'Come out of the ark.'"

The midrash then adds: "Said Rabbi Judah bar Ilai, 'If I had been there, I would have smashed down [the doors of] the ark and taken myself out of it.'"[1]

The moral Rabbi Rabinovitch drew – indeed the only one possible – was that when it comes to rebuilding a shattered world, you do not wait for permission. God gives us permission. He expects us to go on ahead.

This was, of course, part of an ancient tradition, mentioned by Rashi in his commentary (to Gen. 6:9), and central to the Sages' understanding of why God began the Jewish people not with Noah but with Abraham. Noah, says the Torah, "walked with God" (6:9). But God said to Abraham, "Walk on ahead of Me" (Gen. 17:1). So the point was not new, but the drama and power of the midrash were stunning.

Suddenly I understood that this is a significant part of what faith is in Judaism: to have the courage to pioneer, to do something new, to take the road less travelled, to venture out into the unknown. That is what Abraham and Sarah had done when they left their land, their home, and their father's house. It is what the Israelites did in the days of Moses when they journeyed forth into the wilderness, guided only by a pillar of cloud by day and fire by night.

---

1. The midrash seems to be based on the fact that this is the first verse in the Torah where the verb D-B-R (to speak) is used. The root A-M-R (to say) has a similar meaning but there is a slight difference between them; D-B-R usually implies speaking harshly, judgmentally. See also Ibn Ezra ad loc., who senses from the text that Noah was reluctant to leave the ark.

Faith is precisely the courage to take a risk, knowing that "though I walk through the valley of the shadow of death, I will fear no evil, for You are with me" (Ps. 23:4). It took faith to challenge the religions of the ancient world, especially when they were embodied in the greatest empires of their time. It took faith to stay Jewish in the Hellenistic age, when Jews and Judaism must have seemed small and parochial when set against the cosmopolitan culture of ancient Greece and the Alexandrian empire.

It took the faith of Rabbi Yehoshua ben Gamla to build, already in the first century, the world's first-ever system of universal, compulsory education (Bava Batra 21a), and the faith of Rabban Yoḥanan ben Zakkai to realise that Judaism could survive the loss of independence, land, and Temple, on the basis of an academy of scholars and a culture of scholarship.

In the modern age, even though many of Jewry's most distinguished minds either lost or abandoned their faith, nonetheless that ancient reflex survived. How else are we to understand the phenomenon that a tiny minority in Europe and the United States was able to produce so many shapers of the modern mind, each of them a pioneer in his or her own way: Einstein in physics, Durkheim in sociology, Levi-Strauss in anthropology, Mahler and Schoenberg in music, and a whole string of innovative economists from David Ricardo (the law of comparative advantage) to John von Neumann (game theory) to Milton Friedman (monetary theory) to Daniel Kahneman and Amos Tversky (behavioural economics).

They dominated the fields of psychiatry, psychotherapy, and psychoanalysis, from Freud and his circle to Viktor Frankl (logotherapy), Aaron T. Beck (cognitive behavioural therapy), and Martin Seligman (positive psychology). The pioneers of Hollywood and film were almost all Jewish. Even in popular music the achievement is stunning, from Irving Berlin and George Gershwin, masters of the American musical, to Bob Dylan and Leonard Cohen, the two supreme poets of popular music in the twentieth century.

In many cases – such is the fate of innovators – the people concerned had to face a barrage of criticism, disdain, opposition, or disregard. You have to be prepared to be lonely, at best misunderstood, at worst vilified and defamed. As Einstein said, "If my theory of relativity is proven successful, Germany will claim me as a German and France will declare me a citizen of the world. Should my theory prove untrue, France will say that I am a German, and Germany will declare that I am a Jew." To be a pioneer – as Jews know from our history – you have to be prepared to spend a long time in the wilderness.

That was the faith of the early Zionists. They knew early on, some from the 1860s, others after the pogroms of the 1880s, Herzl after the Dreyfus trial, that European Enlightenment and Emancipation had failed, that despite its immense scientific and political achievements, mainland Europe still had no place for the Jew. Some Zionists were religious, others were secular, but most importantly they all knew what the *Midrash Tanhuma* made so clear: When it comes to rebuilding a shattered world or a broken dream, you don't wait for permission from Heaven. Heaven is telling you to go ahead.

That is not carte blanche to do whatever we like. Not all innovation is constructive. Some can be very destructive indeed. But this principle of "walk on ahead," the idea that the Creator wants us, His greatest creation, to be creative, is what makes Judaism unique in the high value it places on the human person and the human condition.

Faith is the courage to take a risk for the sake of God or the Jewish people; to begin a journey to a distant destination knowing that there will be hazards along the way, but knowing also that God is with us, giving us strength if we align our will with His. Faith is not certainty, but the courage to live with uncertainty.

Lekh Lekha

Journey of the Generations

Mark Twain said it most pithily. "When I was a boy of fourteen, my father was so ignorant I could hardly stand to have the old man around. But when I got to be twenty-one, I was astonished at how much the old man had learned in seven years."

Whether Freud was right or wrong about the Oedipus complex, there is surely this much truth to it: that the power and pain of adolescence is that we seek to define ourselves as different, individuated, *someone other than* our parents. When we were young they were the sustaining presence in our lives, our security, our stability, our source of being grounded in the world.

The first and deepest terror we have as very young children is separation anxiety: the absence, especially, of the mother. Young children will play happily so long as mother or care-giver is within sight. Absent that, and there is panic. We are too young to venture into the world on our own. It is precisely the stable, predictable presence of parents in our early years that gives us a basic sense of trust in life.

But then comes the time as we approach adulthood, when we have to learn to make our own way in the world. Those are the years of searching and in some cases, rebellion. They are what make adolescence so fraught. The Hebrew word for youth – the root N-A-R – has these connotations of "awakening" and "shaking." We begin to define ourselves by reference to our friends, our peer-group, rather than our family. Often there is tension between the generations.

The literary theorist Harold Bloom wrote two fascinating books, *The Anxiety of Influence* and *Maps of Misreading*,[1] in which, in Freudian style, he argued that strong poets make space for themselves by deliberately misinterpreting or misunderstanding their predecessors. Otherwise – if you were really in awe of the great poets that came before you – you would be stymied by a sense that everything that could be said has been said, and better than you could possibly do. Creating the space we need to be ourselves often involves an adversarial relationship to those who came before us, and that includes our parents.

One of the great discoveries that tends to come with age is that, having spent what seems like a lifetime of running away from our parents, we have become very much like them – and the further away we ran, the closer we became. Hence the truth in Mark Twain's insight. It needs time and distance to see how much we owe our parents and how much of them lives on in us.

The way the Torah does this in relation to Abraham (or Abram as he was then called) is remarkable in its subtlety. *Lekh Lekha*, and indeed Jewish history, begins with the words, "God said to Abraham, 'Go from your land, your birthplace, and your father's house to a land I will show you'" (Gen. 12:1). This is the boldest beginning of any account of a life in the Hebrew Bible. It seems to come from nowhere. The Torah gives us no portrait of Abraham's childhood, his youth, his relationship with the other members of his family, how he came to marry Sarah, or the qualities of character that made God single him out to become the initiator of what ultimately turned out to be the greatest revolution in the religious history of humankind, what is called nowadays Abrahamic monotheism.

It was this biblical silence that led to the midrashic tradition almost all of us learned as children, that Abraham broke the idols in his father's house. This is Abraham the Revolutionary, the iconoclast, the

---

1. Harold Bloom, *The Anxiety of Influence: A Theory of Poetry* (New York: Oxford University Press, 1973); *A Map of Misreading* (New York: Oxford University Press, 1975).

man of new beginnings who overturned everything his father stood for. This is, if you like, Freud's Abraham.

Perhaps it is only as we grow older that we are able to go back and read the story again, and realise the significance of the passage at the end of the *previous parasha*. It says this:

> Terah took his son Abram, his grandson Lot, son of Haran, and his daughter-in-law Sarai, the wife of his son Abram, and together they set out from Ur of the Chaldeans to go to Canaan. But when they came to Haran, they settled there. (Gen. 11:31)

It turns out, in other words, that Abraham left his father's house *long after* he had left his land and his birthplace. His birthplace was in Ur, in what is today southern Iraq, but he only separated from his father in Haran, in what is now northern Syria. *Terah, Abraham's father, accompanied him for the first half of his journey.* He went with his son at least part of the way.

What actually happened? There are two possibilities. The first is that Abraham received his call in Ur. His father Terah then agreed to go with him, intending to accompany him to the land of Canaan, though he did not complete the journey, perhaps because of age. The second is that the call came to Abraham in Haran, in which case *his father had already begun the journey on his own initiative* by leaving Ur. Either way, the break between Abraham and his father was far less dramatic than we first thought.

I have argued elsewhere (in my book *Not in God's Name*[2]), that biblical narrative is far more subtle than we usually take it to be. It is deliberately written to be understood at different levels at different stages in our moral growth. There is a surface narrative. But there is also, often, a deeper story that we only come to notice and understand when we have reached a certain level of maturity (I call this the concealed counter-narrative). Genesis 11–12 is a classic example.

When we are young we hear the enchanting – indeed empowering – story of Abraham breaking his father's idols, with

---

2. Jonathan Sacks, *Not in God's Name: Confronting Religious Violence* (New York: Schocken Books, 2017).

its message that a child can sometimes be right and a parent wrong, especially when it comes to spirituality and faith. Only much later in life do we hear the far deeper truth – hidden in the guise of a simple genealogy at the end of the previous *parasha* – that Abraham was actually completing a journey his father began.

There is a line in the book of Joshua (24:2) – we read it as part of the Haggada on Seder night – that says, "In the past your ancestors lived beyond the Euphrates River, including Terah the father of Abraham and Nahor. They worshipped other gods." So there was idolatry in Abraham's family background. But Genesis 11 says that it was Terah who took Abraham, not Abraham who took Terah, from Ur to go to the land of Canaan. There was no immediate and radical break between father and son.

Indeed, it is hard to imagine how it could have been otherwise. Abram – Abraham's original name – means "mighty father." Abraham himself was chosen "so that he will direct his children and his household after him to keep the way of the Lord" (Gen. 18:19) – that is, he was chosen to be a model parent. How could a child who rejected the way of his father become a father of children who would not reject his way in turn?[3] It makes more sense to say that Terah already had doubts about idolatry and it was he who inspired Abraham to go further, spiritually and physically. Abraham continued a journey his father had begun, thereby helping Isaac and Jacob, his son and grandson, to chart their own ways of serving God – the same God but encountered in different ways.

Which brings us back to Mark Twain. Often we begin by thinking how different we are from our parents. It takes time for us to appreciate how much they helped us become the people we are. Even when we thought we were running away, we were in fact continuing their journey. Much of what we are is because of what they were.

---

3. Rashi (on Gen. 11:31) says it was to conceal the break between son and father that the Torah records the death of Terah before God's call to Abraham. However, see Nahmanides ad loc.

Vayera

To Bless the Space Between Us

There is a mystery at the heart of the biblical story of Abraham, and it has immense implications for our understanding of Judaism. Who was Abraham and why was he chosen? The answer is far from obvious. Nowhere is he described, as was Noah, as "a righteous man, perfect in his generations" (Gen. 6:9). We have no portrait of him, like the young Moses, physically intervening in conflicts as a protest against injustice. He was not a soldier like David or a visionary like Isaiah. In only one place, near the beginning of our *parasha*, does the Torah say why God singled him out:

> Then the Lord said, "Shall I hide from Abraham what I am about to do? Abraham will surely become a great and powerful nation, and all nations on earth will be blessed through him. For I have chosen him, *so that he will direct his children and his household after him to keep the way of the Lord by doing what is right and just,* so that the Lord will bring about for Abraham what He has promised him." (18:17–19)

Abraham was chosen in order to be a father. Indeed Abraham's original name, *Av ram*, means "mighty father," and his enlarged name, *Avraham*, means "father of many nations."

No sooner do we notice this than we recall that the first person in history to be given a proper name was *Hava, Eve*, because, said Adam, "she is the mother of all life" (3:20). Note that motherhood is drawn attention to in the Torah long before fatherhood (twenty generations to be precise, ten from Adam to Noah, and ten from Noah to Abraham). The reason is that motherhood is a biological phenomenon. It is common to almost all forms of advanced life. Fatherhood is a cultural phenomenon. There is little in biology that supports pair-bonding, monogamy, and faithfulness in marriage, and less still that connects males with their offspring. That is why fatherhood always needs reinforcement from the moral code operative in a society. Absent that, and families fragment very fast indeed, with the burden being overwhelmingly borne by the abandoned mother.

This emphasis on parenthood – motherhood in the case of Eve, fatherhood in that of Abraham – is absolutely central to Jewish spirituality, because what Abrahamic monotheism brought into the world was not just a mathematical reduction of the number of gods from many to one. The God of Israel is not primarily the God of the scientists who set the universe into motion with the Big Bang. It is not the God of the philosophers, whose necessary being undergirds our contingency. Nor is it even the God of the mystics, the *Ein Sof*, the Infinity that frames our finitude. The God of Israel is *the God who loves us and cares for us as a parent loves for and cares for a child.*

Sometimes God is described as our father: "Have we not all one Father? Has not one God created us?" (Mal. 2:10). Sometimes, especially in the late chapters of the book of Isaiah, God is described as a mother: "Like one whom his mother comforts, so shall I comfort you" (Is. 66:13). "Can a woman forget her nursing child and have no compassion on the son of her womb? Even these may forget, but I will not forget you" (ibid. 49:15). The primary attribute of God, especially whenever the four-letter name Hashem is used, is compassion, the Hebrew word for which, *rahamim*, comes from the word *rehem*, meaning "a womb."

Thus our relationship with God is deeply connected with our relationship with our parents, and our understanding of God is deepened if we have had the blessing of children (I love the remark of a young American Jewish mother: "Now that I've become a parent I find that I can relate to God much better: now I know what it's like creating something you can't control").

All of which makes the story of Abraham very hard to understand for two reasons. The first is that *Abraham was the son told by God to leave his father*: "Leave your land, your birthplace, and your father's house" (Gen. 12:1). The second is that *Abraham was the father told by God to sacrifice his son*: "Then God said: Take your son, your only son, whom you love – Isaac – and go to the land of Moriah, and there sacrifice him as a burnt offering on the mountain I will show you" (22:2). How can this make sense? It is hard enough to understand God commanding these things of anyone. How much more so given that God chose Abraham specifically to become a role model of the parent-child, father-son relationship.

The Torah is teaching us something fundamental and counterintuitive. *There has to be separation before there can be connection*. We have to have the space to be ourselves if we are to be good children to our parents, and we have to allow our children the space to be themselves if we are to be good parents.

In the previous essay I argued that Abraham was in fact continuing a journey his father Terah had already begun. However, it takes a certain maturity on our part before we realise this, since our first reading of the narrative seems to suggest that Abraham was about to set out on a journey that was completely new. Abraham, in the famous midrashic tradition, was the iconoclast who took a hammer to his father's idols. Only later in life do we fully appreciate that, despite our adolescent rebellions, there is more of our parents in us than we thought when we were young. But before we can appreciate this there has to be an act of separation.

Likewise in the case of the binding of Isaac. I have long argued that the point of the story is not that Abraham loved God enough to sacrifice his son, but rather that God was teaching Abraham that *we do not own our children,* however much we love them. The first human child was called Cain because his mother Eve said, "With the help of God I have acquired [*kaniti*] a man" (Gen. 4:1). When parents think they own their child, the result is often tragic.

First separate, then join. First individuate, then relate. That is one of the fundamentals of Jewish spirituality. We are not God. God is not us. It is the clarity of the boundaries between heaven and earth that allow us to have a healthy relationship with God. It is true that Jewish mysticism speaks about *bitul hayesh*, the complete nullification of the self in the all-embracing infinite light of God, but that is not the normative mainstream of Jewish spirituality. What is so striking about the heroes and heroines of the Hebrew Bible is that when they speak to God, they remain themselves. God does not overwhelm us. That is the principle the kabbalists called *tzimtzum*, God's self-limitation. *God makes space for us to be ourselves.*

Abraham had to separate himself from his father before he, and we, could understand how much he owed his father. He had to separate from his son so that Isaac could be Isaac and not simply a clone of Abraham. Rabbi Menahem Mendel, the Rebbe of Kotzk, put this inimitably when he said:

> If I am I because I am I, and you are you because you are you, then I am I and you are you. But if I am I because you are you and you are you because I am I, then I am not I and you are not you!

God loves us as a parent loves a child – *but a parent who truly loves their child makes space for the child to develop his or her own identity.* It is the space we create for one another that allows love to be like sunlight to a flower, not like a tree to the plants that grow beneath. The role of love, human and divine, is, in the lovely phrase of Irish poet John O'Donohue, "to bless the space between us."

Ḥayei Sara

Faith in the Future

He was 137 years old. He had been through two traumatic events involving the people most precious to him in the world. The first involved the son for whom he had waited for a lifetime, Isaac. He and Sarah had given up hope, yet God told them both that they would have a son together, and it would be he who would continue the covenant. The years passed. Sarah did not conceive. She had grown old, yet God still insisted they would have a child.

Eventually it came. There was rejoicing. Sarah said: "God has brought me laughter, and everyone who hears about this will laugh with me" (Gen. 21:6). Then came the terrifying moment when God said to Abraham: "Take your son, your only one, the one you love...and offer him as a sacrifice" (22:2). Abraham did not dissent, protest, or delay. Father and son travelled together, and only at the last moment did the command come from heaven saying, "Stop." How does a father, let alone a son, survive a trauma like that?

Then came grief. Sarah, Abraham's beloved wife, died. She had been his constant companion, sharing the journey with him as they left behind all they knew, their land, their birthplace, and their families. Twice she saved Abraham's life by pretending to be his sister.

What does a man of 137 do – the Torah calls him "old and advanced in years" (24:1) – after such a trauma and such a bereavement? We would not be surprised to find that he spent the rest of his days in sadness and memory. He had done what God had asked of him. Yet he could hardly say that God's promises had been fulfilled. Seven times he had been promised the land of Canaan, yet when Sarah died he owned not one square inch of it, not even a place in which to bury his wife. God had promised him many children, a great nation, many nations, as many as the grains of sand on the sea shore and the stars in the sky. Yet he had only one son of the covenant, Isaac, whom he had almost lost, and who was still unmarried at the age of thirty-seven. Abraham had every reason to sit and grieve.

Yet he did not. In one of the most extraordinary sequences of words in the Torah, his grief is described in a mere five Hebrew words: in English, "Abraham came to mourn for Sarah and to weep for her" (23:2). Then immediately we read, "And Abraham rose from his grief." From then on, he engaged in a flurry of activity with two aims in mind: first, to buy a plot of land in which to bury Sarah; second, to find a wife for his son. Note that these correspond precisely to the two divine blessings: of land and descendants. Abraham did not wait for God to act. He understood one of the profoundest truths of Judaism: that *God is waiting for us to act*.

How did Abraham overcome the trauma and the grief? How do you survive almost losing your child and actually losing your life-partner, and still have the energy to keep going? What gave Abraham his resilience, his ability to survive, his spirit intact?

I learned the answer from the people who became my mentors in moral courage, namely the Holocaust survivors I had the privilege to know. How, I wondered, did they keep going, knowing what they knew, seeing what they saw? We know that the British and American soldiers who liberated the camps never forgot what they witnessed. According to Niall Fergusson's biography of Henry Kissinger,[1] who entered the camps as an American soldier, the sight that met his eyes transformed his life. If this was true of those who merely saw Bergen-Belsen and the other camps, how almost infinitely more so, those who lived there and saw so many die there. Yet the survivors I knew had the most tenacious hold on life. I wanted to understand how they kept going.

---

1. Niall Fergusson, *Kissinger: 1923–1968: The Idealist* (London: Penguin Books, 2015).

Eventually I discovered. Most of them did not talk about the past, even to their marriage partners, even to their children. Instead they set about creating a new life in a new land. They learned its language and customs. They found work. They built careers. They married and had children. Having lost their own families, the survivors became an extended family to one another. They looked forward, not back. First they built a future. Only then – sometimes forty or fifty years later – did they speak about the past. That was when they told their story, first to their families, then to the world. *First you have to build a future. Only then can you mourn the past.*

Two people in the Torah looked back, one explicitly, the other by implication. Noah, the most righteous man of his generation, ended his life by making wine and becoming drunk. The Torah does not say why but we can guess. He had lost an entire world. While he and his family were safe on board the ark, everyone else – all his contemporaries – had drowned. It is not hard to imagine this righteous man overwhelmed by grief as he replayed in his mind all that had happened, wondering whether he might have done something to save more lives or avert the catastrophe.

Lot's wife, against the instruction of the angels, actually did look back as the cities of the plain disappeared under fire and brimstone and the anger of God. Immediately she was turned into a pillar of salt – the Torah's graphic description of a woman so overwhelmed by shock and grief as to be unable to move on.

It is the background of these two stories that helps us understand Abraham after the death of Sarah. He set the precedent: first build the future, and only then can you mourn the past. If you reverse the order, you will be held captive by the past. You will be unable to move on. You will become like Lot's wife.

Something of this deep truth drove the work of one of the most remarkable survivors of the Holocaust, the psychotherapist Viktor Frankl. Frankl lived through Auschwitz, dedicating himself to giving other prisoners the will to live. He tells the story in several books, most famously in *Man's Search for Meaning*.[2] He did this by finding for each of them a task that was calling to them, something they had not yet done

---

2. Viktor E. Frankl, *Man's Search for Meaning: An Introduction to Logotherapy*, translated by Ilse Lasch (Boston: Beacon Press, 1992).

but that only they could do. In effect, he gave them a future. This allowed them to survive the present and turn their minds away from the past. Frankl lived his teachings. After the liberation of Auschwitz he built a school of psychotherapy called logotherapy, based on the human search for meaning. It was almost an inversion of the work of Freud. Freudian psychoanalysis had encouraged people to think about their very early past. Frankl taught people to build a future, or more precisely, *to hear the future calling to them.* Like Abraham, Frankl lived a long and good life, gaining worldwide recognition and dying at the age of ninety-two.

Abraham heard the future calling to him. Sarah had died. Isaac was unmarried. Abraham had neither land nor grandchildren. He did not cry out to God in anger or anguish. Instead, he heard the still, small voice saying: *The next step depends on you. You must create a future that I will fill with My spirit.* That is how Abraham survived the shock and grief. God forbid that we experience any of this, but if we do, this is how to survive.

God enters our lives as a call from the future. It is as if we hear Him beckoning to us from the far horizon of time, urging us to take a journey and undertake a task that, in ways we cannot fully understand, we were created for. That is the meaning of the word *vocation,* literally "a calling," a mission, a task to which we are summoned.

We are not here by accident. We are here because God wanted us to be, and because there is a task we were meant to fulfil. Discovering what that is, is not easy, and often takes many years and false starts. But for each of us there is something God is calling on us to do, a future not yet made that awaits our making. It is future-orientation that defines Judaism as a faith, as I explain in the last chapter of my book *Future Tense.*[3]

So much of the anger, hatred, and resentments of this world are brought about by people obsessed by the past and who, like Lot's wife, are unable to move on. There is no good ending to this kind of story, only more tears and more tragedy. The way of Abraham in Ḥayei Sara is different. First build the future. Only then can you mourn the past.

---

3. Jonathan Sacks, *Future Tense: Jews, Judaism, and Israel in the Twenty-first Century* (New York: Schocken Books, 2012).

Toledot

A Father's Love

The boys grew up. Esau became a skilful hunter, a man of the
outdoors; but Jacob was a mild man who stayed at home among
the tents. Isaac, who had a taste for wild game, loved Esau, but
Rebecca loved Jacob. (Gen. 25:27–28)

We have no difficulty understanding why Rebecca loved Jacob. She had
received an oracle from God in which she was told: "Two nations are in
your womb, and two peoples from within you will be separated; one people
will be stronger than the other, and the older will serve the younger" (v. 23).

Jacob was the younger. Rebecca seems to have inferred, correctly
as it turned out, that it would be he who would continue the covenant,
who would stay true to Abraham's heritage, and who would teach it to
his children, carrying the story forward into the future.

The real question is why did Isaac love Esau? Could he not see
that he was a man of the outdoors, a hunter, not a contemplative or a
man of God? Is it conceivable that he loved Esau merely because he had
a taste for wild game? Did his appetite rule his mind and heart? Did
Isaac not know how Esau sold his birthright for a bowl of soup, and how
he subsequently "despised" the birthright itself (vv. 29–34)? Was this
someone with whom to entrust the spiritual patrimony of Abraham?

Isaac surely knew that his elder son was a man of mercurial temperament who lived in the emotions of the moment. Even if this did not trouble him, the next episode involving Esau clearly did: "When Esau was forty years old, he married Judith daughter of Be'eri the Hittite, and also Basemath daughter of Elon the Hittite. They were a source of grief to Isaac and Rebecca" (26:34–35). Esau had made himself at home among the Hittites. He had married two of their women. This was not a man to carry forward the Abrahamic covenant which involved a measure of distance from the Hittites and Canaanites and all they represented in terms of religion, culture, and morality.

Yet Isaac clearly *did* love Esau. Not only does the verse with which we began say so. It remained so. Genesis 27, with its morally challenging story of how Jacob dressed up as Esau and took the blessing that had been meant for him, is remarkable for the picture it paints of the genuine, deep affection between Isaac and Esau. We sense this at the beginning when Isaac asks Esau: "Prepare me the kind of tasty food I like and bring it to me to eat, so that I may give you my blessing before I die" (27:7). This is not Isaac's physical appetite speaking. It is his wish to be filled with the smell and taste he associates with his elder son, so that he can bless him in a mood of focused love.

It is the end of the story, though, that really conveys the depth of feeling between them. Esau enters with the food he has prepared. Slowly Isaac, and then Esau, realise the nature of the deception that has been practised against them. Isaac "trembled violently." Esau "burst out with a loud and bitter cry" (vv. 33–34). It is hard in English to convey the power of these descriptions. The Torah generally says little about people's emotions. During the whole of the trial of the binding of Isaac we are given not the slightest indication of what Abraham or Isaac felt in one of the most fraught episodes in Genesis. The text is, as Erich Auerbach said, "fraught with background," meaning, more is left unsaid than said.[1] The depth of feeling the Torah describes in speaking of Isaac and Esau at that moment is thus rare and almost overwhelming. Father and son share their sense of betrayal, Esau passionately seeking some blessing

---

1. Erich Auerbach, *Mimesis: The Representation of Reality in Western Literature*, translated by Willard R. Trask (Princeton: Princeton UP, 1953).

from his father, and Isaac rousing himself to bless him. The bond of love between them is intense. So the question returns with undiminished force: Why did Isaac love Esau, despite everything, his wildness, his mutability, and his outmarriages?

The Sages gave an explanation. They interpreted the phrase "skilful hunter" (25:27) as meaning that Esau trapped and deceived Isaac. He pretended to be more religious than he was.[2] There is, though, a quite different explanation, closer to the plain sense of the text, and very moving. *Isaac loved Esau because Esau was his son, and that is what fathers do.* They love their children unconditionally. That does not mean that Isaac could not see the faults in Esau's character. It does not imply that he thought Esau the right person to continue the covenant. Nor does it mean he was not pained when Esau married Hittite women. The text explicitly says he was. But it does mean that Isaac knew that *a father must love his son because he is his son.* That is not incompatible with being critical of what he does. But a father does not disown his child, even when he disappoints his expectations. Isaac was teaching us a fundamental lesson in parenthood.

Why Isaac? Because he knew that Abraham had sent his son Ishmael away. He may have known how much that pained Abraham and injured Ishmael. There is a remarkable series of midrashim that suggest that Abraham visited Ishmael even after he sent him away, and others that say it was Isaac who effected the reconciliation.[3] He was determined not to inflict the same fate on Esau.

Likewise, he knew to the very depths of his being the psychological cost on both his father and himself of the trial of the binding. At the beginning of the chapter of Jacob, Esau, and the blessing, the Torah tells us that Isaac was blind. There is a midrash that suggests that it was tears shed by the angels as they watched Abraham bind his son and lift the knife that fell into Isaac's eyes, causing him to go blind in his old age.[4] The trial was surely necessary, otherwise God would not have

---

2. He would ask him questions such as, "Father, how do we tithe salt and straw?" knowing that in fact these were exempt from tithe. Isaac thought that meant that he was scrupulous in his observance of the commandments (Rashi on Gen. 25:27; *Tanḥuma, Toledot*, 8).

3. See Jonathan Sacks, *Not in God's Name: Confronting Religious Violence* (New York: Schocken Books, 2017), 107–124.

4. Genesis Rabba 65:10.

commanded it. But it left wounds, psychological scars, and it left Isaac determined not to have to sacrifice Esau, his own child. In some way, then, Isaac's unconditional love of Esau was a *tikkun* for the rupture in the father-son relationship brought about by the binding.

Thus, though Esau's path was not that of the covenant, Isaac's gift of paternal love helped prepare the way for the next generation, in which all of Jacob's children remained within the fold.

There is a fascinating argument between two mishnaic Sages that has a bearing on this. There is a verse in Deuteronomy (14:1) that says about the Jewish people, "You are children of the Lord your God." Rabbi Judah held that this applied only when Jews behaved in a way worthy of the children of God. Rabbi Meir said that it was unconditional: whether Jews behave like God's children or not, they are still called the children of God.[5]

Rabbi Meir, who believed in unconditional love, acted in accordance with his view. His own teacher, Elisha ben Abuya, eventually lost his faith and became a heretic, yet Rabbi Meir continued to study with him and respect him, maintaining that at the very last moment of his life he had repented and returned to God.[6]

To take seriously the idea, central to Judaism, of *Avinu Malkeinu*, that our King is first and foremost our Parent, is to invest our relationship with God with the most profound emotions. God wrestles with us, as does a parent with a child. We wrestle with Him as a child does with his or her parents. The relationship is sometimes tense, conflictual, even painful, yet what gives it its depth is the knowledge that it is unbreakable. Whatever happens, a parent is still a parent, and a child is still a child. The bond may be deeply damaged but it is never broken beyond repair.

Perhaps that is what Isaac was signalling to all generations by his continuing love for Esau, so unlike him, so different in character and destiny, yet never rejected by him – just as the midrash says that Abraham never rejected Ishmael and found ways of communicating his love.

Unconditional love is not uncritical, but it is unbreakable. That is how we should love our children – for it is how God loves us.

---

5. Kiddushin 36a.
6. Y. Ḥagiga 2:1.

Vayetzeh

How the Light Gets In

Why Jacob? That is the question we find ourselves asking repeatedly as we read the narratives of Genesis. Jacob is not what Noah was: righteous, perfect in his generations, one who walked with God. He did not, like Abraham, leave his land, his birthplace, and his father's house in response to a divine call. He did not, like Isaac, offer himself up as a sacrifice. Nor did he have the burning sense of justice and willingness to intervene that we see in the vignettes of Moses' early life. Yet we are defined for all time as the descendants of Jacob, the children of Israel. Hence the force of the question: Why Jacob?

The answer, it seems to me, is intimated in the beginning of this *parasha*. Jacob was in the middle of a journey from one danger to another. He had left home because Esau had vowed to kill him when Isaac died. He was about to enter the household of his uncle Laban, which would itself present other dangers. Far from home, alone, he was at a point of maximum vulnerability. The sun set. Night fell. Jacob lay down to sleep, and then saw this majestic vision:

> He dreamed and, look, there was a ladder set on the earth, with its top reaching heaven; and look, angels of God were ascending and descending on it. And look, the Lord stood beside him and

said, "I am the Lord, the God of Abraham your father and the God of Isaac; the land on which you lie I will give to you and to your offspring; and your offspring shall be like the dust of the earth, and you shall spread forth to the west and to the east and to the north and to the south; and all the families of the earth shall be blessed through you and through your offspring. And look, I am with you and will keep you wherever you go, and will bring you back to this land; for I will not leave you until I have done what I have promised you." Then Jacob woke from his sleep and said, "Surely the Lord is in this place – and I did not know it!" And he was afraid, and said, "How awesome is this place! This is none other than the house of God, and this is the gate of heaven." (Gen. 28:12–17)

Note the fourfold "and look," in Hebrew *vehinei*, an expression of surprise. Nothing has prepared Jacob for this encounter, a point emphasised in his own words when he says, "the Lord is in this place – and I did not know it." The very verb used at the beginning of the passage, "He came upon a place," in Hebrew *vayifga bamakom*, also means an unexpected encounter. Later, in rabbinic Hebrew, the word *haMakom*, "the Place," came to mean "God." Hence in a poetic way the phrase *vayifga bamakom* could be read as, "Jacob happened on, had an unexpected encounter with, God."

Add to this Jacob's night-time wrestling match with the angel in the following *parasha* and we have an answer to our question. *Jacob is the man who has his deepest spiritual experiences alone, at night, in the face of danger and far from home.* He is the man who meets God when he least expects to, when his mind is on other things, when he is in a state of fear, and possibly on the brink of despair. Jacob is the man who, in liminal space, in the middle of the journey, discovers that "surely the Lord is in this place – and I did not know it!"

Jacob thus became the father of the people who had their closest encounter with God in what Moses was later to describe as "the howling wasteland of a wilderness" (Deut. 32:10). Uniquely, Jews survived a whole series of exiles, and though at first they said, "How can we sing the Lord's song in a strange land?" (Ps. 137:4) they discovered that the

Shekhina, the Divine Presence, was still with them. Though they had lost everything else, they had not lost contact with God. They could still discover that "the Lord is in this place – and I did not know it!" Abraham gave Jews the courage to challenge the idols of the age. Isaac gave them the capacity for self-sacrifice. Moses taught them to be passionate fighters for justice. But Jacob gave them the knowledge that precisely when you feel most alone, God is still with you, giving you the courage to hope and the strength to dream.

The man who gave the most profound poetic expression to this was undoubtedly David in the book of Psalms. Time and again he calls to God from the heart of darkness, afflicted, alone, pained, afraid:

> Save me, O God,
> for the floodwaters are up to my neck.
> Deeper and deeper I sink into the mire;
> I can't find a foothold.
> I am in deep water,
> and the floods overwhelm me. (Ps. 69:2–3)

> From the depths, O Lord,
> I call for Your help. (Ps. 130:1)

Sometimes our deepest spiritual experiences come when we least expect them, when we are closest to despair. It is then that the masks we wear are stripped away. We are at our point of maximum vulnerability – and it is when we are most fully open to God that God is most fully open to us. "The Lord is close to the broken-hearted and saves those who are crushed in spirit" (Ps. 34:18). "My sacrifice, O God, is a broken spirit; a broken and contrite heart You, God, will not despise" (Ps. 51:17). God "heals the broken-hearted and binds up their wounds" (Ps. 147:3).

Rabbi Nahman of Bratslav used to say:

> A person needs to cry to his Father in heaven with a powerful voice from the depths of his heart. Then God will listen to his voice and turn to his cry. And it may be that from this act itself,

all doubts and obstacles that are keeping him back from true service of Hashem will fall from him and be completely nullified.[1]

We find God not only in holy or familiar places but also in the midst of a journey, alone at night. "Though I walk through the valley of the shadow of death I will fear no evil for You are with me" (Ps. 23:4). The most profound of all spiritual experiences, the base of all others, is the knowledge that we are not alone. God is holding us by the hand, sheltering us, lifting us when we fall, forgiving us when we fail, healing the wounds in our soul through the power of His love.

My late father of blessed memory was not a learned Jew. He did not have the chance to become one. He came to Britain as a child and a refugee. He had to leave school young, and besides, the possibilities of Jewish education in those days were limited. Merely surviving took up moot of the family's time. But I saw him walk tall as a Jew, unafraid, even defiant at times, because when he prayed or read the Psalms he felt intensely that God was with him. That simple faith gave him immense dignity and strength of mind.

That was his heritage from Jacob, as it is ours. Though we may fall, we fall into the arms of God. Though others may lose faith in us, and though we may even lose faith in ourselves, God never loses faith in us. And though we may feel utterly alone, we are not. God is there, beside us, within us, urging us to stand and move on, for there is a task to do that we have not yet done and that we were created to fulfil. A singer of our time[2] wrote, "There is a crack in everything. That's how the light gets in." The broken heart lets in the light of God, and becomes the gate of heaven.

---

1. Rabbi Nahman of Bratslav, *Likkutei Maharan* 2:46.
2. Leonard Cohen in "Anthem."

Vayishlaḥ

Feeling the Fear

I t is one of the most enigmatic episodes in the Torah, but also one of the most important, because it was the moment that gave the Jewish people its name: Israel, one who "wrestles with God and with men and prevails" (Gen. 32:28).

Jacob, hearing that his brother Esau was coming to meet him with a force of four hundred men, was terrified. He was, says the Torah, "very afraid and distressed" (32:6). He made three forms of preparation: appeasement, prayer, and war (Rashi on v. 9). He sent Esau a huge gift of cattle and flocks, hoping thereby to appease him. He prayed to God, "Rescue me, I pray, from the hand of my brother" (v. 12). And he made preparation for war, dividing his household into two camps so that one at least would survive.

Yet he remained anxious. Alone at night he wrestled with a stranger until the break of dawn. Who the stranger was is not clear. The text calls him a man. Hosea (Hos. 12:4) called him an angel. The Sages said it was the guardian angel of Esau.[1] Jacob himself seems sure that he has encountered God Himself. He calls the place where the struggle

---

1. Genesis Rabba 77:3.

took place Peniel, saying, "I have seen God face to face and my life was spared" (Gen. 32:30).

There are many interpretations. One, however, is particularly fascinating in terms of both style and substance. It comes from Rashi's grandson, Rabbi Shmuel ben Meir (Rashbam, France, c. 1085–1158). Rashbam had a strikingly original approach to biblical commentary.[2] He felt that the Sages, intent as they were on reading the text for its halakhic ramifications, often failed to penetrate what he called *omek peshuto shel mikra*, the plain sense of the text in its full depth.

Rashbam felt that his grandfather occasionally erred on the side of a midrashic, rather than a "plain" reading of the text. He tells us that he often debated the point with Rashi himself, who admitted that if he had the time he would have written further commentaries to the Torah in the light of new insights into the plain sense that occurred to him "every day." This is a fascinating insight into the mind of Rashi, the greatest and most famous commentator in the entire history of rabbinic scholarship.

All of this is a prelude to Rashbam's remarkable reading of the night-time wrestling match. He takes it as an instance of what Robert Alter has called a *type-scene*,[3] that is, a stylised episode that happens more than once in Tanakh. One obvious example is a young man meeting his future wife at a well, a scene enacted with variations three times in the Torah: in the case of Abraham's servant and Rebecca, Jacob and Rachel, and Moses and Zipporah. There are differences between them, but sufficient similarities to make us realise that we are dealing with a convention. Another example, which occurs many times in Tanakh, is the birth of a hero to a hitherto infertile woman.

Rashbam sees this as the clue to understanding Jacob's night-time fight. He relates it to other episodes in Tanakh, two in particular: the story of Jonah, and the obscure episode in the life of Moses when, on his way back to Egypt, the text says, "When they were in the place where they spent the night along the way, God confronted Moses and

---

2. He expounds on this in his commentary on Genesis 37:2.
3. See Robert Alter, *The Art of Biblical Narrative* (New York: Basic Books, 1981).

wanted to kill him" (Ex. 4:24). Zipporah then saved Moses' life by performing a *brit* on their son (Ex. 4:25–26).[4]

It is the story of Jonah that provides the key to understanding the others. Jonah sought to escape from his mission to go to Nineveh to warn the people that the city was about to be destroyed if they did not repent. Jonah fled in a boat to Tarshish, but God brought a storm that threatened to sink the ship. The prophet was then thrown into the sea and swallowed by a giant fish that later vomited him out alive. Jonah thus realised that flight was impossible.

The same, says Rashbam, applies to Moses who, at the burning bush, repeatedly expressed his reluctance to undertake the task God had set him. Evidently, Moses was still prevaricating even after beginning the journey, which is why God was angry with him.

So it was with Jacob. According to Rashbam, despite God's assurances, he was still afraid of encountering Esau. His courage failed him and he was trying to run away. God sent an angel to stop him doing so.

It is a unique interpretation, sobering in its implications. Here were three great men, Jacob, Moses, and Jonah, yet all three, according to Rashbam, were afraid. Of what? None was a coward.

They were afraid, essentially, of their mission. Moses kept telling God at the burning bush: Who am I? They won't believe in me. I am not a man of words. Jonah was reluctant to deliver a message from God to Israel's enemies. And Jacob had just said to God, "I am unworthy of all the kindness and faith that You have shown me" (Gen. 32:11).

Nor were these the only people in Tanakh who had this kind of fear. So did the prophet Isaiah when he said to God, "I am a man of unclean lips" (Is. 6:5). So did Jeremiah when he said, "I cannot speak: I am a child" (Jer. 1:6).

This is not physical fear. It is the fear that comes from a feeling of personal inadequacy. "Who am I to lead the Jewish people?" asked Moses. "Who am I to deliver the word of God?" asked the prophets. "Who am I to stand before my brother Esau, knowing that I will continue the covenant and he will not?" asked Jacob. Sometimes the greatest

---

4. Rashbam on Genesis 32:29. Rashbam also includes the episode of Balaam, the donkey, and the angel as a further instance of this type-scene.

have the least self-confidence, because they know how immense is the responsibility and how small they feel in relation to it. Courage does not mean having no fear. It means having fear but overcoming it. If that is true of physical courage it is no less true of moral and spiritual courage.

Marianne Williamson's remarks on the subject have become justly famous. She wrote:

> Our deepest fear is not that we are inadequate. Our deepest fear is that we are powerful beyond measure. It is our light, not our darkness that most frightens us. We ask ourselves, Who am I to be brilliant, gorgeous, talented, fabulous? Actually, who are you not to be? You are a child of God. Your playing small does not serve the world. There is nothing enlightened about shrinking so that other people won't feel insecure around you. We are all meant to shine, as children do. We were born to make manifest the glory of God that is within us. It's not just in some of us; it's in everyone. And as we let our own light shine, we unconsciously give other people permission to do the same. As we are liberated from our own fear, our presence automatically liberates others.[5]

Shakespeare said it best: "Be not afraid of greatness: some are born great, some achieve greatness, and some have greatness thrust upon 'em."[6]

I sometimes feel that, consciously or subconsciously, some take flight from Judaism for this very reason. Who are we to be God's witness to the world, a light to the nations, a role model for others? If even spiritual giants like Jacob, Moses, and Jonah sought to flee, how much more so you and I? This *fear of unworthiness* is one that surely most of us have had at some time or other.

The reason it is wrong is not that it is untrue, but that it is irrelevant. Of course we feel inadequate for a great task before we undertake it. It is having the courage to undertake it that makes us great. Leaders grow by leading. Writers grow by writing. Teachers grow by teaching. It is only by overcoming our sense of inadequacy that we throw ourselves

---

5. Marianne Williamson, *A Return to Love* (New York: HarperCollins, 1992), 190.
6. William Shakespeare, *Twelfth Night*, act 2, scene 5.

into the task and find ourselves lifted and enlarged by so doing. In the title of a well-known book,[7] we must "feel the fear and do it anyway." *Be not afraid of greatness*: that is why God wrestled with Jacob, Moses, and Jonah and would not let them escape. We may not be born great, but by being born (or converting to become) a Jew, we have greatness thrust upon us. And as Marianne Williamson rightly said, by liberating ourselves from fear, we help liberate others. That is what we as Jews are meant to do: to have the courage to be different, to challenge the idols of the age, to be true to our faith while seeking to be a blessing to others regardless of their faith.

For we are all children of the man who was given the name of one who *wrestles with God and with men and prevails*. Ours is not an easy task, but what worthwhile mission ever was? We are as great as the challenges we have the courage to undertake. And if, at times, we feel like running away, we should not feel bad about it. So did the greatest.

To feel fear is fine. To give way to it, is not. For God has faith in us even if, at times, even the best lack faith in themselves.

---

7. Susan Jeffers, *Feel the Fear and Do It Anyway* (New York: Random House, 2017).

Vayeshev

How to Change the World

I
n his *Hilkhot Teshuva* (Laws of Repentance), Moses Maimonides makes one of the most empowering statements in religious literature. Having explained that we and the world are judged by the majority of our deeds, he continues:

> Therefore we should see ourselves throughout the year as if our deeds and those of the world are evenly poised between good and bad, so that our next act may change both the balance of our lives and that of the world.[1]

We can make a difference, and it is potentially immense. That should be our mindset, always.

Few statements are more at odds with the way the world seems to us most of the time. Each of us knows that there is only one of us, and that there are seven billion others in the world today. What conceivable difference can we make? We are no more than a wave in the ocean, a grain of sand on the sea shore, dust on the surface of infinity. Is

---

1. Maimonides, *Mishneh Torah, Hilkhot Teshuva* 3:4.

it conceivable that with one act we could change the trajectory of our life, let alone that of humanity as a whole? Our *parasha* tells us that yes, it is.

As the story of Jacob's children unfolds, there is a rapid rise of tension among his children that threatens to spill over into violence. Joseph, eleventh of the twelve, is Jacob's favourite son. He was, says the Torah, the child of Jacob's old age. More significantly, he was the first child of Jacob's beloved wife Rachel. Jacob "loved him more" than his other sons (Gen. 37:3), and they knew it and resented it. They were jealous of their father's love. They were provoked by Joseph's dreams of greatness. The sight of the multi-coloured robe Jacob had given him as a token of his love provoked them to anger.

Then came the moment of opportunity. The brothers were away far from home tending the flocks when Joseph appeared in the distance, sent by Jacob to see how they were doing. Their envy and anger reached boiling point, and they resolved to take violent revenge. "'Here comes that dreamer!' they said to each other. 'Come now, let's kill him and throw him into one of these cisterns and say that a wild animal devoured him. Then we'll see what comes of his dreams'" (vv. 19–20).

Only one of the brothers disagreed: Reuben. He knew that what they were proposing was very wrong, and he protested. At this point the Torah does something extraordinary. It makes a statement that cannot be literally true, and we, reading the story, know this. The text says, "And Reuben heard and saved him [Joseph] from them" (v. 21).

We know this cannot be true because of what happens next. Reuben, realising that he is only one against many, devises a stratagem. He says, Let us not kill him. Let us throw him alive into one of the cisterns and let him die. That way, we will not be directly guilty of murder. His intention was to come back to the cistern later, when the others were elsewhere, and rescue Joseph. When the Torah says, "And Reuben heard and saved him from them," it is using the principle that "God accounts a good intention as a deed."[2] Reuben wanted to save Joseph and intended to do so, but in fact he failed. The moment passed, and by the time he acted, it was already too late. Returning to the cistern, he found Joseph already gone, sold as a slave.

---

2. Tosefta, *Pe'ah* 1:4.

On this, a midrash says:

> Had Reuben known that the Holy One blessed be He would write about him, "And Reuben heard and saved him from them," he would have lifted Joseph bodily onto his shoulders and taken him back to his father.[3]

What does this mean?

Consider what would have happened had Reuben actually acted at that moment. Joseph would not have been sold as a slave. He would not have been taken to Egypt. He would not have worked in Potiphar's house. He would not have attracted Potiphar's wife. He would not have been thrown into prison on a false charge. He would not have interpreted the dreams of the butler and baker, nor would he have done the same two years later for Pharaoh. He would not have been made viceroy of Egypt. He would not have brought his family to stay there.

To be sure, God had already told Abraham many years earlier, "Know for certain that for four hundred years your descendants will be strangers in a country not their own, and they will be enslaved and mistreated there" (Gen. 15:13). The Israelites would have become slaves, come what may. But at least they would not have had this happen as a result of their own family dysfunctions. An entire chapter of Jewish guilt and shame might have been avoided.

If only Reuben had known what we know. *If only he had been able to read the book.* But we never can read the book that tells of the long-term consequences of our acts. We never know how much we affect the lives of others.

There is a story I find very moving, about how in 1966 an eleven-year-old African-American boy moved with his family to a hitherto white neighbourhood in Washington.[4] Sitting with his brothers and sisters on the front step of the house, he waited to see how they would be greeted. They were not. Passers-by turned to look at them but no one gave them

---

3. *Tanḥuma, Vayeshev*, 13.
4. Stephen Carter, *Civility* (New York: Basic Books, 1999), 61–75.

a smile or even a glance of recognition. All the fearful stories he had heard about how whites treated blacks seemed to be coming true. Years later, writing about those first days in their new home, he says, "I knew we were not welcome here. I knew we would not be liked here. I knew we would have no friends here. I knew we should not have moved here."

As he was thinking those thoughts, a woman passed by on the other side of the road. She turned to the children and with a broad smile said, "Welcome!" Disappearing into the house, she emerged minutes later with a tray laden with drinks and cream cheese and jelly sandwiches which she brought over to the children, making them feel at home. That moment – the young man later wrote – changed his life. It gave him a sense of belonging where there was none before. It made him realise, at a time when race relations in the United States were still fraught, that a black family could feel at home in a white area and that there could be relationships that were colour-blind. Over the years, he learned to admire much about the woman across the street, but it was that first spontaneous act of greeting that became, for him, a definitive memory. It broke down a wall of separation and turned strangers into friends.

The young man, Stephen Carter, eventually became a law professor at Yale and wrote a book about what he learned that day. He called it *Civility*. The name of the woman, he tells us, was Sara Kestenbaum, and she died all too young. He adds that it was no coincidence that she was a religious Jew. "In the Jewish tradition," he notes, such civility is called "*hessed* – the doing of acts of kindness – which is in turn derived from the understanding that human beings are made in the image of God."

"Civility," he adds, "itself may be seen as part of *hessed*: it does indeed require kindnesses toward our fellow citizens, including the ones who are strangers, and even when it is hard."

He adds:

> To this day, I can close my eyes and feel on my tongue the smooth, slick sweetness of the cream cheese and jelly sandwiches that I gobbled on that summer afternoon when I discovered how a single act of genuine and unassuming civility can change a life forever.

A single life, says the Mishna, is like a universe.[5] Change a life, and you begin to change the universe. That is how we make a difference: one life at a time, one day at a time, one act at a time. We never know in advance what effect a single act may have. Sometimes we never know it at all. Sara Kestenbaum, like Reuben, never did have the chance to read the book that told the story of the long-term consequences of that moment. But she acted. She did not hesitate. Neither, said Maimonides, should we. Our next act might tilt the balance of someone else's life as well as our own.

We are not inconsequential. We can make a difference to our world. When we do so, we become God's partners in the work of redemption, bringing the world that is a little closer to the world that ought to be.

---

5. Mishna Sanhedrin 4:5 (original manuscript text).

Miketz

To Wait Without Despair

Something extraordinary happens between the previous *parasha* and this one. It is almost as if the pause of a week between them were itself part of the story.

Recall *Parashat Vayeshev* about the childhood of Joseph, focusing not on *what* happened but on *who made it* happen. Throughout the entire roller-coaster ride of Joseph's early life he is described as passive, not active; the done-to, not the doer; the object, not the subject, of verbs.

It was his father who loved him and gave him the richly embroidered cloak. It was his brothers who envied and hated him. He had dreams, but we do not dream because we want to but because, in some mysterious way still not yet fully understood, they come unbidden into our sleeping mind.

His brothers, tending their flocks far from home, plotted to kill him. They threw him into a pit. He was sold as a slave. In Potiphar's house he rose to a position of seniority, but the text goes out of its way to say that this was not because of Joseph himself, but because of God:

> *God was with Joseph*, and he became a successful man; he was in the house of his Egyptian master. His master saw that *God was*

> *with him,* and that *God caused all that he did* to prosper in his
> hands. (Gen. 39:2–3)

Potiphar's wife tried to seduce him, and failed, but here too, Joseph was
passive, not active. He did not seek her, she sought him. Eventually, "she
caught hold of his garment, saying, 'Lie with me!' But he left his garment in her hand, and fled and ran outside" (v. 12). Using the garment
as evidence, she had him imprisoned on a totally false charge. There was
nothing Joseph could do to establish his innocence.

In prison, again he became a leader, a manager, but again the
Torah goes out of its way to attribute this not to Joseph but to divine
intervention:

> *God was with Joseph* and showed him kindness. *He gave him favour
> in the sight of the chief jailer....* Whatever was done there, God
> was the one who did it. The chief jailer paid no heed to anything
> that was in Joseph's care, because *God was with him;* and *whatever
> he did, God made it prosper.* (vv. 21–23)

There he met Pharaoh's chief butler and baker. They had dreams, and
Joseph interpreted them, but insisted that it is not he but God who was
doing so: "Joseph said to them, '*Do not interpretations belong to God?*
Please tell them to me'" (40:8).

There is nothing like this anywhere else in Tanakh. Whatever
happened to Joseph was the result of someone else's deed: those of his
father, his brothers, his master's wife, the chief jailer, or God Himself.
Joseph was the ball thrown by hands other than his own.

Then, for essentially the first time in the whole story, Joseph
decided to take fate into his own hands. Knowing that the chief butler
was about to be restored to his position, he asked him to bring his case
to the attention of Pharaoh:

> Remember me when it is well with you; please do me the kind-
> ness to make mention of me to Pharaoh, and so get me out of
> this place. For indeed I was stolen out of the land of the Hebrews;

and here also I have done nothing that they should have put me into prison. (vv. 14–15)

A double injustice had been done, and Joseph saw this as his one chance of regaining his freedom. But the end of the *parasha* delivers a devastating blow: "The chief cupbearer *did not remember* Joseph, and *forgot* him" (v. 23). The anticlimax is intense, emphasised by the double verb, "did not remember" and "forgot." We sense Joseph waiting day after day for news. None comes. His last, best hope has gone. He will never go free. Or so it seems.

To understand the power of this anticlimax, we must remember that only since the invention of printing and the availability of books have we been able to tell what happens next merely by turning a page. For many centuries, there were no printed books. People knew the biblical story primarily by *listening* to it week by week. Those who were hearing the story for the first time had to wait a week to discover what Joseph's fate would be.

The *parasha* break is thus a kind of real-life equivalent to the delay Joseph experienced in jail, which, as this *parasha* begins by telling us, took "two whole years." It was then that Pharaoh had two dreams that no one in the court could interpret, prompting the chief butler to remember the man he had met in prison. Joseph was brought to Pharaoh, and within hours was transformed from zero to hero: from prisoner-without-hope to viceroy of the greatest empire of the ancient world.

Why this extraordinary chain of events? It is telling us something important, but what? Surely this: *God answers our prayers, but often not when we thought or how we thought.* Joseph sought to get out of prison, and he did get out of prison. But not immediately, and not because the butler kept his promise.

The story is telling us something fundamental about the relationship between our dreams and our achievements. Joseph was the great dreamer of the Torah, and his dreams for the most part came true. But not in a way he or anyone else could have anticipated. At the end of the previous *parasha* – with Joseph still in prison – it seemed as if those dreams had ended in ignominious failure. We have to wait for a week, as he had to wait for two years, before discovering that it was not so.

There is no achievement without effort. That is the first principle. God saved Noah from the flood, but first Noah had to build the ark. God promised Abraham the land, but first he had to buy the cave of Machpelah in which to bury Sarah. God promised the Israelites the land, but they had to fight the battles. Joseph became a leader, as he dreamed he would. But first he had to hone his practical and administrative skills, first in Potiphar's house, then in prison. Even when God assures us that something will happen, it will not happen without our effort. A divine promise is not a *substitute for* human responsibility. To the contrary, it is a *call to* responsibility.

But effort alone is not enough. We need *siyata diShemaya*, "the help of Heaven." We need the humility to acknowledge that we are dependent on forces not under our control. No one in Genesis invoked God more often than Joseph. As Rashi (on Gen. 39:3) says, "God's name was constantly in his mouth." He credited God for each of his successes. He recognised that without God he could not have done what he did. Out of that humility came patience.

Those who have achieved great things have often had this unusual combination of characteristics. On the one hand they work hard. They labour, they practise, they strive. On the other, they know that it will not be their hand alone that writes the script. It is not our efforts alone that decide the outcome. So we pray, and God answers our prayers – but not always when or how we expected. (And of course, sometimes the answer is No.)

The Talmud (Nidda 70b) says it simply. It asks: What should you do to become rich? It answers: Work hard and behave honestly. But, says the Talmud, many have tried this and did not become rich. Back comes the answer: You must pray to God from whom all wealth comes. In which case, asks the Talmud, why work hard? Because, answers the Talmud: *The one without the other is insufficient.* We need both: human effort and divine favour. We have to be, in a certain sense, patient *and* impatient – impatient with ourselves but patient in waiting for God to bless our endeavours.

The week-long delay between Joseph's failed attempt to get out of jail and his eventual success is there to teach us this delicate balance. If we work hard enough, God grants us success – but not when we want but, rather, when the time is right.

Vayigash

Reframing

Maimonides called his ideal type of human being – the sage – a *rofe nefashot*, a "healer of souls."[1] Today we call such a person a *psychotherapist*, a word coined relatively recently from the Greek word *psyche*, meaning "soul," and *therapeia*, "healing." It is astonishing how many of the pioneering soul-healers in modern times have been Jewish.

Almost all the early psychoanalysts were; among them Sigmund Freud, Alfred Adler, Otto Rank, and Melanie Klein. So overwhelming was this, that psychoanalysis was known in Nazi Germany as the "Jewish science." More recent Jewish contributions include Solomon Asch on conformity, Lawrence Kohlberg on developmental psychology, and Bruno Bettelheim on child psychology. From Leon Festinger came the concept of cognitive dissonance, from Howard Gardner the idea of multiple intelligences, and from Peter Salovey and Daniel Goleman, emotional intelligence. Abraham Maslow gave us new insight into motivation, as did Walter Mischel into self-control via the famous "marshmallow test." Daniel Kahneman and Amos Tversky gave us prospect theory and behavioural economics. Most recently, Jonathan Haidt and

---

1. Maimonides, *Shemona Perakim*, ch. 4.

Joshua Green have pioneered empirical study of the moral emotions. The list goes on and on.

To my mind, though, one of the most important Jewish contributions came from three outstanding figures: Viktor Frankl, Aaron T. Beck, and Martin Seligman. Frankl created the method known as logotherapy, based on the search for meaning. Beck was the joint creator of the most successful form of treatment, cognitive behavioural therapy. Seligman gave us positive psychology, that is, psychology not just as a cure for depression but as a means of achieving happiness or flourishing through acquired optimism.

These are very different approaches but they have one thing in common. They are based on the belief – set out much earlier in Chabad Hasidism, in Rabbi Schneur Zalman of Liadi's *Tanya* – that *if we change the way we think, we will change the way we feel.* This was, at the outset, a revolutionary proposition in sharp contrast to other theories of the human psyche. There were those who believed that our characters are determined by genetic factors. Others thought our emotional life was governed by early childhood experiences and unconscious drives. Others again, most famously Ivan Pavlov, believed that human behaviour is determined by conditioning. In all of these theories our inner freedom is severely circumscribed. Who we are, and how we feel, are largely dictated by factors other than the conscious mind.

It was Viktor Frankl who showed there is another way – and he did so under some of the worst conditions ever endured by human beings: in Auschwitz. As a prisoner there Frankl discovered that the Nazis took away almost everything that made people human: their possessions, their clothes, their hair, their very names. Before being sent to Auschwitz, Frankl had been a therapist specialising in curing people who had suicidal tendencies. In the camp he devoted himself, as far as he could, to giving his fellow prisoners the will to live, knowing that if they lost it, they would soon die.

There he made the fundamental discovery for which he later became famous:

> We who lived in concentration camps can remember the men who walked through the huts comforting others, giving away

their last piece of bread. They may have been few in number, but they offer sufficient proof that everything can be taken from a man but one thing: *the last of the human freedoms – to choose one's attitude in any given set of circumstances, to choose one's own way.*[2]

What made the difference, what gave people the will to live, was the belief that there was a task for them to perform, a mission for them to accomplish, that they had not yet completed and that was waiting for them to do in the future. Frankl discovered that *"it did not really matter what we expected from life, but rather what life expected from us."*[3] There were people in the camp who had so lost hope that they had nothing more to expect from life. Frankl was able to get them to see that "life was still expecting something from them." One, for example, had a child still alive in a foreign country, who was waiting for him. Another came to see that he had books to produce that no one else could write. Through this sense of a future calling to them, Frankl was able to help them to discover their purpose in life, even in the valley of the shadow of death.

The mental shift this involved came to be known, especially in cognitive behavioural therapy, as *reframing.* Just as a painting can look different when placed in a different frame, so can a life. The facts don't change, but the way we perceive them does. Frankl writes that he was able to survive Auschwitz by daily seeing himself as if he were in a university, giving a lecture on the psychology of the concentration camp. Everything that was happening to him was transformed, by this one act of the mind, into a series of illustrations of the points he was making in the lecture. "By this method, I succeeded somehow in rising above the situation, above the sufferings of the moment, and I observed them as if they were already of the past."[4] Reframing tells us that though we cannot always change the circumstances in which we find ourselves, *we can change the way we see them, and this itself changes the way we feel.*

2. Viktor Frankl, *Man's Search for Meaning: An Introduction to Logotherapy,* translated by Ilse Lasch (Boston: Beacon Press, 1992), 75.
3. Ibid., 85.
4. Ibid., 82.

Yet this modern discovery is really a re-discovery, because the first great re-framer in history was Joseph, as described in this *parasha* and the next. Recall the facts. He had been sold into slavery by his brothers. He had lost his freedom for thirteen years, and been separated from his family for twenty-two years. It would be understandable if he felt toward his brothers resentment and a desire for revenge. Yet he rose above such feelings, and did so precisely by shifting his experiences into a different frame. Here is what he says to his brothers when he first discloses his identity to them:

> I am your brother, Joseph, whom you sold into Egypt. And now do not be distressed, or angry with yourselves, because you sold me here; for *God sent me* before you to preserve life... *God sent me* before you to preserve for you a remnant on earth, and to keep alive for you many survivors. So *it was not you who sent me here, but God.* (Gen. 45:4–8)

And this is what he says years later, after their father Jacob has died and the brothers fear that he may now take revenge:

> Do not be afraid! Am I in the place of God? *Though you intended to do harm to me, God intended it for good*, in order to preserve a numerous people, as He is doing today. So have no fear; I myself will provide for you and your little ones. (50:19–21)

Joseph had reframed his entire past. He no longer saw himself as a man wronged by his brothers. He had come to see himself as a man charged with a life-saving mission by God. Everything that had happened to him was necessary so that he could achieve his purpose in life: to save an entire region from starvation during a famine, and to provide a safe haven for his family.

This single act of reframing allowed Joseph to live without a burning sense of anger and injustice. It enabled him to forgive his brothers and be reconciled with them. It transformed the negative energies of feelings about the past into focused attention to the future. Joseph, without knowing it, had become the precursor of one of the great movements in psychotherapy in the modern world. He showed the power of reframing. We cannot change the past. But by changing the way we *think about* the past, we can change the future.

Whatever situation we are in, by reframing it we can change our entire response, giving us the strength to survive, the courage to persist, and the resilience to emerge, on the far side of darkness, into the light of a new and better day.

Vayeḥi

On Not Predicting
the Future

Jacob was on his deathbed. He summoned his children. He wanted to bless them before he died. But the text begins with a strange semi-repetition:

> Gather around so I can tell you what will happen to you in days to come.
> Assemble and listen, sons of Jacob; listen to your father Israel. (Gen. 49:1–2)

This seems to be saying the same thing twice, with one difference. In the first sentence, there is a reference to "what will happen to you in the days to come" (literally, "at the end of days"). This is missing from the second sentence.

Rashi, following the Talmud,[1] says that "Jacob wished to reveal what would happen in the future, but the Divine Presence was removed from him." He tried to foresee the future but found he could not.

---

1. Rashi on Genesis 49:1; Pesaḥim 56a; Genesis Rabba 99:5.

This is no minor detail. It is a fundamental feature of Jewish spirituality. We believe that we cannot predict the future when it comes to human beings. We *make* the future by our choices. The script has not yet been written. The future is radically open.

This was a major difference between ancient Israel and ancient Greece. The Greeks believed in fate, *moira*, even blind fate, *ananke*. When the Delphic oracle told Laius that he would have a son who would kill him, he took every precaution to make sure it did not happen. When the child was born, Laius nailed him by his feet to a rock and left him to die. A passing shepherd found and saved him, and he was eventually raised by the king and queen of Corinth. Because his feet were permanently misshapen, he came to be known as Oedipus (the "swollen-footed").

The rest of the story is well known. Everything the oracle foresaw happened, and every act designed to avoid it actually helped bring it about. Once the oracle has been spoken and fate has been sealed, all attempts to avoid it are in vain. This cluster of ideas lies at the heart of one of the great Greek contributions to civilization: *tragedy*.

Astonishingly, given the many centuries of Jewish suffering, biblical Hebrew has no word for tragedy. The word *ason* means "a mishap, a disaster, a calamity" but not tragedy in the classic sense. A tragedy is a drama with a sad outcome involving a hero destined to experience downfall or destruction through a character flaw or a conflict with an overpowering force, such as fate. Judaism has no word for this, because we do not believe in fate as something blind, inevitable, and inexorable. We are free. We can choose. As Isaac Bashevis Singer wittily said: "We *must* be free: we have no choice!"[2]

Rarely is this more powerfully asserted than in the *UNetaneh Tokef* prayer we say on Rosh HaShana and Yom Kippur. Even after we have said, "On Rosh HaShana it is written and on Yom Kippur it is sealed...who will live and who will die," we still go on to say, "But *teshuva*, prayer, and charity *avert the evil of the decree*." There is no sentence

---

2. Quoted in slightly varying forms, as "We have to believe in free will. We've got no choice" attributed to L. Tiger, *Optimism: The Biology of Hope* (New York: Simon & Schuster, 1979).

against which we cannot appeal, no verdict we cannot mitigate by showing that we have repented and changed.

There is a classic example of this in Tanakh.

> In those days Hezekiah became ill and was at the point of death. The prophet Isaiah son of Amoz went to him and said, "This is what the Lord says: Put your house in order, because you are going to die; you will not recover." Hezekiah turned his face to the wall and prayed to the Lord, "Remember, Lord, how I have walked before You faithfully and with wholehearted devotion and have done what is good in Your eyes." And Hezekiah wept bitterly. Before Isaiah had left the middle court, the word of the Lord came to him: "Go back and tell Hezekiah, the ruler of My people: This is what the Lord, God of your father David, says: I have heard your prayer and seen your tears; I will heal you." (II Kings 20:1–5; Is. 38:1–5)

The prophet Isaiah had told King Hezekiah he would not recover, but he did. He lived for another fifteen years. God heard his prayer and granted him stay of execution. From this the Talmud infers, "Even if a sharp sword rests upon your neck, you should not desist from prayer."[3] We pray for a good fate but we do not reconcile ourselves to fatalism.

Hence there is a fundamental difference between a prophecy and a prediction. *If a prediction comes true, it has succeeded. If a prophecy comes true, it has failed.* A prophet delivers not a prediction but a warning. He or she does not simply say, "This will happen," but rather, "This will happen *unless* you change." The prophet speaks to human freedom, not to the inevitability of fate.

I was once present at a gathering where Bernard Lewis, the great scholar of Islam, was asked to predict the outcome of a certain American foreign policy intervention. He gave a magnificent reply. "I am a historian, so I only make predictions about the past. What is more, I am a retired historian, so even my past is passé." This was a profoundly Jewish answer.

---

3. Berakhot 10a.

In the twenty-first century we know much at a macro- and micro-level. We look up and see a universe of a hundred billion galaxies each of a hundred billion stars. We look down and see a human body containing a hundred trillion cells, each with a double copy of the human genome, 3.1 billion letters long, enough if transcribed to fill a library of five thousand books. But there remains one thing we do not know and will never know: what tomorrow will bring. The past, said L. P. Hartley, is a foreign country. But the future is an undiscovered one. That is why predictions so often fail.

That is the essential difference between nature and *human* nature. The ancient Mesopotamians could make accurate predictions about the movement of planets, yet even today, despite brain-scans and neuroscience, we are still not able to predict what people will do. Often, they take us by surprise.

The reason is that we are free. We choose, we make mistakes, we learn, we change, we grow. The failure at school becomes the winner of a Nobel Prize. The leader who disappointed, suddenly shows courage and wisdom in a crisis. The driven businessman has an intimation of mortality and decides to devote the rest of his life to helping the poor. Some of the most successful people I ever met were written off by their teachers at school and told they would never amount to anything. We constantly defy predictions. This is something science has not yet explained and perhaps never will. Some believe freedom is an illusion. But it isn't. It's what makes us human.

We are free because we are not merely objects. We are subjects. We respond not just to physical events but to the way we perceive those events. We have minds, not just brains. We have thoughts, not just sensations. We react but we can also choose not to react. There is something about us that is irreducible to material, physical causes and effects.

The way our ancestors spoke about this remains true and profound. We are free because God is free, and He made us in His image. That is what is meant by the three words God told Moses at the burning bush when he asked God for His name. God replied, *Ehyeh asher Ehyeh.* This is often translated as "I am what I am," but what it really means is, "I will be who and how I choose to be." I am the God of freedom. I cannot be predicted. Note that God says this at the start of Moses' mission to lead a people from slavery to freedom. He wanted the Israelites to become living testimony to the power of freedom. Do not believe that the future is written. It isn't. There is no fate we cannot change, no prediction we cannot defy. We are not predestined to fail; neither are we pre-ordained to succeed. We do not predict the future, because we make the future – by our choices, our willpower, our persistence, and our determination to survive.

The proof is the Jewish people itself. The first reference to Israel outside the Bible is engraved on the Merneptah stele, inscribed around 1225 BCE by Pharaoh Merneptah IV, Ramses II's successor. It reads: "Israel is laid waste; her seed is no more." It was, in short, an obituary. The Jewish people have been written off many times by their enemies, but they remain, after almost four millennia, still young and strong.

That is why, when Jacob wanted to tell his children what would happen to them in the future, the divine spirit was taken away from him. Our children continue to surprise us, as we continue to surprise others. Made in the image of God, we are free. Sustained by the blessings of God, we can become greater than anyone, even ourselves, could foresee.

Exodus
שמות

Shemot

Turning Curses
into Blessings

Genesis ends on an almost serene note. Jacob has found his long-lost son. The family has been reunited. Joseph has forgiven his brothers. Under his protection and influence the family has settled in Goshen, one of the most prosperous regions of Egypt. They now have homes, property, food, the protection of Joseph, and the favour of Pharaoh. It must have seemed one of the golden moments of Abraham's family's history.

Then, as has happened so often since, "There arose a new Pharaoh who did not know Joseph" (Ex. 1:8). There was a political climate change. The family fell out of favour. Pharaoh told his advisers: "Look, the Israelite people are becoming too numerous and strong for us"[1] – the first time the word "people" is used in the Torah with reference to the children of Israel. "Let us deal shrewdly with them,

---

1. This is the first intimation in history of what in modern times took the form of the Russian forgery, the *Protocols of the Elders of Zion*. In the Diaspora, Jews – powerless – were often seen as all-powerful. What this usually means, when translated, is: How is it that Jews manage to evade the pariah status we have assigned to them?

so that they may not increase" (vv. 9–10). And so the whole mechanism of oppression moves into operation: forced labour that turns into slavery that becomes attempted genocide. The story is engraved in our memory. We tell it every year, and in summary form in our prayers, every day. It is part of what it is to be a Jew. Yet there is one phrase that shines out from the narrative: *"But the more they were oppressed, the more they increased and the more they spread."* That, no less than oppression itself, is part of what it means to be a Jew. The worse things get, the stronger we become. Jews are the people who not only survive but thrive in adversity.

Jewish history is not merely a story of Jews enduring catastrophes that might have spelled the end to less tenacious groups. It is that after every disaster, Jews renewed themselves. They discovered some hitherto hidden reservoir of spirit that fuelled new forms of collective self-expression as the carriers of God's message to the world.

Every tragedy begat new creativity. After the division of the kingdom following the death of Solomon came the great literary prophets, Amos and Hosea, Isaiah and Jeremiah. Out of the destruction of the First Temple and the Babylonian exile came the renewal of Torah in the life of the nation, beginning with Ezekiel and culminating in the vast educational programme brought back to Israel by Ezra and Nehemiah. From the destruction of the Second Temple came the immense literature of rabbinic Judaism, until then preserved mostly in the form of an oral tradition: Mishna, Midrash and Gemara.

From the Crusades came the Hasidei Ashkenaz, the North European school of piety and spirituality. Following the Spanish expulsion came the mystic circle of Safed: Lurianic Kabbala and all it inspired by way of poetry and prayer. From East European persecution and poverty came the hasidic movement and its revival of grass-roots Judaism through a seemingly endless flow of story and song. And from the worst tragedy of all in human terms, the Holocaust, came the rebirth of the State of Israel, the greatest collective Jewish affirmation of life in more than two thousand years.

It is well known that the Chinese ideogram for "crisis" also means "opportunity." Any civilisation that can see the blessing within the curse, the fragment of light within the heart of darkness, has within it the capacity to endure. Hebrew goes one better. The word for crisis, *mashber*, also means "a child-birth chair." Written into the semantics of Jewish consciousness is the idea that the pain of hard times is a collective form of the contractions of a woman giving birth. Something new is being born. That is the mindset of a people of whom it can be said that "the more they were oppressed, the more they increased and the more they spread."

Where did it come from, this Jewish ability to turn weakness into strength, adversity into advantage, darkness into light? It goes back to the moment in which our people received its name, Israel. It was then, as Jacob wrestled alone at night with an angel, that as dawn broke his adversary begged him to let him go. "I will not let you go until you bless me," said Jacob (Gen. 32:26). That is the source of our peculiar, distinctive obstinacy. We may have fought all night. We may be tired and on the brink of exhaustion. We may find ourselves limping, as did Jacob. Yet we will not let our adversary go until we have extracted a blessing from the encounter. This turned out to be not a minor and temporary concession. It became the basis of his new name and our identity. Israel, the people who "wrestled with God and man and prevailed" (v. 28), is the nation that grows stronger with each conflict and catastrophe.

I was reminded of this unusual national characteristic by an article that appeared in the British press in October 2015. Israel at the time was suffering from a wave of terrorist attacks that saw Palestinians murdering innocent civilians in streets and bus stations throughout the country. It began with these words: "Israel is an astonishing country, buzzing with energy and confidence, a magnet for talent and investment – a cauldron of innovation." It spoke of its world-class excellence in aerospace, clean-tech, irrigation systems, software, cyber-security, pharmaceuticals, and defence systems.[2]

"All this," the writer went on to say, "derives from brainpower, for Israel has no natural resources and is surrounded by hostile neighbours." The country is living proof of "the power of technical education, immigration, and the benefits of the right sort of military service." Yet this

---

2. Luke Johnson, "Animal Spirits: Israel and Its Tribe of Risk-Taking Entrepreneurs," *Sunday Times*, October 4, 2015.

cannot be all, since Jews have consistently overachieved, wherever they were and whenever they were given the chance. He goes through the various suggested explanations: the strength of Jewish families, their passion for education, a desire for self-employment, risk-taking as a way of life, and even ancient history. The Levant was home to the world's first agricultural societies and earliest traders. Perhaps, then, the disposition to enterprise was written, thousands of years ago, into Jewish DNA. Ultimately, though, he concludes that it has to do with "culture and communities."

A key element of that culture has to do with the Jewish response to crisis. To every adverse circumstance, those who have inherited Jacob's sensibilities insist: "I will not let you go until you bless me." That is how Jews, encountering the Negev, found ways of making the desert bloom. Seeing a barren, neglected landscape elsewhere, they planted trees and forests. Faced with hostile armies on all their borders, they developed military technologies they then turned to peaceful use. War and terror forced them to develop medical expertise and world-leading skills in dealing with the aftermath of trauma. They found ways of turning every curse into a blessing. The historian Paul Johnson, as always, put it eloquently:

> Over 4,000 years the Jews proved themselves not only great survivors but extraordinarily skilful in adapting to the societies among which fate had thrust them, and in gathering whatever human comforts they had to offer. No people has been more fertile in enriching poverty or humanising wealth, or in turning misfortune to creative account.[3]

There is something profoundly spiritual as well as robustly practical about this ability to transform the bad moments of life into a spur to creativity. It is as if, deep within us, a voice was saying, "You are in this situation, bad though it is, because there is a task to perform, a skill to acquire, a strength to develop, a lesson to learn, an evil to redeem, a shard of light to be rescued, a blessing to be uncovered, for I have chosen you to give

---

3. Paul Johnson, *The History of the Jews* (London: Weidenfeld and Nicolson, 1987), 58.

testimony to humankind that out of suffering can come great blessings if you wrestle with it for long enough and with unshakeable faith."

In an age in which people of violence are committing acts of brutality in the name of the God of compassion, the people of Israel are proving daily that this is not the way of the God of Abraham, the God of life and the sanctity of life. And whenever we who are a part of that people lose heart, and wonder when it will ever end, we should recall the words: "The more they were oppressed, the more they increased and the more they spread." A people of whom that can be said can be injured, but can never be defeated. God's way is the way of life.

Va'era

Spirits in a Material World

The Torah sometimes says something of fundamental importance in what seems like a minor and incidental comment. There is a fine example of this near the beginning of this *parasha*.

In the previous *parasha*, we read of how Moses was sent by God to lead the Israelites to freedom, and how his initial efforts met with failure. Not only did Pharaoh not agree to let the people go; he made the working conditions of the Israelites even worse. They had to make the same number of bricks as before, but now they had to gather their own straw. The people complained to Pharaoh, then they complained to Moses, then Moses complained to God. "Why have You brought trouble to this people? Why did You send me?" (Ex. 5:22)

At the beginning of this *parasha* God tells Moses that he will indeed bring the Israelites to freedom, and tells him to announce this to the people. Then we read this:

So Moses told this to the Israelites but they did not listen to him, *because their spirit was broken and because the labour was harsh.* (6:9)

The italicised phrase seems simple enough. The people did not listen to Moses because he had brought them messages from God before which had done nothing to improve their situation. They were busy trying to survive day by day. They had no time for utopian promises that seemed to have no grounding in reality. Moses had failed to deliver in the past. They had no reason to think he would do so in the future. So far, so straightforward.

But there is something more subtle going on beneath the surface. When Moses first met God at the burning bush, God told him to lead, and Moses kept refusing on the grounds that the people would not listen to him. He was not a man of words. He was slow of speech and tongue. He was a man of "uncircumcised lips" (6:30). He lacked eloquence. He could not sway crowds. He was not an inspirational leader.

It turned out, though, that Moses was both right and wrong, right that they did not listen to him, but wrong about why. It had nothing to do with his failures as a leader or a public speaker. In fact, it had nothing to do with Moses at all. They did not listen "because their spirit was broken and because the labour was harsh." In other words: *If you want to improve people's spiritual situation, first improve their physical situation.* That is one of the most humanising aspects of Judaism.

Maimonides emphasises this in *The Guide for the Perplexed*.[1] The Torah, he says, has two aims: the well-being of the soul and the well-being of the body. The well-being of the soul is something inward and spiritual, but the well-being of the body requires a strong society and economy, where there is the rule of law, division of labour, and the promotion of trade. We have bodily well-being when all our physical needs are supplied, but none of us can do this on his own. We specialise and exchange. That is why we need a good, strong, just society.

Spiritual achievement, says Maimonides, is higher than material achievement, but we need to ensure the latter first, because "a person suffering from great hunger, thirst, heat or cold, cannot grasp an idea even if it is communicated by others, much less can he arrive at it by his own reasoning." In other words, if we lack basic physical needs, there is no way we can reach spiritual heights. When people's spirits are broken

---

1. Maimonides, *The Guide for the Perplexed*, III:27.

by harsh labour they cannot listen to a Moses. If you want to improve people's spiritual situation, first improve their physical conditions.

This idea was given classic expression in modern times by two New York Jewish psychologists, Abraham Maslow (1908–1970) and Frederick Herzberg (1923–2000). Maslow was fascinated by the question of why many people never reached their full potential. He also believed – as, later, did Martin Seligman, creator of positive psychology – that psychology should focus not only on the cure of illness but also on the positive promotion of mental health. His most famous contribution to the study of the human mind was his "hierarchy of needs."

We are not a mere bundle of wants and desires. There is a clear order to our concerns. Maslow enumerated five levels. First are our *physiological* needs: for food and shelter, the basic requirements of survival. Next come *safety* needs: protection against harm done to us by others. Third is our need for *love and belonging*. Above that comes our desire for *recognition and esteem,* and higher still is *self-actualisation*: fulfilling our potential, becoming the person we feel we could and should be. In his later years Maslow added a yet higher stage: *self-transcendence,* rising beyond the self through altruism and spirituality.

Herzberg simplified this whole structure by distinguishing between physical and psychological factors. He called the first, *Adam needs,* and the second *Abraham needs.* Herzberg was particularly interested in what motivates people at work. What he realised in the late 1950s – an idea revived more recently by American-Israeli economist Dan Ariely – is that money, salary, and financial rewards (stock options and the like) is not the only motivator. People do not necessarily work better, harder, or more creatively, the more you pay them. Money works up to a certain level, but beyond that the real motivator is the challenge to grow, create, find meaning, and to invest your highest talents in a great cause. Money speaks to our Adam needs, but meaning speaks to our Abraham needs.

There is a truth here that Jews and Judaism have tended to note and live by more fully than many other civilisations and faiths. Most religions are *cultures of acceptance.* There is poverty, hunger, and disease on earth because that is the way the world is; that is how God made it and wants it. Yes, we can find happiness, nirvana, or bliss, but to achieve it you must escape from the world, by meditation, or retreating to a monastery, or by drugs, or trance, or by waiting patiently for the joy that awaits us in the world to come. Religion anaesthetises us to pain. That isn't Judaism at all. When it comes to the poverty and pain of the world, ours is a *religion of protest*, not acceptance. God does not want people to be poor, hungry, sick, oppressed, uneducated, deprived of rights, or subject to abuse. He has made us His agents in this cause. He wants us to be His partners in the work of redemption. That is why so many Jews have become doctors fighting disease, lawyers fighting injustice, or educators fighting ignorance. It is surely why they have produced so many pioneering (and Nobel Prize-winning) economists. As Michael Novak (citing Irving Kristol) writes:

> Jewish thought has always felt comfortable with a certain well-ordered worldliness, whereas the Christian has always felt a pull to otherworldliness. Jewish thought has had a candid orientation toward private property, whereas Catholic thought – articulated from an early period chiefly among priests and monks – has persistently tried to direct the attention of its adherents beyond the activities and interests of this world to the next. As a result, tutored by the law and the prophets, ordinary Jews have long felt more at home in this world, while ordinary Catholics have regarded this world as a valley of temptation and as a distraction from their proper business, which is preparation for the world to come.[2]

God is to be found in this world, not just the next. But for us to climb to spiritual heights we must first have satisfied our material needs. Abraham was greater than Adam, but Adam came before Abraham. When the physical world is harsh, the human spirit is broken, and people cannot then hear the word of God, even when delivered by a Moses.

---

2. Michael Novak, *This Hemisphere of Liberty* (Washington, DC: American Enterprise Institute, 1990), 64.

Levi Yitzhak of Berditchev said it well: "Don't worry about the state of someone else's soul and the needs of your body. Worry about the needs of someone else's body and the state of your own soul."

Alleviating poverty, curing disease, ensuring the rule of law, and respect for human rights: these are spiritual tasks no less than prayer and Torah study. To be sure, the latter are higher, but the former are prior. People cannot hear God's message if their spirit is broken and their labour harsh.

Bo

The Spiritual Child

The American writer Bruce Feiler published a best-selling book entitled *The Secrets of Happy Families.*[1] It's an engaging work that uses research largely drawn from fields like team building, problem solving, and conflict resolution to show how management techniques can also be used at home to help make families cohesive units that make space for personal growth.

At the end, however, he makes a very striking and unexpected point: "The single most important thing you can do for your family may be the simplest of all: develop a strong family narrative." He quotes a study from Emory University that the more children know about their family's story, "the stronger their sense of control over their lives, the higher their self-esteem, the more successfully they believe their family functions."[2]

A family narrative connects children to something larger than themselves. It helps them make sense of how they fit into the world that

1. Bruce Feiler, *The Secrets of Happy Families* (New York: William Morrow, 2013).
2. Ibid., 274. Feiler does not cite the source, but see: Jennifer G. Bohanek, Kelly A. Marin, Robyn Fivush, and Marshall P. Duke, "Family Narrative Interaction and Children's Sense of Self," *Family Process* 45.1 (2006): 39–54.

existed before they were born. It gives them the starting point of an identity. That in turn becomes the basis of confidence. It enables children to say: This is who I am. This is the story of which I am a part. These are the people who came before me and whose descendant I am. These are the roots of which I am the stem reaching upward toward the sun.

Nowhere was this point made more dramatically than by Moses in this *parasha*. The tenth plague is about to strike. Moses knows that this will be the last. Pharaoh will not merely let the people go. He will urge them to leave. So, on God's command, he prepares the people for freedom. But he does so in a way that is unique. He does not talk about liberty. He does not speak about breaking the chains of bondage. He does not even mention the arduous journey that lies ahead. Nor does he enlist their enthusiasm by giving them a glimpse of the destination, the Promised Land that God swore to Abraham, Isaac, and Jacob, the land of milk and honey.

He talks about children. Three times in the course of the *parasha* he turns to the theme:

> *And when your children ask you,* "What do you mean by this rite?" you shall say.... (Ex. 12:26–27)

> *And you shall explain to your child* on that day, "It is because of what the Lord did for me when I went free from Egypt." (13:8)

> *And when, in time to come, your child asks you,* saying, "What does this mean?" you shall say to him.... (v. 14)

This is wonderfully counter-intuitive. He doesn't speak about tomorrow but about the distant future. He does not celebrate the moment of liberation. Instead he wants to ensure that it will form part of the people's memory until the end of time. He wants each generation to pass on the story to the next. He wants Jewish parents to become educators, and Jewish children to be guardians of the past for the sake of the future. Inspired by God, Moses taught the Israelites the lesson arrived at via a different route by the Chinese: *If you plan for a year, plant rice. If you plan for a decade, plant a tree. If you plan for a century, educate a child.*

Jews became famous throughout the ages for putting education first. Where others built castles and palaces, Jews built schools and houses of study. From this flowed all the familiar achievements in which we take collective pride: the fact that Jews knew their texts even in ages of mass illiteracy; the record of Jewish scholarship and intellect; the astonishing over-representation of Jews among the shapers of the modern mind; the Jewish reputation, sometimes admired, sometimes feared, sometimes caricatured for mental agility, argument, debate, and the ability to see all sides of a disagreement.

But Moses' point wasn't simply this. God never commanded us: Thou shall win a Nobel Prize. What he wanted us to teach our children was a story. He wanted us to help our children understand who they are, where they came from, what happened to their ancestors to make them the distinctive people they became, and what moments in their history shaped their lives and dreams. He wanted us to give our children an identity by turning history into memory, and memory itself into a sense of responsibility. Jews were not summoned to be a nation of intellectuals. They were called on to be actors in a drama of redemption, a people invited by God to bring blessings into the world by the way they lived and sanctified life.

For some time now, along with many others in the West, we have sometimes neglected this deeply spiritual element of education. That is what makes Lisa Miller's recent book *The Spiritual Child*[3] an important reminder of a forgotten truth. Professor Miller teaches psychology and education at Columbia University and co-edits the journal *Spirituality in Clinical Practice*. Her book is not about Judaism or even religion as such, but specifically about the importance of parents encouraging the spirituality of the child.

Children are naturally spiritual. They are fascinated by the vastness of the universe and our place in it. They have the same sense of wonder that we find in some of the greatest of the psalms. They love stories, songs, and rituals. They like the shape and structure they give to time, and relationships, and the moral life. To be sure, sceptics and

---

3. Lisa Miller, *The Spiritual Child: The New Science on Parenting for Health and Lifelong Thriving* (New York: St Martin's Press, 2015).

atheists have often derided religion as a child's view of reality, but that only serves to strengthen the corollary, that a child's view of reality is instinctively, intuitively religious. Deprive a child of that by ridiculing faith, abandoning ritual, and focusing instead on academic achievement and other forms of success, and you starve him or her of some of the most important elements of emotional and psychological well-being. As Professor Miller shows, the research evidence is compelling. Children who grow up in homes where spirituality is part of the atmosphere at home are less likely to succumb to depression, substance abuse, aggression, and high-risk behaviours including physical risk-taking and "a sexuality devoid of emotional intimacy." Spirituality plays a part in a child's resilience, physical and mental health, and healing. It is a key dimension of adolescence and its intense search for identity and purpose. The teenage years often take the form of a spiritual quest. And when there is a cross generational bond through which children and parents come to share a sense of connection to something larger, an enormous inner strength is born. Indeed, the parent-child relationship, especially in Judaism, mirrors the relationship between God and us.

That is why Moses so often emphasises the role of the *question* in the process of education: "When your child asks you, saying..." – a feature ritualised at the Seder table in the form of the *Ma Nishtana*. Judaism is a questioning and argumentative faith, in which even the greatest ask questions of God, and in which the rabbis of the Mishna and Midrash constantly disagree. Rigid doctrinal faith that discourages questions, calling instead for blind obedience and submission, is psychologically damaging and fails to prepare a child for the complexity of real life. What is more, the Torah is careful, in the first paragraph of the *Shema*, to say, "You shall love the Lord your God" *before* saying, "You shall teach these things diligently to your children." Parenthood works when your children see that you love what you want them to learn.

The long walk to freedom, suggests this *parasha*, is not just a matter of history and politics, let alone miracles. It has to do with the relationship between parents and children. It is about telling the story and passing it on across the generations. It is about a sense of God's presence in our lives. It is about making space for transcendence, wonder, gratitude, humility, empathy, love, forgiveness, and compassion, ornamented by ritual, song, and prayer. These help to give a child confidence, trust, and hope, along with a sense of identity, belonging, and at-home-ness in the universe.

You cannot build a healthy society out of emotionally unhealthy families and angry and conflicted children. Faith begins in families. Hope is born in the home.

Beshallaḥ

Renewable Energy

T he first translation of the Torah into another language – Greek – took place in around the second century BCE, in Egypt during the reign of Ptolemy II. It is known as the Septuagint, in Hebrew *HaShivim*, because it was done by a team of seventy scholars. The Talmud, however, says that at various points the Sages at work on the project deliberately mistranslated certain texts because they believed that a literal translation would simply be unintelligible to a Greek readership. One of these texts was the phrase, "On the seventh day God finished all the work He had made." Instead, the translators wrote, "On the sixth day God finished."[1]

What was it that they thought the Greeks would not understand? How did the idea that God made the universe in six days make more sense than that He did so in seven? It seems puzzling, yet the answer is simple. The Greeks could not understand the seventh day, Shabbat, as itself part of the work of creation. What is creative about resting? What do we achieve by *not* making, *not* working, *not* inventing? The idea seems to make no sense at all.

Indeed, we have the independent testimony of the Greek writers of that period, that one of the things they ridiculed in Judaism was

---

1. Megilla 9a.

Shabbat. One day in seven Jews do not work, they said, because they are lazy. The idea that the day itself might have independent value was apparently beyond their comprehension. Oddly enough, within a very short period of time, the empire of Alexander the Great began to crumble, just as had the earlier city state of Athens that gave rise to some of the greatest thinkers and writers in history. Civilisations, like individuals, can suffer from burnout. It's what happens when you don't have a day of rest written into your schedule. As Ahad HaAm said, "More than the Jewish people has kept Shabbat, Shabbat has kept the Jewish people." Rest one day in seven and you won't burn out.

Shabbat, which we encounter for the first time in this *parasha*, is one of the greatest institutions the world has ever known. It changed the way the world thought about time. Prior to Judaism, people measured time either by the sun – the solar calendar of 365 days aligning us with the seasons – or by the moon, that is, by months ("month" comes from the word "moon") of roughly thirty days. The idea of the seven-day week – which has no counterpart in nature – was born in the Torah and spread throughout the world via Christianity and Islam, both of which borrowed it from Judaism, marking the difference simply by having it on a different day. We have years because of the sun, months because of the moon, and weeks because of the Jews.

What Shabbat did and still does is to create space within our lives and within society as a whole in which we are truly free. Free from the pressures of work; free from the demands of ruthless employers; free from the siren calls of a consumer society urging us to spend our way to happiness; free to be ourselves in the company of those we love. Somehow this one day has renewed its meaning in generation after generation, despite the most profound economic and industrial change. In Moses' day it meant freedom from slavery to Pharaoh. In the nineteenth and early twentieth century it meant freedom from sweatshop working conditions of long hours for little pay. In ours, it means freedom from emails, smartphones, and the demands of 24/7 availability.

What our *parasha* tells us is that Shabbat was among the first commands the Israelites received on leaving Egypt. Having complained about the lack of food, God told them that He would send them manna from heaven, but they were not to gather it on the seventh day. Instead, a double portion would fall on the sixth. That is why to this day we have two challot on Shabbat, in memory of that time.

Not only was Shabbat culturally unprecedented. Conceptually, it was so as well. Throughout history people have dreamed of an ideal world. We call such visions, utopias, from the Greek *ou* meaning "no" and *topos* meaning "place."[2] They are called that because no such dream has ever come true, except in one instance, namely Shabbat. Shabbat is "utopia now," because on it we create, for twenty-five hours a week, a world in which there are no hierarchies, no employers and employees, no buyers and sellers, no inequalities of wealth or power, no production, no traffic, no din of the factory or clamour of the marketplace. It is "the still point of the turning world," a pause between symphonic movements, a break between the chapters of our days, an equivalent in time of the open countryside between towns where you can feel the breeze and hear the song of birds. Shabbat is utopia, not as it will be at the end of time but rather, as we rehearse for it now in the midst of time.

God wanted the Israelites to begin their one-day-in-seven rehearsal of freedom almost as soon as they left Egypt, because real freedom, of the seven-days-in-seven kind, takes time, centuries, millennia. The Torah regards slavery as wrong,[3] but it did not abolish it immediately because people were not yet ready for this. Neither Britain nor America abolished it until the nineteenth century, and even then not without a struggle. Yet the outcome was inevitable once Shabbat

---

2. The word was coined in 1516 by Sir Thomas More, who used it as the title of his book.

3. On the wrongness of slavery from a Torah perspective, see the important analysis in Rabbi N. L. Rabinovitch, *Mesilot BiLevavam* (Maaleh Adumim: Maaliyot, 2015), 38–45. The basis of the argument is the view, central to both the Written Torah and the Mishna, that all humans share the same ontological dignity as the image and likeness of God. This was in the sharpest possible contrast to the views, for instance, of Plato and Aristotle. Rabbi Rabinovitch analyses the views of the Sages, and of Maimonides and Me'iri, on the phrase "They shall be your slaves forever" (Lev. 25:46). Note also the quote he brings from Job 31:13–15, "If I have denied justice to any of my servants…when they had a grievance against me, what will I do when God confronts me? What will I answer when called to account? Did not He who made me in the womb make them? Did not the same One form us both within our mothers?"

had been set in motion, because slaves who know freedom one day in seven will eventually rise against their chains.

The human spirit needs time to breathe, to inhale, to grow. The first rule in time management is to distinguish between matters that are *important*, and those that are merely *urgent*. Under pressure, the things that are important but not urgent tend to get crowded out. Yet these are often what matter most to our happiness and sense of a life well lived. Shabbat is time dedicated to the things that are important but not urgent: family, friends, community, a sense of sanctity, prayer in which we thank God for the good things in our life, and Torah reading in which we retell the long, dramatic story of our people and our journey. Shabbat is when we celebrate *shalom bayit* – the peace that comes from love and lives in the home blessed by the *Shekhina*, the presence of God you can almost feel in the candlelight, the wine, and the special bread. This is a beauty created not by Michelangelo or Leonardo but by each of us: a serene island of time in the midst of the often-raging sea of a restless world.

I once took part, together with the Dalai Lama, in a seminar (organised by the Elijah Institute) in Amritsar, Northern India, the sacred city of the Sikhs. In the course of the talks, delivered to an audience of two thousand Sikh students, one of the Sikh leaders turned to the students and said: "What we need is what the Jews have: Shabbat!" Just imagine, he said, a day dedicated every week to family and home and relationships. He could see its beauty. We can live its reality.

The ancient Greeks could not understand how a day of rest could be part of creation. Yet it is so, for without rest for the body, peace for the mind, silence for the soul, and a renewal of our bonds of identity and love, the creative process eventually withers and dies. It suffers entropy, the principle that all systems lose energy over time. The Jewish people did not lose energy over time, and remains as vital and creative as it ever was. The reason is Shabbat: humanity's greatest source of renewable energy, the day that gives us the strength to keep on creating.

Yitro

To Thank Before We Think

T he Ten Commandments are the most famous religious and moral code in history. Until recently they adorned American courtrooms. They still adorn most synagogue arks. Rembrandt gave them their classic artistic expression in his portrait of Moses, about to break the tablets on seeing the golden calf. John Rogers Herbert's massive painting of Moses bringing down the tablets of law dominates the main committee room of the House of Lords. The twin tablets with their ten commands are the enduring symbol of eternal law under the sovereignty of God.

It is worth remembering, of course, that the "ten commandments" are *not* Ten Commandments. The Torah calls them *aseret hadevarim* (Ex. 34:28), and tradition terms them *aseret hadibrot*, meaning the "ten words" or "ten utterances." We can understand this better in the light of documentary discoveries in the twentieth century, especially Hittite covenants or "suzerainty treaties" dating back to 1400–1200 BCE, that is, around the time of Moses and the exodus. These treaties often contained a twofold statement of the laws laid down in the treaty, first in general outline, then in specific detail. That is precisely the relationship between the "ten utterances" and the detailed commands of *Parashat Mishpatim* (Ex. 22–23). The former are the general outline, the basic principles of the law.

Usually they are portrayed, graphically and substantively, as two sets of five, the first dealing with relationships between us and God (including honouring our parents since they, like God, brought us into being), the second with the relations between us and our fellow humans.

However, it also makes sense to see them as three groups of three. The first three (one God, no other God, do not take God's name in vain) are about God, the Author and Authority of the laws. The second set (keep Shabbat, honour parents, do not murder) are about createdness. Shabbat reminds us of the birth of the universe. Our parents brought us into being. Murder is forbidden because we are all created in God's image (Gen. 9:6). The third three (don't commit adultery, don't steal, don't bear false witness) are about the basic institutions of society: the sanctity of marriage, the integrity of private property, and the administration of justice. Lose any of these and freedom begins to crumble.

This structure serves to emphasise what a strange command the tenth is: "Do not be envious of your neighbour's house. Do not be envious of your neighbour's wife, his slave, his maid, his ox, his donkey, or anything else that is your neighbour's." At least on the surface this is different from all the other rules, which involve speech or action.[1] Envy, covetousness, desiring what someone else has, is an emotion, not a thought, a word, or a deed. And surely we can't help our emotions. They used to be called the "passions," precisely because we are passive in relation to them. So how can envy be forbidden at all? Surely it only makes sense to command or forbid matters that are within our control. In any case, why should the occasional spasm of envy matter if it does not lead to anything harmful to other people?

Here, it seems to me, the Torah is conveying a series of fundamental truths we forget at our peril. First, as we have been reminded

---

1. To be sure, Maimonides held that the first command is to believe in God. *Halakhot Gedolot* as understood by Nahmanides, however, disagreed and maintained that the verse "I am the Lord who brought you out of the land of Egypt" is not a command but a prelude to the commands.

by cognitive behavioural therapy, what we believe affects what we feel.[2] Narcissists, for instance, are quick to take offence because they think other people are talking about or "dissing" (disrespecting) them, whereas often other people aren't interested in us at all. Their belief is false, but that does not stop them feeling angry and resentful.

Second, envy is one of the prime drivers of violence in society. It is what led Iago to mislead Othello with tragic consequences. Closer to home, it is what led Cain to murder Abel. It is what led Abraham and then Isaac to fear for their lives when famine forced them temporarily to leave home. They believed that, married as they were to attractive women, the local rulers would kill them so that they could take their wives into their harem.

Most poignantly, envy lay at the heart of the hatred of the brothers for Joseph. They resented his special treatment at the hands of their father, the richly embroidered cloak he wore, and his dreams of becoming the ruler of them all. That is what led them to contemplate killing him and eventually to sell him as a slave.

Rene Girard, in his classic *Violence and the Sacred*,[3] says that the most basic cause of violence is mimetic desire, that is, the desire to have what someone else has, which is ultimately the desire to be what someone else is. Envy can lead to breaking many of the other commands: it can move people to adultery, theft, false testimony, and even murder.[4]

Jews have especial reason to fear envy. It surely played a part in the existence of antisemitism throughout the centuries. Non-Jews envied Jews their ability to prosper in adversity – the strange phenomenon we noted in *Parashat Shemot* that "the more they afflicted them the more they grew and the more they spread." They also and especially envied them their sense of chosenness (despite the fact that virtually

---

2. This has long been part of Jewish thought. It is at the heart of Chabad philosophy as set out in Rabbi Schneur Zalman of Liadi's masterpiece, *Tanya*. Likewise, Ibn Ezra in his commentary to this verse says that we only covet what we feel to be within our reach. We do not envy those we know we could never become.

3. René Girard, *Violence and the Sacred* (Baltimore: John Hopkins University Press, 1979).

4. See Helmut Schoeck's classic, *Envy: a Theory of Social Behaviour* (New York: Harcourt, Brace & World, 1969). See also Joseph Epstein, *Envy* (New York: New York Public Library, 2003).

every other nation in history has seen itself as chosen).[5] It is absolutely essential that we, as Jews, should conduct ourselves with an extra measure of humility and modesty.

So the prohibition of envy is not odd at all. It is the most basic force undermining the social harmony and order that are the aim of the Ten Commandments as a whole. Not only though do they forbid it; they also help us rise above it. It is precisely the first three commands, reminding us of God's presence in history and our lives, and the second three, reminding us of our createdness, that help us rise above envy.

We are here because God wanted us to be. We have what God wanted us to have. Why then should we seek what others have? If what matters most in our lives is how we appear in the eyes of God, why should we want anything else merely because someone else has it? It is when we *stop* defining ourselves in relation to God and start defining ourselves in relation to other people that competition, strife, covetousness, and envy enter our minds, and they lead only to unhappiness.

If your new car makes me envious, I may be motivated to buy a more expensive model that I never needed in the first place, which will give me satisfaction for a few days until I discover another neighbour who has an even more costly vehicle, and so it goes. Should I succeed in satisfying my own envy, I will do so only at the cost of provoking yours, in a cycle of conspicuous consumption that has no natural end. Hence the bumper sticker: "He who has the most toys when he dies, wins." The operative word here is "toys," for this is the ethic of the kindergarten, and it should have no place in a mature life.

The antidote to envy is gratitude. "Who is rich?" asked Ben Zoma, and replied, "One who rejoices in what he has." There is a beautiful Jewish practice that, performed daily, is life-transforming. The first words we say on waking are *Modeh ani lefanekha*, "I thank You, living and eternal King." *We thank before we think.*

Judaism is gratitude with attitude. Cured of letting other people's happiness diminish our own, we release a wave of positive energy allowing us to celebrate what we have instead of thinking about what other people have, and to be what we are instead of wanting to be what we are not.

---

5. See Anthony Smith, *Chosen Peoples* (Oxford: Oxford University Press, 2003).

Mishpatim

Doing and Hearing

O ne of the most famous phrases in the Torah makes its appearance in this *parasha*. It has often been used to characterise Jewish faith as a whole. It consists of two words: *naaseh venishma*, literally, "we will do and we will hear" (Ex. 24:7). What does this mean and why does it matter?

There are two famous interpretations, one ancient, the other modern. The first appears in the Babylonian Talmud,[1] where it is taken to describe the enthusiasm and whole-heartedness with which the Israelites accepted the covenant with God at Mount Sinai. When they said to Moses, "All that the Lord has spoken we will do and we will hear," they were saying, in effect: Whatever God asks of us, we will do – saying this *before they had heard any of the commandments*. The words, "We will hear," imply that they had not yet heard – neither the Ten Commandments, nor the detailed laws that followed as set out in our *parasha*. So keen were they to signal their assent to God that they agreed to His demands before knowing what they were.[2]

---

1. Shabbat 88a–b.
2. There are, of course, quite different interpretations of the Israelites' assent. According to one, God "suspended the mountain over them," giving them no choice but to agree or die (Shabbat 88a).

This reading, adopted also by Rashi in his commentary to the Torah, is difficult because it depends on reading the narrative out of chronological sequence (using the principle that "there is no before and after in the Torah"). The events of chapter 24, according to this interpretation, happened before chapter 20, the account of the revelation at Mount Sinai and the Ten Commandments. Ibn Ezra, Rashbam, and Nahmanides all disagree and read the chapters in chronological sequence. For them, the words *naaseh venishma* mean not, "we will do and we will hear," but simply, "we will do and we will obey."

The second interpretation – not the plain sense of the text but important nonetheless – has been given often in modern Jewish thought. On this view *naaseh venishma* means, "We will do and we will *understand*."[3] From this they derive the conclusion that we can only understand Judaism by doing it, by performing the commands and living a Jewish life. In the beginning is the deed.[4] Only then comes the grasp, the insight, the comprehension.

This is a signal and substantive point. The modern Western mind tends to put things in the opposite order. We seek to understand what we are committing ourselves to before making the commitment. That is fine when what is at stake is signing a contract, buying a new mobile phone, or purchasing a subscription, but not when making a deep existential commitment. The only way to understand leadership is to lead. The only way to understand marriage is to get married. The only way to understand whether a certain career path is right for you is to actually try it for an extended period. Those who hover on the edge of a commitment, reluctant to make a decision until all the facts are in, will eventually find that life has passed them by.[5] The only way to understand a

---

3. The word already carries this meaning in biblical Hebrew as in the story of the Tower of Babel, where God says, "Come let us confuse their language so that people will not be able to understand their neighbour."
4. This is the famous phrase from Goethe's *Faust*.
5. This is similar to the point made by Bernard Williams in his famous essay, "Moral Luck," that there are certain decisions – his example is Gauguin's decision to leave his career and family and go to Tahiti to paint – about which we cannot know whether they are the right decision until after we have taken them and seen how they work out. All such existential decisions involve risk.

way of life is to take the risk of living it.[6] So: *Naaseh venishma,* "We will do and eventually, through extended practice and long exposure, we will understand."

In my introduction to this book I suggested a quite different, third interpretation, based on the fact that the Israelites are described by the Torah as ratifying the covenant three times: once before they heard the commandments and twice afterward. There is a fascinating difference between the way the Torah describes the first two of these responses and the third:

> The people all *responded together,* "We will do [*naaseh*] everything the Lord has said." (Ex. 19:8)

> When Moses went and told the people all the Lord's words and laws, they *responded with one voice,* "Everything the Lord has said we will do [*naaseh*]." (24:3)

> Then he took the Book of the Covenant and read it to the people. They *responded,* "We will do and hear [*naaseh venishma*] everything the Lord has said." (24:7)

The first two responses, which refer only to action (*naaseh*), are given unanimously. The people respond "together." They do so "with one voice." The third, which refers not only to doing but also to hearing (*nishma*), involves no unanimity. "Hearing" here means many things: listening, paying attention, understanding, absorbing, internalising, responding, and obeying. It refers, in other words, to *the spiritual, inward dimension of Judaism.*

From this, an important consequence follows. Judaism is a *community of doing* rather than of "hearing." There is an authoritative code

---

6. This, incidentally, is the Verstehen approach to sociology and anthropology; namely that cultures cannot be fully understood from the outside. They need to be experienced from within. That is one of the key differences between the social sciences and the natural sciences.

of Jewish law. When it comes to halakha, the way of Jewish doing, we seek consensus.

By contrast, though there are undoubtedly principles of Jewish faith, *when it comes to spirituality there is no single normative Jewish approach.* Judaism has had its priests and prophets, its rationalists and mystics, its philosophers and poets. Tanakh, the Hebrew Bible, speaks in a multiplicity of voices. Isaiah was not Ezekiel. The book of Proverbs comes from a different mindset than the books of Amos and Hosea. The Torah contains law and narrative, history and mystic vision, ritual and prayer. There are norms about how to act as Jews. But there are few about how to think and feel as Jews.

We experience God in different ways. Some find Him in nature, in what Wordsworth called "a sense sublime / Of something far more deeply interfused, / Whose dwelling is the light of setting suns, / And the round ocean and the living air."[7] Others find Him in interpersonal emotion, in the experience of loving and being loved – what R. Akiva meant when he said that in a true marriage, "the Divine Presence is between" husband and wife.

Some find God in the prophetic call: "Let justice roll down like a river, and righteousness like a never-failing stream" (Amos 5:24). Others find Him in study, "rejoicing in the words of Your Torah ... for they are our life and the length of our days; on them we will meditate day and night."[8] Yet others find Him in prayer, discovering that God is close to all who call on Him in truth.

There are those who find God in joy, dancing and singing as did King David when he brought the Holy Ark into Jerusalem. Others – or the same people at different points in their life – find Him in the depths, in tears and remorse, and a broken heart. Einstein found God in the "fearful symmetry" and ordered complexity of the universe. Rav Kook found Him in the harmony of diversity. Rav Soloveitchik found Him in the loneliness of being as it reaches out to the soul of Being itself.

---

7. William Wordsworth, "Lines Composed a Few Miles Above Tintern Abbey, on Revisiting the Banks of the Wye during a Tour, July 13, 1798."
8. From the blessing before *Shema* said in the evening prayer.

There is a normative way of performing the holy deed, but there are many ways of hearing the holy voice, encountering the sacred presence, feeling at one and the same time how small we are yet how great the universe we inhabit, how insignificant we must seem when set against the vastness of space and the myriads of stars, yet how momentously significant we are, knowing that God has set His image and likeness upon us and placed us here, in this place, at this time, with these gifts, in these circumstances, with a task to perform if we are able to discern it. We can find God on the heights and in the depths, in loneliness and togetherness, in love and fear, in gratitude and need, in dazzling light and in the midst of deep darkness. We can find God by seeking Him, but sometimes He finds us when we least expect it.

That is the difference between *naaseh* and *nishma*. We do the Godly deed "together." We respond to His commands "with one voice." But we hear God's presence in many ways, for though God is one, we are all different, and we encounter Him each in our own way.

Teruma

The Gift of Giving

I t was the first Israelite house of worship, the first home Jews made for God. But the very idea is fraught with paradox, even contradiction. How can you build a house for God? He is bigger than anything we can imagine, let alone build.

King Solomon made this point when he inaugurated another house of God, the First Temple: "But will God really dwell on earth? The heavens, even the highest heaven, cannot contain You. How much less this house I have built!" (I Kings 8:27). So did Isaiah in the name of God Himself: "Heaven is My throne, and the earth is My footstool. What house can you build for Me? Where will My resting place be?" (Is. 66:1).

Not only does it seem impossible to build a home for God. It should be unnecessary. The God of everywhere can be accessed anywhere, as readily in the deepest pit as on the highest mountain, in a city slum as in a palace lined with marble and gold.

The answer, and it is fundamental, is that God does not live in buildings. He lives in builders. He lives not in structures of stone but in the human heart. What the Jewish Sages and mystics pointed was that in our *parasha* God says, "Let them build Me a sanctuary that I may dwell in *them*" (Ex. 25:8), not "that I may dwell in *it*."

Why then did God command the people to make a sanctuary at all? The answer given by most commentators, and hinted at by the Torah itself, is that God gave the command specifically after the sin of the golden calf.

The people made the calf after Moses had been on the mountain for forty days to receive the Torah. So long as Moses was in their midst, the people knew that he communicated with God, and God with him, and therefore God was accessible, close. But when he was absent for nearly six weeks, they panicked. Who else could bridge the gap between the people and God? How could they hear God's instructions? Through what intermediary could they make contact with the Divine Presence?

That is why God said to Moses, "Let them build Me a sanctuary that I may dwell among them." The key word here is the verb SH-KH-N, to dwell. Never before had it been used in connection with God. It eventually became a keyword of Judaism itself. From it came the word *Mishkan* meaning a sanctuary, and *Shekhina*, the Divine Presence.

Central to its meaning is the idea of closeness. *Shakhen* in Hebrew means a neighbour, the person who lives next door. What the Israelites needed and what God gave them was a way of feeling as close to God as to our next-door neighbour.

That is what the patriarchs and matriarchs had. God spoke to Abraham, Isaac, and Jacob, Sarah, Rebecca, Rachel, and Leah intimately, like a friend. He told Abraham and Sarah that they would have a child. He explained to Rebecca why she was suffering such acute pain in pregnancy. He appeared to Jacob at key moments in his life telling him not to be afraid.

That is not what the Israelites had experienced until now. They had seen God bringing plagues on the Egyptians. They had seen Him divide the sea. They had seen Him send manna from heaven and water from a rock. They had heard His commanding voice at Mount Sinai and found it almost unbearable. They said to Moses, "Speak to us yourself and we will listen. But do not have God speak to us or we will die." God had appeared to them as an overwhelming presence, an irresistible force, a light so bright that to look at it makes you blind, a voice so strong it makes you go deaf.

So for God to be accessible, not just to the pioneers of faith – the patriarchs and matriarchs – but to every member of a large nation, was a challenge, as it were, for God Himself. He had to do what the Jewish mystics called *tzimtzum*, "contract" Himself, screen His light, soften His voice, hide His glory within a thick cloud, and allow the infinite to take on the dimensions of the finite.

But that, as it were, was the easy part. The difficult part had nothing to do with God and everything to do with us. How do we come to sense the presence of God? It isn't difficult to do so standing at the foot of Mount Everest or seeing the Grand Canyon. You do not have to be very religious, or even religious at all, to feel awe in the presence of the sublime. The psychologist Abraham Maslow, whom we encountered in *Parashat Va'era*, spoke about "peak experiences," and saw them as the essence of the spiritual encounter.

But how do you feel the presence of God in the midst of everyday life? Not from the top of Mount Sinai but from the plain beneath? Not when it is surrounded by thunder and lightning as it was at the great revelation, but today, just a day among days?

That is the life-transforming secret of the name of the *parasha*, *Teruma*. It means "a contribution." God said to Moses: "Tell the Israelites to take for Me a contribution. You are to receive the contribution for Me from everyone whose heart prompts them to give" (25:2). The best way of encountering God is to give.

The very act of giving flows from, or leads to, the understanding that what we give is part of what we were given. It is a way of giving thanks, an act of gratitude. That is the difference in the human mind between the presence of God and the absence of God.

If God is present, it means that what we have is His. He created the universe. He made us. He gave us life. He breathed into us the very air we breathe. All around us is the majesty, the plenitude, of God's generosity: the light of the sun, the gold of the stone, the green of the leaves, the song of the birds. This is what we feel reading the great creation psalms we recite every day in the morning service. The world is God's art gallery and His masterpieces are everywhere.

When life is a given, you acknowledge this by giving back.

But *if life is not a given because there is no Giver,* if the universe came into existence only because of a random fluctuation in the quantum field, if there is nothing in the universe that knows we exist, if there is nothing to the human body but a string of letters in the genetic code, and to the human mind but electrical impulses in the brain, if our moral convictions are self-serving means of self-preservation, and our spiritual aspirations mere delusions, then it is difficult to feel gratitude for the gift of life. There is no gift if there is no giver. There is only a series of meaningless accidents, and it is difficult to feel gratitude for an accident.

The Torah therefore tells us something simple and practical. Give, and you will come to see life as a gift. *You don't need to be able to prove God exists. All you need is to be thankful that you exist – and the rest will follow.*

That is how God came to be close to the Israelites through the building of the sanctuary. It wasn't the quality of the wood and metals and drapes. It wasn't the glitter of jewels on the breastplate of the high priest. It wasn't the beauty of the architecture or the smell of the sacrifices. It was the fact that it was built out of the gifts of "everyone whose heart prompts them to give" (25:2). *Where people give voluntarily to one another and to holy causes, that is where the Divine Presence rests.*

Hence the special word that gives its name to this *parasha*: *Teruma*. I've translated it as "a contribution" but it actually has a subtly different meaning for which there is no simple English equivalent. It means "something you lift up" by dedicating it to a sacred cause. *You lift it up, then it lifts you up.* The best way of scaling the spiritual heights is simply to give in gratitude for the fact that you have been given.

God doesn't live in a house of stone. He lives in the hearts of those who give.

Tetzaveh

Inspiration and Perspiration

Beethoven rose each morning at dawn and made himself coffee. He was fastidious about this: each cup had to be made with exactly sixty beans, which he counted out each time. He would then sit at his desk and compose until 2:00 p.m. or 3:00 p.m. in the afternoon. Subsequently he would go for a long walk, taking with him a pencil and some sheets of music paper to record any ideas that came to him on the way. Each night after supper he would have a beer, smoke a pipe, and go to bed early, 10:00 p.m. at the latest.

Anthony Trollope who as his day job worked for the Post Office, paid a groom to wake him every day at 5:00 a.m. By 5:30 a.m. he would be at his desk, and he then proceeded to write for exactly three hours, working against the clock to produce 250 words each quarter-hour. This way he wrote forty-seven novels, many of them three volumes in length, as well as sixteen other books. If he finished a novel before the day's three hours were over, he would immediately take a fresh piece of paper and begin the next.

Immanuel Kant, the most brilliant philosopher of modern times, was famous for his routine. As Heinrich Heine put it, "Getting up, drinking coffee, writing, giving lectures, eating, taking a walk, everything had its set time, and the neighbours knew precisely that the time was 3:30 p.m. when Kant stepped outside his door with his grey coat and the Spanish stick in his hand."

These details, together with more than 150 other examples drawn from the great philosophers, artists, composers, and writers come from a book by Mason Currey entitled *Daily Rituals: How Great Minds Make Time, Find Inspiration, and Get to Work*.[1] The book's point is simple. Most creative people have daily rituals. These form the soil in which the seeds of their invention grow.

In some cases they deliberately took on jobs they did not need to do, simply to establish structure and routine in their lives. A typical example was the poet Wallace Stevens, who took a position as an insurance lawyer at the Hartford Accident and Indemnity Company where he worked until his death. He said that having a job was one of the best things that could happen to him because "it introduces discipline and regularity into one's life."

Note the paradox. These were all innovators, pioneers, groundbreakers, trail-blazers, who formulated new ideas, originated new forms of expression, did things no one had done before in quite that way. They broke the mould. They changed the landscape. They ventured into the unknown.

Yet their daily lives were the opposite: ritualised and routine. One could even call them boring. Why so? Because – the saying is famous, though we don't know who first said it – *genius is one per cent inspiration, ninety-nine per cent perspiration*. The paradigm-shifting scientific discovery, the path-breaking research, the wildly successful new product, the brilliant novel, the award-winning film are almost always the result of many years of long hours and attention to detail. Being creative involves hard work.

The ancient Hebrew word for hard work is *avoda*. It is also the word that means "serving God." *What applies in the arts, sciences, business, and industry, applies equally to the life of the spirit.* Achieving any form of spiritual growth requires sustained effort and daily rituals.

---

1. Mason Currey, *Daily Rituals* (New York: Knopf, 2013).

Hence the remarkable aggadic passage in which various Sages put forward their idea of *klal gadol baTorah*, "the great principle of the Torah." Ben Azzai says it is the verse, "This is the book of the chronicles of man: On the day that God created man, He made him in the likeness of God" (Gen. 5:1). Ben Zoma says that there is a more embracing principle, "Listen, Israel, the Lord our God, the Lord is one" (Deut. 6:4). Ben Nannas says there is a yet more embracing principle: "Love your neighbour as yourself" (Lev. 19:18). Ben Pazzi says we find a more embracing principle still. He quotes a verse from this *parasha*: "One sheep shall be offered in the morning, and a second in the afternoon" (Ex. 29:39) – or, as we might say nowadays, *Shaḥarit, Minḥa,* and *Maariv*. In a word: "routine." The passage concludes: The law follows Ben Pazzi.[2]

The meaning of Ben Pazzi's statement is clear: all the high ideals in the world – the human person as God's image, belief in God's unity, and the love of neighbour – count for little until they are turned into habits of action that become habits of the heart. We can all recall moments of insight when we had a great idea, a transformative thought, the glimpse of a project that could change our lives. A day, a week, or a year later the thought has been forgotten or become a distant memory, at best a might-have-been.

The people who change the world, whether in small or epic ways, are those who turn peak experiences into daily routines, who know that the details matter, and who have developed the discipline of hard work, sustained over time.

Judaism's greatness is that it takes high ideals and exalted visions – image of God, faith in God, love of neighbour – and turns them into patterns of behaviour. Halakha (Jewish law) involves a set of routines that – like those of the great creative minds – reconfigures the brain, giving discipline to our lives and changing the way we feel, think, and act.

Much of Judaism must seem to outsiders, and sometimes to insiders also, boring, prosaic, mundane, repetitive, routine, obsessed with details, and bereft for the most part of drama or inspiration. Yet that is

---

2. The passage is cited in the introduction to the commentary *HaKotev* on *Ein Yaakov*, the collected aggadic passages of the Talmud. It is also quoted by Maharal in *Netivot Olam, Ahavat Re'a* 1.

precisely what writing the novel, composing the symphony, directing the film, perfecting the killer app, or building a billion-dollar business is, most of the time. It is a matter of hard work, focused attention, and daily rituals. That is where all sustainable greatness comes from.

We have developed in the West a strange view of religious experience: that it's what overwhelms you when something happens completely outside the run of normal experience. You climb a mountain and look down. You are miraculously saved from danger. You find yourself part of a vast and cheering crowd. It's how the German Lutheran theologian Rudolf Otto (1869–1937) defined "the holy": as a mystery (*mysterium*) both terrifying (*tremendum*) and fascinating (*fascinans*). You are awed by the presence of something vast. We have all had such experiences.

But that is all they are: experiences. They linger in the memory, but they are not part of everyday life. They are not woven into the texture of our character. They do not affect what we do or achieve or become. Judaism is about changing us so that we become creative artists whose greatest creation is our own life.[3] And that needs daily rituals: *Shaḥarit, Minḥa, Maariv*, the food we eat, the way we behave at work or in the home, the choreography of holiness which is the special contribution of the priestly dimension of Judaism, set out in this *parasha* and throughout the book of Leviticus.

These rituals have an effect. We now know through PET and fMRI scans that repeated spiritual exercise reconfigures the brain. It gives us inner resilience. It makes us more grateful. It gives us a sense of basic trust in the source of our being. It shapes our identity, the way we act and talk and think. Ritual is to spiritual greatness what practice is to a tennis player, daily writing disciplines are to a novelist, and reading company accounts are to Warren Buffett. They are the precondition of high achievement. Serving God is *avoda*, which means hard work.

If you seek sudden inspiration, then work at it every day for a year or a lifetime. That is how it comes. As a famous golfer is said to have said when asked for the secret of his success: "I was just lucky. But the funny thing is that the harder I practise, the luckier I become." The more you seek spiritual heights, the more you need the ritual and routine of halakha, the Jewish "way" to God.

---

3. A point made by Rabbi Joseph Soloveitchik in his book *Halakhic Man*.

Ki Tissa

The Closeness of God

T he more I study the Torah, the more conscious I become of the immense mystery of Exodus 33. This is the chapter set in the middle of the golden calf narrative, between chapter 32 describing the sin and its consequences, and chapter 34, God's revelation to Moses of the "thirteen attributes of mercy," the second set of tablets, and the renewal of the covenant. It is, I believe, this mystery that frames the shape of Jewish spirituality.

What makes chapter 33 perplexing is, first, that it is not clear what it is about. What was Moses doing? In the previous chapter he had already prayed twice for the people to be forgiven. In chapter 34 he prays for forgiveness again. What then was he trying to achieve in chapter 33?

Second, Moses' requests are strange. He says, "Show me now Your ways" and "Show me now Your glory" (33:13, 33:18). These seem more requests for metaphysical understanding or mystical experience than for forgiveness. They have to do with Moses as an individual, not with the people on whose behalf he was praying. This was a moment of national crisis. God was angry. The people were traumatised. The whole nation was in disarray. This was not the time for Moses to ask for a seminar in theology.

Third, more than once the narrative seems to be going backward in time. In verse 4, for example, it says, "No man put on his ornaments," then in the next verse God says, "Now, then, remove your ornaments." In verse 14, God says, "My presence will go with you." In verse 15, Moses says, "If Your presence does not go with us, do not make us leave this place." In both cases, time seems to be reversed: the second sentence is responded to by the one before. The Torah is clearly drawing our attention to something, but what?

Add to this the mystery of the calf itself – was it or was it not an idol? The text states that the people said, "This, Israel, is your God who brought you out of Egypt" (32:4). But it also says that they sought the calf because they did not know what had happened to *Moses*. Were they seeking a replacement for him or for God? What was their sin?

Surrounding it all is the larger mystery of the precise sequence of events involved in the long passages about the *Mishkan*, before and after the golden calf. What was the relationship between the Sanctuary and the calf?

At the heart of the mystery is the odd and troubling detail of verses 7–11. This tells us that Moses took his tent and pitched it *outside the camp*. What has this to do with the subject at hand, namely the relationship between God and the people after the golden calf? In any case, it was surely the worst possible thing for Moses to do at that time under those circumstances. God had just announced that "I will not go in your midst" (33:3). At this, the people were deeply distressed. They "went into mourning" (33:4). For Moses, then, to leave the camp must have been doubly demoralising. At times of collective distress, a leader has to be close to the people, not distant.

There are many ways of reading this cryptic text, but it seems to me that the most powerful and simple interpretation is this. Moses was making his most audacious prayer, so audacious that the Torah does not state it directly and explicitly. We have to reconstruct it from anomalies and clues within the text itself.

The previous chapter implied that the people panicked because of the absence of Moses, their leader. God Himself implied as much when He said to Moses, "Go down, because *your* people, whom *you* brought up out of Egypt, have become corrupt" (32:7). The suggestion is that Moses' absence or distance was the cause of the sin. He should have stayed closer to the people. Moses took the point. He did go down. He did punish the guilty. He did pray for God to forgive the people. That was the theme of chapter 32. But in chapter 33, having restored order to the people, Moses now began on an entirely new line of approach. He was, in effect, saying to God: What the people need is not for *me* to be close to them. I am just a human, here today, gone tomorrow. But You are eternal. You are their God. They need *You* to be close to them.

It was as if Moses was saying: Until now, they have experienced You as a terrifying, elemental force, delivering plague after plague to the Egyptians, bringing the world's greatest empire to its knees, dividing the sea, overturning the very order of nature itself. At Mount Sinai, merely hearing Your voice, they were so overwhelmed that they said, if we continue to hear the voice, "we will die" (Ex. 20:16). The people needed, said Moses, to experience not the *greatness* of God but the *closeness* of God, not God heard in thunder and lightning at the top of the mountain, but as a perpetual presence in the valley below.

That is why Moses removed his tent and pitched it outside the camp, as if to say to God: It is not my presence the people need in their midst, but Yours. That is why Moses sought to understand the very nature of God Himself. Is it possible for God to be close to where people are? Can transcendence become immanence? Can the God who is vaster than the universe live within the universe in a predictable, comprehensible way, not just in the form of miraculous intervention?

To this, God replied in a highly structured way. First, He said, you cannot understand My ways. "I will be gracious to whom I will be gracious and I will show mercy to whom I will show mercy" (33:19). There is an element of divine justice that must always elude human comprehension. We cannot fully enter into the mind of another human being, how much less so the mind of the Creator Himself.

Second, "You cannot see My face, for no one can see Me and live" (33:20). Humans can at best "see My back." Even when God intervenes in history, we can see this only in retrospect, looking back. Steven Hawking was wrong.[1] Even if we decode every scientific mystery, we still will not know the mind of God.

---

1. He famously said, at the end of *A Brief History of Time* (New York: Bantam Books, 1988), that if we were to reach a full scientific understanding of the cosmos, we would "know the mind of God."

However, third, you *can* see My "glory." That is what Moses asked for once he realised that he could never know God's "ways" or see His "face." That is what God caused to pass by as Moses stood "in a cleft of the rock" (v. 22). We do not know at this stage, exactly what is meant by God's glory, but we discover this at the very end of the book of Exodus. Chapters 35–40 describe how the Israelites built the *Mishkan*. When it is finished and assembled we read this:

> Then the cloud covered the tent of meeting, and *the glory of the Lord* filled the *Mishkan*. Moses could not enter the tent of meeting because the cloud had settled on it, and *the glory of the Lord* filled the *Mishkan*. (40:34–35)

We now understand the entire drama set in motion by the making of the golden calf. Moses pleaded with God to come closer to the people, so that they would encounter Him, not only at unrepeatable moments in the form of miracles, but regularly, on a daily basis, and not only as a force that threatens to obliterate all it touches, but as a presence that can be sensed in the heart of the camp.

That is why God commanded Moses to instruct the people to build the Mishkan. It is what He meant when He said: "Let them make Me a sanctuary and I will dwell (*veshakhanti*) among them" (25:8). It is from this verb that we get the word *Mishkan*, "Tabernacle," and the post-biblical word *Shekhina*, meaning the Divine Presence. Applied to God, as discussed above in *Parashat Teruma*, it means "the presence that is close." If this is so – and it is the way Judah Halevi understood the text[2] – then the entire institution of the *Mishkan* was a divine response to the sin of the golden calf, and an acceptance by God of Moses' plea that He come close to the people. We cannot see God's *face*; we cannot understand God's *ways*; but we can encounter God's *glory* whenever we build a home for His presence here on earth.

That is the ongoing miracle of Jewish spirituality. No one before the birth of Judaism ever envisaged God in such abstract and awe-inspiring ways: God is more distant than the furthest star and more eternal than

2. Judah Halevi, *The Kuzari*, 1:97.

time itself. Yet no religion has ever felt God to be closer. In Tanakh the prophets argue with God. In the book of Psalms King David speaks to Him in terms of utmost intimacy. In the Talmud God listens to the debates between the Sages and accepts their rulings even when they go against a heavenly voice. God's relationship with Israel, said the prophets, is like that between a parent and a child, or between a husband and a wife. In the Song of Songs it is like that between two infatuated lovers. The Zohar, key text of Jewish mysticism, uses the most daring language of passion, as does *Yedid Nefesh*, the poem attributed to the sixteenth-century Safed kabbalist, Rabbi Elazar Azikri.

That is one of the striking differences between the synagogues and the cathedrals of the Middle Ages. *In a cathedral you sense the vastness of God and the smallness of humankind. But in the Altneushul in Prague or the synagogues of the Ari and Rabbi Joseph Karo in Safed, you sense the closeness of God and the potential greatness of humankind.* Many nations worship God, but Jews are the only people to count themselves His close relatives ("My child, My firstborn, Israel" – Ex. 4:22).

Between the lines of Exodus 33, if we listen attentively enough, we sense the emergence of one of the most distinctive and paradoxical features of Jewish spirituality. No religion has ever held God higher, but none has ever felt Him closer. That is what Moses sought and achieved in chapter 33, in his most daring conversation with God.

Vayak'hel

The Social Animal

At the beginning of this *parasha* Moses performs a *tikkun*, a mending of the past, namely the sin of the golden calf. The Torah signals this by using essentially the same word at the beginning of both episodes. It eventually became a key word in Jewish spirituality: K-H-L, "to gather, assemble, congregate." From it we get the words *kahal* and *kehilla*, meaning "community." Far from being merely an ancient concern, it remains at the heart of our humanity. As we will see, recent scientific research confirms the extraordinary power of communities and social networks to shape our lives.

First, the biblical story. The episode of the golden calf began with these words: "When the people saw that Moses was so long in coming down from the mountain, they gathered themselves [*vayikahel*] around Aaron" (Ex. 32:1). At the beginning of this *parasha*, having won God's forgiveness and brought down a second set of tablets, Moses began the work of rededicating the people: "Moses assembled [*vayak'hel*] the entire Israelite congregation" (Ex. 35:1). They had sinned as a community. Now they were about to be reconstituted as a community. Jewish spirituality is first and foremost a communal spirituality.

Note, too, exactly what Moses does in this *parasha*. He directs their attention to the two great centres of community in Judaism, one in space, the other in time. The one in time is Shabbat. The one in space was the

Mishkan, the Tabernacle, that led eventually to the Temple and later to the synagogue. These are where the *kehilla* lives most powerfully: on Shabbat when we lay aside our private devices and desires and come together as a community; and the synagogue, where community has its home. Judaism attaches immense significance to the individual. Every life is like a universe. Each one of us, though we are all in God's image, is different, therefore unique and irreplaceable. Yet the first time the words "not good" appear in the Torah are in the verse, "It is not good for man to be alone" (Gen. 2:18). Much of Judaism is about the shape and structure of our togetherness. It values the individual but does not endorse individualism.

Ours is a religion of community. Our holiest prayers can only be said in the presence of a *minyan*, the minimum definition of a community. When we pray, we do so as a community. Martin Buber spoke of I-and-Thou, but Judaism is really a matter of We-and-Thou. Hence, to atone for the sin the Israelites committed as a community, Moses sought to consecrate community in time and place.

This has become one of the fundamental differences between tradition and the contemporary culture of the West. We can trace this in the titles of three landmark books about American society. In 1950, David Riesman, Nathan Glazer, and Reuel Denney published an insightful book about the changing character of Americans, called *The Lonely Crowd*. In 2000, Robert Putnam of Harvard published *Bowling Alone*, an account of how more Americans than ever were going ten-pin bowling, but fewer were joining bowling clubs and leagues. In 2011, Sherry Turkle of MIT published a book on the impact of smartphones and social networking software called *Alone Together*.

Listen to those titles. They are each about the advancing tide of loneliness, successive stages in the long, extended breakdown of community in modern life. Robert Bellah put it eloquently when he wrote that "social ecology is damaged not only by war, genocide, and political repression. It is also damaged by the destruction of the subtle ties that bind human beings to one another, leaving them frightened and alone."[1]

---

1. Robert Bellah et al., *Habits of the Heart: Individualism and Commitment in American Life* (Berkeley: University of California Press, 1985), 284.

That is why the two themes of *Parashat Vayak'hel* – Shabbat and the *Mishkan*, today the synagogue – remain powerfully contemporary. They are antidotes to the attenuation of community. They help restore "the subtle ties that bind human beings to one another." They reconnect us to community.

Consider Shabbat. Michael Walzer, the Princeton political philosopher, draws attention to the difference between holidays and holy days (or as he puts it, between vacations and Shabbat).[2] The idea of a vacation as a private holiday is relatively recent. Walzer dates it to the 1870s. Its essence is its individualist (or familial) character. "Everyone plans his own vacation, goes where he wants to go, does what he wants to do." Shabbat, by contrast, is essentially collective: "You, your son and daughter, your male and female servant, your ox, your donkey, your other animals, and the stranger in your gates" (Deut. 5:14). It is public, shared, the property of us all. A vacation is a commodity. We buy it. Shabbat is not something we buy. It is available to each on the same terms: "enjoined for everyone, enjoyed by everyone." We take vacations as individuals or families. We celebrate Shabbat as a community.

Something similar is true about the synagogue – the Jewish institution, unique in its day, that was eventually adopted by Christianity and Islam in the form of the church and mosque. We noted above Robert Putnam's argument in *Bowling Alone*, that Americans were becoming more individualistic. There was a loss, he said, of "social capital," that is, the ties that bind us together in shared responsibility for the common good.

A decade later, Putnam revised his thesis.[3] Social capital, he said, still exists, and you can find it in churches and synagogues. Regular attendees at a place of worship were – so his research showed – more likely than others to give money to charity, engage in voluntary work, donate blood, spend time with someone who is depressed, offer a seat to a stranger, help find someone a job, and many other measures of civic, moral, and philanthropic activism. They are, quite simply, more public spirited than others. *Regular attendance at a house of worship is the most*

---

2. Michael Walzer, *Spheres of Justice* (Oxford: Blackwell, 1983), 190–96.
3. Robert Putnam and David E. Campbell, *American Grace: How Religion Divides and Unites Us* (New York: Simon & Schuster, 2010).

accurate predictor of altruism, more so than any other factor, including gender, education, income, race, region, marital status, ideology, and age. Most fascinating of his findings is that the key factor is *being part of a religious community*. What turned out *not* to be relevant is what you believe. The research findings suggest that an atheist who goes regularly to a house of worship (perhaps to accompany a spouse or a child) is more likely to volunteer in a soup kitchen than a fervent believer who prays alone. The key factor again is community.

This may well be one of the most important functions of religion in a secular age, namely, keeping community alive. Most of us need community. We are social animals. Evolutionary biologists have suggested recently that the huge increase in brain size represented by Homo sapiens was specifically to allow us to form more extended social networks. It is the human capacity to co-operate in large teams – rather than the power of reason – that marks us off from other animals. As the Torah says, it is not good to be alone.

Recent research has shown something else as well. Who you associate with has a powerful impact on what you do and become. In 2009 Nicholas Christakis and James Fowler statistically analysed a group of 5,124 subjects and their 53,228 ties to friends, family, and work colleagues. They found that if a friend takes up smoking, it makes it significantly more likely (by 36 per cent) that you will. The same applies to drinking, slenderness, obesity, and many other behavioural patterns.[4] We become like the people we are close to.

A study of students at Dartmouth College in the year 2000 found that if you share a room with someone with good study habits, it will probably raise your own performance. A 2006 Princeton study showed that if your sibling has a child, it makes it 15 per cent more likely that you will too within the next two years. There is such a thing as "social contagion." We are profoundly influenced by our friends – as indeed Maimonides states in his law code, the *Mishneh Torah*.[5]

---

4. Nicholas Christakis and James H. Fowler, *Connected: The Surprising Power of Our Social Networks and How They Shape Our Lives* (New York: Little, Brown, 2009).
5. See Maimonides, *Mishneh Torah, Hilkhot Deot* 6:1.

Which brings us back to Moses and *Vayak'hel*. By placing community at the heart of the religious life and by giving it a home in space and time – the synagogue and Shabbat – Moses was showing the power of community for good, as the episode of the golden calf had shown its power for bad. Jewish spirituality is for the most part profoundly communal. Hence my definition of Jewish faith: the redemption of our solitude.

Pekudei

Don't Sit: Walk

Sitting is the new smoking. So goes the new health mantra. Spend too much time at a desk or in front of a screen and you are at risk of significant danger to your health. The World Health Organisation has identified physical inactivity as the fourth greatest health hazard today, ahead of obesity. In the words of Dr. James Levine, one of the world's leading experts on the subject, and the man credited with coining the mantra, "We are sitting ourselves to death."

The reason is that we were not made to sit still. Our bodies were made for movement, standing, walking, and running. If we fail to give the body regular exercise, it can easily malfunction and put us at risk of serious illness. The question is: Does the same apply to the soul, the spirit, the mind?

It is fascinating to look at the sequence of verbs in the very first verse of the book of Psalms: "Happy is the man who does not *walk* in the counsel of the ungodly, or *stand* in the way of sinners, or *sit* in the seat of the scornful" (Ps. 1:1). That is a picture of the bad life, lived in pursuit of the wrong values. Note how the bad man begins by walking, then stands, then sits. A bad life *immobilises*. That is the point of the famous verses in Hallel:

Their idols are silver and gold, the work of men's hands. They
have mouths, but do not speak, eyes but do not see, ears but do
not hear, noses but do not smell. They have hands but cannot
feel, feet but cannot walk, nor can they make a sound with their
throats. *Those who make them will be like them*; so will all who
trust in them. (Ps. 115:4–8)

If you live for lifeless things, you will become lifeless.

Except in the House of the Lord, Jews do not sit. Jewish life
began with two momentous journeys, Abraham from Mesopotamia
and Moses and the Israelites from Egypt. *"Walk on ahead of Me* and
be blameless," said God to Abraham (Gen. 17:1). At the age of ninety-
nine, having just been circumcised, Abraham saw three strangers
passing by and *"ran* to meet them" (ibid. 18:2). On the verse, "Jacob
dwelled [*vayeshev*, the verb that also means "to sit"] in the land where
his father had stayed" (ibid. 37:1), Rashi, citing the Sages, commented:
"Jacob sought to live in tranquillity, but immediately there broke in on
him the troubles of Joseph." The righteous do not sit still. They do not
have a quiet life.

Rarely is the point made with more subtlety than at the end of
this *parasha* and the book of Exodus as a whole. The Tabernacle had
been made and assembled. The closing verses tell us about the relationship between it and the "cloud of glory" that filled the Tent of Meeting. The Tabernacle was made to be portable.[1] It could be dismantled
and its parts carried as the Israelites travelled on the next stage of their
journey. When the time came for them to move on, the cloud moved
from the Tent of Meeting to a position outside the camp, signalling the
direction the Israelites were to take. This is how the Torah describes it:

When the cloud lifted from above the tabernacle, the Israelites
went onward *in all their journeys,* but if the cloud did not lift,

---

1. This was especially true of the ark. It was carried by staves that passed through rings
   on the side of the ark. It was forbidden to remove the staves, even when the Israelites
   were encamped (Ex. 25:15). The ark already had to be ready to travel at a moment's
   notice. See the commentary of S. R. Hirsch ad loc.

they did not set out until the day it lifted. So the cloud of the Lord was over the tabernacle by day, and fire was in the cloud by night, in the sight of all the house of Israel *in all their journeys*. (Ex. 40:36–38)

There is a significant difference between the two occurrences of the phrase "in all their journeys." In the first, the words are meant literally. When the cloud lifted, the Israelites knew they were about to begin a new stage of their journey. However, in the second instance, they *cannot* be meant literally. The cloud was *not* "over the Tabernacle" in all their journeys. To the contrary, it was there only when they *stopped* journeying and instead pitched camp. During the journeys the cloud went on ahead. Rashi notes this and makes the following comment:

> A place where they encamped is also called *massa*, "a journey"... because from the place of encampment they always set out again on a new journey, therefore they are all called "journeys."

The point is linguistic, but the message is remarkable. In a few brief words, Rashi has summarised an existential truth about Jewish identity. *To be a Jew is to travel.* Judaism is a journey, not a destination. Even a place of rest, an encampment, is still called a journey. The patriarchs lived, not in houses but in tents.[2] The first time we are told that a patriarch built a house, proves the point: "Jacob travelled to Sukkot. There he built himself a house and made shelters [*sukkot*] for his livestock. That is why he called the place Sukkot" (Gen. 33:17).

The verse is astonishing. *Jacob has just become the first member of the covenantal family to build a house, yet he does not call the place "House"* (as in Bet-El or Bet-Leḥem). *He calls it "cattle-sheds."* It is as if Jacob, consciously or unconsciously, already knew that to live the life of the covenant means to be ready to move on, to travel, to journey, to grow.

One might have thought that all this applied only to the time before the Israelites crossed the Jordan and entered the Promised Land.

---

2. Note that Lot, in Sodom, lived in a house (Gen. 19:2). So did Laban (Gen. 24:23).

Yet the Torah tells us otherwise: "The land shall not be sold in perpetuity because the land is Mine: you are *strangers and temporary residents* as far as I am concerned" (Lev. 25:23).

If we live as if the land is permanently ours, our stay there will be temporary. If we live as if it is only temporarily so, we will live there permanently. In this world of time and change, growth and decay, only God and His word are permanent. One of the most poignant lines in the book of Psalms – a verse cherished by the French-Jewish philosopher Emmanuel Levinas – says, "I am a stranger on earth. Do not hide your commands from me" (Ps. 119:19). To be a Jew is to stay light on your feet, ready to begin the next stage of the journey, literally or metaphorically. An Englishman's home is his castle, they used to say. But a Jew's home is a tent, a tabernacle, a sukka. We know that life on earth is a temporary dwelling. That is why we value each moment and its newness.

Recently a distinguished British Jew, (Lord) George Weidenfeld, died at the age of ninety-six. He was a successful publisher, a friend and confidant of European leaders, an inveterate fighter for peace, and a passionate Zionist. In 1949–50, he was political adviser and Chief of Cabinet to Chaim Weizmann, first president of Israel. One of his last acts was to help rescue 20,000 Christian refugees fleeing from ISIS in Syria. He was alert and active, even hyperactive, to the very end of a long and distinguished life.

In an interview with *The Times* on his ninety-second birthday he was asked the following question: "Most people in their nineties slow down. You seem to be speeding up. Why is that?" He replied, "When you get to ninety-two, you begin to see the door about to close. I have so much to do before the door closes that the older I get, the harder I have to work." That is a good formula for staying young.

Like our bodies, our souls were not made for sitting still. We were made for moving, walking, travelling, learning, searching, striving, growing, knowing that it is not for us to complete the work but neither may we stand aside from it. In Judaism, as the book of Exodus reminds us in its closing words, even an encampment is called a journey. In matters spiritual, not just physical, sitting is the new smoking.

Leviticus
ויקרא

Vayikra

The Pursuit of Meaning

The American Declaration of Independence speaks of the inalienable rights of life, liberty, and the pursuit of happiness. Recently, following the pioneering work of Martin Seligman, founder of positive psychology, there have been hundreds of books published on happiness. Yet there is something more fundamental still to the sense of a life well-lived, namely, *meaning.* The two seem similar. It's easy to suppose that people who find meaning are happy, and people who are happy have found meaning. But the two are not the same, nor do they always overlap.

Happiness is largely a matter of satisfying needs and wants. Meaning, by contrast, is about a sense of purpose in life, especially by making positive contributions to the lives of others. Happiness is largely about how you feel in the present. Meaning is about how you judge your life as a whole: past, present, and future.

Happiness is associated with *taking,* meaning with *giving.* Individuals who suffer stress, worry, or anxiety are not happy, but they may be living lives rich with meaning. Past misfortunes reduce present happiness, but people often connect such moments with the discovery of meaning. Furthermore, happiness is not unique to humans. Animals also experience contentment when their wants and needs are satisfied. But meaning is a distinctively human phenomenon. It has to do not with *nature* but with *culture*. It is not about what happens to us, but about *how we interpret* what happens to us. There can be happiness without meaning, and there can be meaning in the absence of happiness, even in the midst of darkness and pain.[1]

In a fascinating article in *The Atlantic*, "There's More to Life Than Being Happy,"[2] Emily Smith argued that the pursuit of happiness can result in a relatively shallow, self-absorbed, even selfish life. What makes the pursuit of meaning different is that it is about the search for something larger than the self.

No one did more to put the question of meaning into modern discourse than the late Viktor Frankl, who has figured prominently in these essays on spirituality.[3] In the three years he spent in Auschwitz, Frankl survived and helped others to survive by inspiring them to discover a purpose in life even in the midst of hell on earth. He knew that in the camps, those who lost the will to live died. It was there that he formulated the ideas he later turned into a new type of psychotherapy based on what he called "man's search for meaning." His book of that title, written in the course of nine days in 1946, has sold more than ten million copies throughout the world, and ranks as one of the most influential works of the twentieth century.

Frankl used to say that the way to find meaning was not to ask what we want from life. Instead we should ask what life wants from us. We are each, he said, unique: in our gifts, our abilities, our skills and talents, and in the circumstances of our life. For each of us, then, there is a task only we can do. This does not mean that we are better than others. But if we believe we are here for a reason, then there is a *tikkun*, a mending, only we can perform; a fragment of light only we can redeem; an act of kindness, or courage, or generosity, or hospitality only we can perform; even a word of encouragement or a smile only we can give,

1. See Roy F. Baumeister, Kathleen D. Vohs, Jennifer Aaker, and Emily N.Garbinsky, "Some Key Differences between a Happy Life and a Meaningful Life," *Journal of Positive Psychology*, vol. 8, issue 6 (2013): 505–16.
2. Emily Smith, "There's More to Life Than Being Happy," *The Atlantic*, Jan. 9, 2013.
3. See in particular the essay above on *Parashat Vayigash*, "Reframing."

because we are here, in this place, at this time, facing this person at this moment in their lives.

"Life is a task," he used to say, and added, "The religious man differs from the apparently irreligious man only by experiencing his existence not simply as a task, but as a mission." He or she is aware of being summoned, called, by a Source. "For thousands of years that source has been called God."[4]

That is the significance of the word that gives our *parasha*, and the third book of the Torah, its name: *Vayikra*, "And He called." The precise meaning of this opening verse is difficult to understand. Literally translated it reads: "And He called to Moses, and God spoke to him from the Tent of Meeting, saying...." The first phrase seems to be redundant. If we are told that God spoke to Moses, why say in addition, "And He called"? Rashi explains as follows:

> *And He called to Moses*: Every [time God communicated with Moses, whether signalled by the expression] "And He spoke," or "and He said," or "and He commanded," it was always preceded by [God] calling [to Moses by name].[5]

"Calling" is an expression of endearment. It is the expression employed by the ministering angels, as it says, "And one called to the other" (Is. 6:3).

Vayikra, Rashi is telling us, means *to be called to a task in love*. This is the source of one of the key ideas of Western thought, namely the concept of a *vocation* or a *calling*, that is, the choice of a career or way of life not just because you want to do it, or because it offers certain benefits, but because you feel *summoned* to it. You feel this is your meaning and mission in life. This is what you were placed on earth to do.

There are many such calls in Tanakh. There was the call Abraham heard to leave his land and family (Gen. 12:1). There was the call to Moses at the burning bush (Ex. 3:4). There was the one experienced

---

4. Viktor Frankl, *The Doctor and the Soul: from Psychotherapy to Logotherapy* (New York: A. A. Knopf, 1965), 13.
5. Rashi on Leviticus 1:1.

by Isaiah when he saw in a mystical vision God enthroned and surrounded by angels:

> Then I heard the voice of the Lord saying, "Whom shall I send? And who will go for us?" And I said, "Here am I. Send me!" (Is. 6:8)

One of the most touching is the story of the young Samuel, dedicated by his mother Hannah to serve in the sanctuary at Shiloh where he acted as an assistant to Eli the priest. In bed at night he heard a voice calling his name. He assumed it was Eli. He ran to see what he wanted but Eli told him he had not called. This happened a second time and then a third, and by then Eli realised that it was God calling the child. He told Samuel that the next time the voice called his name, he should reply, "Speak, Lord, for Your servant is listening." It did not occur to the child that it might be God summoning him to a mission, but it was. Thus began his career as a prophet, judge, and anointer of Israel's first two kings, Saul and David (I Sam. 3).

When we see a wrong to be righted, a sickness to be healed, a need to be met, and we feel it speaking to us, that is when we come as close as we can in a post-prophetic age to hearing *Vayikra*, God's call. And why does the word appear here, at the beginning of the third and central book of the Torah? Because the book of Leviticus is about sacrifices, and a vocation is about sacrifices. *We are willing to make sacrifices when we feel they are part of the task we are called on to do.*

From the perspective of eternity, we may sometimes be overwhelmed by a sense of our own insignificance. We are no more than a wave in the ocean, a grain of sand on the sea shore, a speck of dust on the surface of infinity. *Yet we are here because God wanted us to be, because there is a task He wants us to perform.* The search for meaning is the quest for this task.

Each of us is unique. Even genetically identical twins are different. There are things only we can do, we who are what we are, in this time, this place, and these circumstances. For each of us God has a task: work to perform, a kindness to show, a gift to give, love to share, loneliness to ease, pain to heal, or broken lives to help mend. Discerning that task, hearing *Vayikra*, God's call, is one of the great spiritual challenges for each of us.

How do we know what it is? Some years ago, in *To Heal a Fractured World*, I offered this as a guide, and it still seems to me to make sense: Where what we want to do meets what needs to be done, that is where God wants us to be.

Tzav

Understanding Sacrifice

O ne of the most difficult elements of the Torah and the way of
life it prescribes is the phenomenon of animal sacrifices – for obvious reasons.
First, Jews and Judaism have survived without them for almost two thousand years. Second, virtually all the prophets were critical of them, not least
Jeremiah in the *haftara* for *Parashat Tzav*.[1] None of the prophets sought to
abolish sacrifices, but they were severely critical of those who offered them
while at the same time oppressing or exploiting their fellow human beings.
What disturbed them – what disturbed God in whose name they spoke –
was that evidently some people thought of sacrifices as a kind of bribe: if
we make a generous enough gift to God then He may overlook our crimes
and misdemeanours. This is an idea radically incompatible with Judaism.

Then again, along with monarchy, sacrifices were among the least
distinctive features of Judaism in ancient times. Every ancient religion
in those days, every cult and sect, had its altars and sacrifices. Finally, it
remains remarkable how simply and smoothly the Sages were able to

---

1. Jeremiah 7:22: "When I freed your fathers from the land of Egypt, I did not speak
   with them or command them concerning burnt offerings or sacrifice" – a remarkable
   statement. See Rashi and Radak ad loc., and especially Maimonides, *Guide for the
   Perplexed*, III:32.

construct substitutes for sacrifice, three in particular: prayer, study, and *tzedaka*. Prayer, particularly *Shaḥarit, Minḥa*, and *Musaf*, took the place of the regular offerings. One who studies the laws of sacrifice is as if he had brought a sacrifice. And one who gives to charity brings, as it were, a financial sacrifice, acknowledging that all we have we owe to God.

So, though we pray daily for the rebuilding of the Temple and the restoration of sacrifices, the principle of sacrifice itself remains hard to understand. Many theories have been advanced by anthropologists, psychologists, and Bible scholars as to what the sacrifices represented, but most are based on the questionable assumption that sacrifice is essentially the same act across cultures. This is poor scholarship. Always seek to understand a practice in terms of the distinctive beliefs of the culture in which it takes place. What could sacrifice possibly mean in a religion in which God is the creator and owner of all?

What, then, was sacrifice in Judaism and why does it remain important, at least as an idea, even today? The simplest answer – though it does not explain the details of the different kinds of offering – is this: *We love what we are willing to make sacrifices for.* That is why, when they were a nation of farmers and shepherds, the Israelites demonstrated their love of God by bringing Him a symbolic gift of their flocks and herds, their grain and fruit; that is, their livelihood. To love is to thank. To love is to want to bring an offering to the Beloved. To love is to give.[2] Sacrifice is the choreography of love.

This is true in many aspects of life. A happily married couple is constantly making sacrifices for one another. Parents make huge sacrifices for their children. People drawn to a calling – to heal the sick, or care for the poor, or fight for justice for the weak against the strong – often sacrifice remunerative careers for the sake of their ideals. In ages of patriotism, people make sacrifices for their country. In strong communities people make sacrifices for one another when someone is in distress or needs help. Sacrifice is the superglue of relationship. It bonds us to one another.

That is why, in the biblical age, sacrifices were so important – not as they were in other faiths but precisely because at the beating heart of

---

2. The verb "to love," A-H-V, is related to the verbs H-V-H, H-V-V, and Y-H-V, all of which have the sense of giving, bringing, or offering.

Tzav: Understanding Sacrifice

Judaism is love: "You shall love the Lord your God with all your heart, and with all your soul, and with all your might." In other faiths the driving motive behind sacrifice was fear: fear of the anger and power of the gods. In Judaism it was love.

We see this in the Hebrew word for sacrifice itself: the noun *korban*, and the verb *lehakriv*, which mean "to come, or bring close." The name of God invariably used in connection with the sacrifices is *Hashem*, God in His aspect of love and compassion, never *Elokim*, God as justice and distance. The word *Elokim* occurs only five times in the whole book of Leviticus, and always in the context of other nations. The word *Hashem* appears 209 times. And as we saw in the previous *parasha*, the very name of the book, *Vayikra*, means to summon in love. Where there is love, there is sacrifice.

Once we realise this we begin to understand how deeply relevant the concept of sacrifice is in the twenty-first century. The major institutions of the modern world – the liberal democratic state and the free-market economy – were predicated on the model of the *rational actor*, that is, one who acts to maximise the benefits to him- or herself.

Hobbes' account of the social contract was that it is in the interests of each of us to hand over some of our rights to a central power charged with ensuring the rule of law and the defence of the realm. Adam Smith's insight into the market economy was that if we each act to maximise our own advantage, the result is the growth of the commonwealth. Modern politics and economics were built on the foundation of the rational pursuit of self-interest.

There was nothing wrong with this. It was done for the highest of motives. It was an attempt to create peace in a Europe that had for centuries been ravaged by war. The democratic state and the market economy were serious attempts to harness the power of self-interest to combat the destructive passions that led to violence.[3] The fact that politics and economics were based on self-interest did not negate the possibility that families and communities were sustained by altruism. It was a good system, not a bad one.

3. The classic text is A. O. Hirschman, *The Passions and the Interests* (Princeton University Press, 1977).

Now, however, after several centuries, the idea of love as sacrifice has grown thin in many areas of life. We see this specifically in relationships. Throughout the West, fewer people are getting married, those who do are getting married later, and almost half of marriages end in divorce. Throughout Europe, indigenous populations are in decline. To have a stable population, a country must have an average birth-rate of 2.1 children per female. In 2015 the average birth-rate throughout the European Union was 1.55. In Spain it was 1.27. Germany has the lowest birth-rate of any country in the world.[4] That is why the population of Europe is today rendered stable only on the basis of unprecedented rates of immigration.

Lose the concept of sacrifice within a society, and sooner or later marriage falters, parenthood declines, and the society slowly ages and dies. My late predecessor, Lord Jakobovits, had a lovely way of putting this. The Talmud says that when a man divorces his first wife, "the altar sheds tears" (Gittin 90b). What is the connection between the altar and a marriage? Both, he said, are about sacrifices. Marriages fail when the partners are unwilling to make sacrifices for one another.

Jews and Judaism survived despite the many sacrifices people had to make for it. In the eleventh century Judah Halevi expressed something close to awe at the fact that Jews stayed Jewish despite the fact that "with a word lightly spoken" they could have converted to the majority faith and lived a life of relative ease.[5] Equally possible though is that Judaism survived *because* of those sacrifices. Where people make sacrifices for their ideals, the ideals stay strong. Sacrifice is an expression of love.

Not all sacrifice is holy. Today's suicide bombers sacrifice their lives and those of their victims in a way I have argued is sacrilege.[6] Indeed, the very existence of animal sacrifice in the Torah may have been a way of preventing people from offering human sacrifice in the form of violence and war. But the principle of sacrifice remains. It is the gift we bring to what and whom we love.

---

4. *The Observer*, August 23, 2015.
5. Judah Halevi, *The Kuzari*, 4:23.
6. See Jonathan Sacks, *Not in God's Name: Confronting Religious Violence* (New York: Schocken Books, 2017).

Shemini

The Dangers of Enthusiasm

Excavating the history of words can sometimes be as revealing as excavating the ruins of an ancient city. Take the English word "enthusiasm." Today we see this as something positive. One dictionary defines it as "a feeling of energetic interest in a particular subject or activity and an eagerness to be involved in it." People with enthusiasm have passion, zest, and excitement, and this can be contagious. It is one of the gifts of a great teacher or leader. People follow people of passion. If you want to influence others, cultivate enthusiasm.

But the word did not always have a favourable connotation. Originally it referred to someone possessed by a spirit or demon. In the seventeenth century in England, it came to refer to extreme and revolutionary Protestant sects, and more generally to the Puritans who fought the English Civil War. It became a synonym for religious extremism, zealotry, and fanaticism. It was looked on as irrational, volatile, and dangerous.

David Hume (1711–1776), the Scottish philosopher, wrote a fascinating essay on the subject.[1] He begins by noting that "the corruption of the best things produces the worst," and that is especially true of religion.

---

1. David Hume, "Of Superstition and Enthusiasm," in *Essays Moral, Political, and Literary* (1742–1754).

There are, he says, two ways in which religion can go wrong: through superstition and through enthusiasm. These are quite different phenomena. Superstition is driven by ignorance and fear. We can sometimes have irrational anxieties and terrors, and we deal with them by resorting to equally irrational remedies. Enthusiasm is the opposite. It is the result of over-confidence. The enthusiast, in a state of high religious rapture, comes to believe that he is being inspired by God Himself, and is thus empowered to disregard reason and restraint.

Enthusiasm "thinks itself sufficiently qualified to approach the Divinity, without any human mediator." The person in its grip is so full of what he takes to be holy rapture that he feels able to override the rules by which priestly conduct is normally governed. "The fanatic consecrates himself and bestows on his own person a sacred character, much superior to what forms and ceremonious institutions can confer on any other." Rules and regulations, thinks the enthusiast, are for ordinary people, not for us. We, inspired by God, know better. That, said Hume, can be very dangerous indeed.

We now have a precise description of the sin for which Nadav and Avihu, the two elder sons of Aaron, died. Clearly the Torah regards their death as highly significant because it refers to it on no less than four occasions (Lev. 10:1–2, 16:1; Num. 3:4, 26:61). It was a shocking tragedy, occurring as it did on the day of the inauguration of the service of the *Mishkan*, a moment that should have been one of the great celebrations in Jewish history.

The Sages themselves were puzzled by the episode. The text itself merely says that "they offered unauthorised fire [*esh zara*] before the Lord, that He had not commanded. So fire came out from the presence of the Lord and consumed them, and they died before the Lord" (Lev. 10:1–2). Evidently the Sages felt that there must have been something else, some further sin or character flaw, to justify so dire and drastic a punishment.

Putting together clues in the biblical text, some speculated that they were guilty of entering the Holy of Holies;[2] that they had given

---

2. This is based on the statement in Leviticus 16:1, that the two sons of Aaron died when "they drew near before the Lord," implying that they had come too close, i.e., they had entered the Holy of Holies.

a ruling of their own accord without consulting Moses or Aaron; that they had become intoxicated; that they were not properly robed; that they had not purified themselves with water from the laver; that they were so self-important that they had not married, thinking no woman was good enough for them; or that they were impatient for Moses and Aaron to die so they could become the leaders of Israel.

Some speculated that the sin for which they were punished did not happen on that day at all. It had occurred months earlier at Mount Sinai. The text says that Nadav and Avihu along with seventy elders ascended the mountain and "saw the God of Israel." God "did not raise His hand against the leaders of the Israelites; they saw God, and they ate and drank" (Ex. 24:10–11). The implication is that they deserved punishment then for not averting their eyes, or for eating and drinking at so sacred an encounter. But God delayed the punishment so as not to cause grief on the day He made a covenant with the people.[3]

These are all midrashic interpretations: true, valid and important but not the plain sense of the verse. The text is clear. On each of the three occasions where their death is mentioned, the Torah says merely that they offered "unauthorised fire." The sin was that they did something that had not been commanded. They did so, surely, for the highest motives. Moses said to Aaron immediately after they died that this is what God had meant when He said, "Among those who are near Me I will be sanctified" (Lev. 10:3). A midrash says that Moses was comforting his brother by saying, "They were closer to God than you or I."[4]

The history of the word "enthusiasm," though, helps us understand the episode. Nadav and Avihu were "enthusiasts," not in the contemporary sense but in the sense in which the word was used in the seventeenth and eighteenth centuries. Enthusiasts were people who, full of religious passion, believed that God was inspiring them to do deeds in defiance of law and convention. They were very holy but they were also potentially very dangerous. David Hume in particular saw that enthusiasm in this sense is diametrically opposed to the mindset of priesthood. In his words, "All enthusiasts have been free from the yoke of ecclesiastics,

---

3. The seventy elders were punished later. See Rashi on Exodus 24:10.
4. *Midrash Aggada* (Buber) ad loc.

and have expressed great independence of devotion; with a contempt of forms, ceremonies, and traditions."

Priests understand the power, and thus the potential danger, of the sacred. That is why holy places, times, and rituals must be guarded with rules, the way a nuclear power station must be protected by the most careful insulation. Think of the accidents that have occurred when this has failed: Chernobyl, for example, or Fukushima in Japan in 2011. The results can be devastating and lasting.

To bring unauthorised fire to the Tabernacle might seem a small offence, but a single unauthorised act in the realm of the holy causes a breach in the laws around the sacred that can grow in time to a gaping hole. Enthusiasm, harmless though it might be in some of its manifestations, can quickly become extremism, fanaticism, and religiously motivated violence. That is what happened in Europe during the wars of religion in the sixteenth and seventeenth centuries, and it is happening in some religions today. As David Hume observed: "Human reason and even morality are rejected [by enthusiasts] as fallacious guides, and the fanatic madman delivers himself over blindly" to what he believes to be divine inspiration, but what may in fact be overheated self-importance or frenzied rage.

We now understand in detail that the human brain contains two different systems, what Daniel Kahneman calls "thinking fast and slow." The fast brain, the limbic system, gives rise to emotions, particularly in response to fear. The slow brain, the prefrontal cortex, is rational, deliberative, and capable of thinking through the long-term consequences of alternative courses of action. It is no accident that we have both systems. Without instinctive responses triggered by danger we would not survive. But without the slower, deliberative brain we would find ourselves time and again engaging in destructive and self-destructive behaviour. Individual happiness and the survival of civilisation depend on striking a delicate balance between the two.

Precisely because it gives rise to such intense passions, religious life in particular needs the constraints of law and ritual, the entire intricate minuet of worship, so that the fire of faith is contained, giving light and a glimpse of the glory of God. Otherwise it can eventually become a raging inferno, spreading destruction and claiming lives. After many centuries in the West, we have tamed enthusiasm to the point where we can think of it as a positive force. We should never forget, however, that it was not always so. That is why Judaism contains so many laws and so much attention to detail – and the closer we come to God, the more we need.

The Power of Shame

On December 20, 2013, a young woman, Justine Sacco, was waiting in Heathrow airport before boarding a flight to Africa. To while away the time she sent a tweet in questionable taste about the hazards of catching AIDS. There was no immediate response, and she boarded the plane unaware of the storm that was about to break. Eleven hours later, on landing, she discovered that she had become an international cause célèbre. Her tweet and responses to it had gone viral. Over the next eleven days she would be googled more than a million times. She was branded a racist and dismissed from her job. Overnight she had become a pariah.[1]

The new social media have brought about a return to an ancient phenomenon, public shaming. Two recent books, Jon Ronson's *So You've Been Publicly Shamed*, and Jennifer Jacquet's *Is Shame Necessary?*[2] have discussed it. Jacquet believes it is a good thing. It can be a way of getting public corporations to behave more responsibly, for example. Ronson highlights the dangers. It is one thing to be shamed by the community

---

1. Jon Ronson, *So You've Been Publicly Shamed* (London: Picador, 2015), 63–86.
2. Jennifer Jacquet, *Is Shame Necessary? New Uses for an Old Tool* (London: Allen Lane, 2015).

of which you are a part, quite another by a global network of strangers who know nothing about you or the context in which your act took place. That is more like a lynch mob than the pursuit of justice.

Either way, this gives us a way of understanding the otherwise bewildering phenomenon of *tzaraat*, the condition dealt with at length in the previous *parasha* and this one. It has been variously translated as leprosy, skin disease, or scaly infection. Yet there are formidable problems in identifying it with any known disease. First, its symptoms do not correspond to Hansen's disease, otherwise known as leprosy. Second, as described in the Torah it affects not only human beings but also the walls of houses, furniture, and clothes. There is no known medical condition that has this property.

Besides, the Torah is a book about holiness and right conduct. It is not a medical text. Even if it were, as Rabbi David Zvi Hoffmann points out in his commentary, the procedures to be carried out do not correspond to those that would be done if *tzaraat* were a contagious disease. Finally, *tzaraat* as described in the Torah is a condition that brings not sickness, but rather impurity, *tuma*. Health and purity are different things altogether.

The Sages decoded the mystery by relating our *parasha* to the instances in the Torah where someone was actually afflicted by *tzaraat*. One happened when Miriam spoke against her brother Moses (Num. 12:1–15). Another occurred when Moses at the burning bush said to God that the Israelites would not believe in him. His hand briefly turned "as leprous as snow" (Ex. 4:7). The Sages regarded *tzaraat* as a punishment for *lashon hara*, evil speech, speaking negatively about or denigrating another person.

This helped them explain why the symptoms of *tzaraat* – mould, discolouration – could affect walls, furniture, clothes, and human skin. These were a sequence of warnings or punishments. First God warned the offender by sending a sign of decay to the walls of his house. If the offender repented, the condition stopped there. If he failed to do so, his furniture was affected, then his clothes, and finally his skin.

How are we to understand this? Why was "evil speech" regarded as so serious an offence that it took these strange phenomena to point to its existence? And why was it punished this way and not another?

It was the anthropologist Ruth Benedict and her book about Japanese culture, *The Chrysanthemum and the Sword*, that popularised a distinction between two kinds of society: *guilt cultures* and *shame cultures*.[3] Ancient Greece, like Japan, was a shame culture. Judaism and the religions influenced by it (most obviously, Calvinism) were guilt cultures. The differences between them are substantial.

In shame cultures, what matters is the judgment of others. Acting morally means conforming to public roles, rules, and expectations. You do what other people expect you to do. You follow society's conventions. If you fail to do so, society punishes you by subjecting you to shame, ridicule, disapproval, humiliation, and ostracism. In guilt cultures what matters is not what other people think but what the voice of conscience tells you. Living morally means acting in accordance with internalised moral imperatives: "You shall" and "You shall not." What matters is what you know to be right and wrong.

People in shame cultures are *other-directed*. They care about how they appear in the eyes of others, or as we would say today, about their "image." People in guilt cultures are *inner-directed*. They care about what they know about themselves in moments of absolute honesty. Even if your public image is undamaged, if you know you have done wrong, it will make you feel uneasy. You will wake up at night, troubled. "O coward conscience, how dost thou afflict me!" says Shakespeare's Richard III. "My conscience hath a thousand several tongues / And every tongue brings in a several tale /And every tale condemns me for a villain."[4] Shame is public humiliation. Guilt is inner torment.

The emergence of a guilt culture in Judaism flowed from its understanding of the relationship between God and humankind. In Judaism we are not actors on a stage with society as the audience and the judge. We can fool society; we cannot fool God. All pretence and pride, every mask and persona, the cosmetic cultivation of public image are irrelevant: "The Lord does not look at the things people look at. People look at the outward appearance, but the Lord looks at

---

3. For more on the theme of shame and guilt cultures, see above, *Parashat Bereshit*, "The Art of Listening."

4. William Shakespeare, *Richard III*, act 5, scene 3.

the heart" (I Sam. 16:7). Shame cultures are collective and conformist. By contrast, Judaism, the archetypal guilt culture, emphasises the individual and his or her relationship with God. What matters is not whether we conform to the culture of the age but whether we do what is good, just, and right.

This makes the law of *tzaraat* fascinating, because according to the Sages' interpretation, it constitutes one of the rare instances in the Torah of *punishment by shame rather than guilt*. The appearance of mould or discolouration on the walls of a house was a public signal of private wrongdoing. It was a way of saying to everyone who lived or visited there, "Bad things have been said in this place." Little by little the signals came ever closer to the culprit, appearing next on his bed or chair, then on his clothes, then on his skin, until eventually he found himself diagnosed as defiled:

> When a person has the mark of the defiling disease, his clothing must have a tear in it, he must go without a haircut, and he must cover his head down to his lips. "Unclean! Unclean!" he must call out. As long as he has the mark, he shall remain unclean. Since he is unclean, he must remain alone, and his place shall be outside the camp. (Lev. 13:45–46)

These are quintessential expressions of shame. First is the *stigma*: the public marks of disgrace or dishonour (the torn clothes, unkempt hair, etc.). Then comes the *ostracism*: temporary exclusion from the normal affairs of society. These have nothing to do with illness and everything to do with social disapproval. This is what makes the law of *tzaraat* so hard to understand at first: it is one of the rare appearances of public shame in a non-shame, guilt-based culture.[5] It happened, though, not because society had expressed its disapproval but because God was signalling that it should do so.

Why specifically in the case of *lashon hara*, "evil speech"? Because *speech is what holds society together*. Anthropologists have argued that

---

5. Another according to Rabban Yoḥanan ben Zakkai was the ceremony in which a slave who did not wish to go free after the completion of six years of service, had his ear pierced against a doorpost (Ex. 20:6). See Rashi ad loc., and Kiddushin 22b.

language evolved among humans precisely in order to strengthen the bonds between them so that they could co-operate in larger groupings than any other animal. What sustains co-operation is *trust*. This allows and encourages me to make sacrifices for the group, knowing that others can be relied on to do likewise. This is precisely why *lashon hara* is so destructive. It undermines trust. It makes people suspicious about one another. It weakens the bonds that hold the group together. If unchecked, *lashon hara* will destroy any group it attacks: a family, a team, a community, even a nation. Hence its uniquely malicious character: it uses the power of language to weaken the very thing language was brought into being to create, namely, the trust that sustains the social bond.

That is why the punishment for *lashon hara* was to be temporarily excluded from society by *public exposure* (the signs that appear on walls, furniture, clothes, and skin), *stigmatisation and shame* (the torn clothes etc.), and *ostracism* (being forced to live outside the camp). It is difficult, perhaps impossible, to punish the malicious gossiper using the normal conventions of law, courts, and the establishment of guilt. This can be done in the case of *motzi shem ra*, libel or slander, because these are all cases of *making a false statement*. *Lashon hara* is more subtle. It is done not by falsehood but by insinuation. There are many ways of harming a person's reputation without actually telling a lie. Someone accused of *lashon hara* can easily say, "I didn't say it, I didn't mean it, and even if I did, I did not say anything that was untrue." The best way of dealing with people who poison relationships without actually uttering falsehoods is by naming, shaming, and shunning them.

That, according to the Sages, is what *tzaraat* miraculously did in ancient times. It no longer exists in the form described in the Torah. But the use of the internet and social media as instruments of public shaming illustrates both the power and the danger of a culture of shame. Only rarely does the Torah invoke it, and in the case of the *metzora* only by an act of God, not society. Yet the moral of the *metzora* remains. Malicious gossip, *lashon hara*, undermines relationships, erodes the social bond, and damages trust. It deserves to be exposed and shamed.

Never speak ill of others, and stay far from those who do.

The Courage to Admit Mistakes

Some years ago I was visited by the then American ambassador to the Court of St James, Philip Lader. He told me of a fascinating project he and his wife had initiated in 1981. They had come to realise that many of their contemporaries would find themselves in positions of influence and power in the not-too-distant future. He thought it would be useful and creative if they were to come together for a study retreat every so often to share ideas, listen to experts, and form friendships, thinking through collectively the challenges they would face in the coming years. So they created what they called Renaissance Weekends. They still happen.

The most interesting thing he told me was that they discovered that the participants, all exceptionally gifted people, found one thing particularly difficult, namely, *admitting that they made mistakes*. The Laders understood that this was something important they had to learn. Leaders, above all, should be capable of acknowledging when and how they had erred, and how to put it right. They came up with a brilliant idea. They set aside a session at each Weekend for a talk given by a recognised star in some field, on the subject of "My biggest blooper." Being

English, not American, I had to ask for a translation. I discovered that a blooper is an embarrassing mistake. A gaffe. A faux pas. A bungle. A boo-boo. A fashla. A balagan. Something you shouldn't have done and are ashamed to admit you did.

This, in essence, is what Yom Kippur is in Judaism. In Tabernacle and Temple times, it was the day when the holiest man in Israel, the high priest, made atonement, first for his own sins, then for the sins of his "house," then for the sins of all Israel. From the day the Temple was destroyed, we have had no high priest nor the rites he performed, but we still have the day, and the ability to confess and pray for forgiveness. It is so much easier to admit your sins, failings, and mistakes when other people are doing likewise. If a high priest, or the other members of our congregation, can admit to sins, so can we.

I have argued elsewhere (in the Introduction to the *Koren Yom Kippur Maḥzor*) that the move from the first Yom Kippur to the second was one of the great transitions in Jewish spirituality. The first Yom Kippur was the culmination of Moses' efforts to secure forgiveness for the people after the sin of the golden calf (Ex. 32–34). The process, which began on the seventeenth of Tammuz, ended on the tenth of Tishrei – the day that later became Yom Kippur. That was the day when Moses descended the mountain with the second set of tablets, the visible sign that God had reaffirmed His covenant with the people. The second Yom Kippur, one year later, initiated the series of rites set out in this *parasha* (Lev. 16), conducted in the *Mishkan* by Aaron in his role as high priest.

The differences between the two were immense. Moses acted as a prophet. Aaron functioned as a priest. Moses was following his heart and mind, improvising in response to God's response to his words. Aaron was following a precisely choreographed ritual, every detail of which was set out in advance. Moses' encounter was ad hoc, a unique, unrepeatable drama between heaven and earth. Aaron's was the opposite. The rules he was following never changed throughout the generations, so long as the Temple stood.

Moses' prayers on behalf of the people were full of audacity, what the Sages called *ḥutzpa kelapei shemaya,* "audacity toward heaven," reaching a climax in the astonishing words, "Now, please forgive their sin – but if not, then blot me out of the book You have written" (Ex. 32:32).

Aaron's behaviour by contrast was marked by obedience, humility, and confession. There were purification rituals, sin offerings, and atonements, for his own sins and those of his "house" as well as those of the people. The move from Yom Kippur 1 to Yom Kippur 2 was a classic instance of what Max Weber called the "routinization of charisma," that is, taking a unique moment and translating it into ritual, turning a "peak experience" into a regular part of life. Few moments in the Torah rival in intensity the dialogue between Moses and God after the golden calf. But the question thereafter was: How could we achieve forgiveness – we who no longer have a Moses, or prophets, or direct access to God? Great moments change history. But what changes us is the unspectacular habit of doing certain acts again and again until they reconfigure the brain and change our habits of the heart. We are shaped by the rituals we repeatedly perform.

Besides which, Moses' intercession with God did not, in and of itself, induce a penitential mood among the people. Yes, he performed a series of dramatic acts to demonstrate to the people their guilt. But we have no evidence that they internalised it. Aaron's acts were different. They involved confession, atonement, and a search for spiritual purification. They involved a candid acknowledgment of the sins and failures of the people, and they began with the high priest himself.

The effect of Yom Kippur – extended into the prayers of much of the rest of the year by way of *taḥanun* (supplicatory prayers), *vidui* (confession), and *seliḥot* (prayers for forgiveness) – was to create a culture in which people are not ashamed or embarrassed to say, "I got it wrong, I sinned, I made mistakes." That is what we do in the litany of wrongs we enumerate on Yom Kippur in two alphabetical lists, one beginning *Ashamnu, bagadnu*, the other beginning *Al ḥet sheḥatanu*.

As Philip Lader discovered, the capacity to admit mistakes is anything but widespread. We rationalise. We justify. We deny. We blame others. There have been several powerful books on the subject in recent years, among them Matthew Syed, *Black Box Thinking: The Surprising Truth About Success (and Why Some People Never Learn from Their Mistakes)*; Kathryn Schulz, *Being Wrong: Adventures in the Margins of Error*; and Carol Tavris and Elliot Aronson, *Mistakes Were Made, But Not By Me*.

Politicians find it hard to admit mistakes. So do doctors: preventable medical error causes more than 400,000 deaths every year in the United States. So do bankers and economists. The financial crash of 2008 was predicted by Warren Buffett as early as 2002. It happened despite the warnings of several experts that the level of mortgage lending and the leveraging of debt was unsustainable. Tavris and Aronson tell a similar story about the police. Once they have identified a suspect, they are reluctant to admit evidence of his or her innocence. And so it goes.

The avoidance strategies are almost endless. People say, it wasn't a mistake. Or, given the circumstances, it was the best that could have been done. Or it was a small mistake. Or it was unavoidable given what we knew at the time. Or someone else was to blame. We were given the wrong facts. We were faultily advised. So people bluff it out, or engage in denial, or see themselves as victims.

We have an almost infinite capacity for interpreting the facts to vindicate ourselves. As the Sages said in the context of the laws of purity, "No one can see his own blemishes, his own impurities." We are our own best advocates in the court of self-esteem. Rare is the individual with the courage to say, as the high priest did, or as King David did after the prophet Nathan confronted him with his guilt in relation to Uriah and Batsheva, *ḥatati*, "I have sinned."

Judaism helps us admit our mistakes in three ways. First is the knowledge that God forgives. He does not ask us never to sin. He knew in advance that His gift of freedom of choice would sometimes be misused. All He asks of us is that we acknowledge our mistakes, learn from them, confess, and resolve not to do them again.

Second is Judaism's clear separation between the sinner and the sin. We can condemn an act without losing faith in the agent.

Third is the aura Yom Kippur spreads over the rest of the year. It helps create a culture of honesty in which we are not ashamed to acknowledge the wrongs we have done. And despite the fact that, technically, Yom Kippur focuses on sins between us and God, a simple reading of the confessions in *Ashamnu* and *Al Ḥet* shows us that, actually, most of the sins we confess are about our dealings with other people.

What Philip Lader discovered about his high-flying contemporaries, Judaism internalised long ago. Seeing the best admit that they too make mistakes is deeply empowering for the rest of us. The first Jew to admit he made a mistake was Judah, who had wrongly accused Tamar of sexual misconduct, and then, realising he had been wrong, said, "She is more righteous than I" (Gen. 38:26).

It is surely more than mere coincidence that the name Judah comes from the same root as *vidui*, "confession." In other words, the very fact that we are called Jews – *Yehudim* – means that we are the people who have the courage to admit our wrongs.

Honest self-criticism is one of the unmistakable marks of spiritual greatness.

Kedoshim

In Search of Jewish Identity

The other day I was having a conversation with a Jewish intellectual and the question came up, as it often does, as to the nature of Jewish identity. What are we? What makes us Jewish? This has been one of the persisting debates about Jewish life ever since the nineteenth century. Until then, people by and large knew who and what Jews were. They were the heirs of an ancient nation who, in the Sinai desert long ago, made a covenant with God and, with greater or lesser success, tried to live by it ever since. They were God's people.

Needless to say, this upset others. The Greeks thought they were the superior race. They called non-Greeks "barbarians," a word intended to resemble the sound made by sheep. The Romans likewise thought themselves better than others, Christians and Muslims both held, in their different ways, that they, not the Jews, were the true chosen of God. The result was many centuries of persecution. So when Jews were given the chance to become citizens of the newly secular nation states of Europe, they seized it with open arms. In many cases they abandoned their faith and religious practice. But they were still regarded as Jews.

What, though, did this mean? It could not mean that they were a people dedicated to God, since many of them no longer believed in

God or acted as if they did. So it came to mean a race. Benjamin Disraeli,[1] converted to Christianity by his father as a young child, thought of his identity in those terms. He once wrote, "All is race – there is no other truth," and said about himself, in response to a taunt by the Irish politician Daniel O'Connell, "Yes, I am a Jew, and when the ancestors of the right honourable gentleman were brutal savages in an unknown island, mine were priests in the temple of Solomon."

The trouble was that hostility to Jews did not cease despite all that Europe claimed by way of enlightenment, reason, the pursuit of science, and emancipation. It could now, though, no longer be defined by religion, since neither Jews nor Europeans used that as the basis of identity. So Jews became hated for their race, and in the 1870s a new word was coined to express this: antisemitism. This was dangerous. So long as Jews were defined by religion, Christians could work to convert them. You can change your religion. But you cannot change your race. Antisemites could only work, therefore, for the expulsion or extermination of the Jews.

Ever since the Holocaust it has become taboo to use the word "race" in polite society in the West. Yet secular Jewish identity persists, and there seems no other way of referring to it. So a new term has come to be used instead: ethnicity, which means roughly what "race" meant in the nineteenth century. The Wikipedia definition of ethnicity is "a category of people who identify with each other based on common ancestral, social, cultural, or national experiences."

The trouble is that ethnicity is where we came from, not where we are going to. It involves culture and cuisine, a set of memories meaningful to parents but ever less so to their children. In any case, there is no one Jewish ethnicity; there are ethnicities in the plural. That is what makes Sephardic Jews different from their Ashkenazic cousins, and Sephardic Jews from North Africa and the Middle East different from those whose families originally came from Spain and Portugal.

Besides which, what is often thought of as Jewish ethnicity is often not even Jewish in origin. It is a lingering trace of what Jews absorbed

---

1. Benjamin Disraeli twice served as prime minister of the United Kingdom: 1868, 1874–1880.

from a local non-Jewish culture: Polish dress, Russian music, North African food, and the German-Jewish dialect known as Yiddish along with its Spanish-Jewish counterpart Ladino. Ethnicity is often a set of borrowings thought of as Jewish because their origins have been forgotten. Judaism is not an ethnicity and Jews are not an ethnic group. Go to the Western Wall in Jerusalem and you will see Jews of every colour and culture under the sun, the Beta Israel from Ethiopia, the Bene Israel from India, Bukharan Jews from central Asia, Iraqi, Berber, Egyptian, Kurdish, and Libyan Jews, the Temanim from Yemen, alongside American Jews from Russia, South African Jews from Lithuania, and British Jews from German-speaking Poland. Their food, music, dress, customs, and conventions are all different. Jewishness is not an ethnicity but a bricolage of multiple ethnicities.

Besides which, ethnicity does not last. If Jews are merely an ethnic group, they will experience the fate of all such groups, which is that they disappear over time. Like the grandchildren of Irish, Polish, German, and Norwegian immigrants to America, they merge into the melting pot. Ethnicity lasts for three generations, for as long as children can remember immigrant grandparents and their distinctive ways. Then it begins to fade, for there is no reason for it not to. If Jews had been no more than an ethnicity, they would have died out long ago, along with the Canaanites, Perizzites, and Jebusites, known only to students of antiquity and having left no mark on the civilisation of the West.

So when, in 2000, a British Jewish research institute proposed that Jews in Britain be defined as an ethnic group and not a religious community, it took a non-Jewish journalist, Andrew Marr, to state the obvious: "All this is shallow water," he wrote, "and the further in you wade, the shallower it gets." He continued:

> The Jews have always had stories for the rest of us. They have had their Bible, one of the great imaginative works of the human spirit. They have been victim of the worst modernity can do, a mirror for Western madness. Above all they have had the story of their cultural and genetic survival from the Roman Empire to the 2000s, weaving and thriving amid uncomprehending, hostile European tribes.

This story, their post-Bible, their epic of bodies, not words, involved an intense competitive hardening of generations which threw up, in the end, a blaze of individual geniuses in Europe and America. Outside painting, Morris dancing and rap music, it's hard to think of many areas of Western endeavour where Jews haven't been disproportionately successful. For non-Jews, who don't believe in a people being chosen by God, the lesson is that generations of people living on their wits and hard work, outside the more comfortable mainstream certainties, will seed Einsteins and Wittgensteins, Trotskys and Seiffs. Culture matters…. The Jews really have been different; they have enriched the world and challenged it.[2]

Marr himself is neither Jewish nor a religious believer, but his insight points us in the direction of this *parasha*, which contains one of the most important sentences in Judaism: "Speak to the whole assembly of Israel and say to them: Be holy because I, the Lord your God, am holy" (Lev. 19:2). Jews were and remain the people summoned to holiness.

What does this mean? Rashi reads it in context. The previous chapter was about forbidden sexual relationships. So is the next chapter. So he understands it as meaning, be careful not to put yourself in the way of temptation to forbidden sex. Nahmanides reads it more broadly. The Torah forbids certain activities and permits others. When it says "be holy" it means, according to Nahmanides, practise self-restraint even in the domain of the permitted. Don't be a glutton, even if what you are eating is kosher. Don't be an alcoholic, even if what you are drinking is kosher wine. Don't be, in his famous phrase, a *naval bireshut haTorah*, "a scoundrel with Torah license."

These are localised interpretations. They are what the verse means in its immediate context. But it clearly means something larger as well, and the chapter itself tells us what this is. To be holy is to love your neighbour and to love the stranger. It means not stealing, lying, or deceiving others. It means not standing idly by when someone else's life is in danger. It means not cursing the deaf or putting a stumbling block before

2. Andrew Marr, *The Observer*, Sunday, May 14, 2000.

the blind, that is, insulting or taking advantage of others even when they are completely unaware of it – because God is not unaware of it.

It means not planting your field with different kinds of seed, not crossbreeding your livestock, or wearing clothes made of a forbidden mixture of wool and linen – or as we would put it nowadays, respecting the integrity of the environment. It means not conforming with whatever happens to be the idolatry of the time – and every age has its idols. It means being honest in business, doing justice, treating your employees well, and sharing your blessings (in those days, parts of the harvest) with others.

It means not hating people, not bearing a grudge, or taking revenge. If someone has done you wrong, don't hate them. Remonstrate with them. Let them know what they have done and how it has hurt you, give them a chance to apologise and make amends, and then forgive them.

Above all, "be holy" means: Have the courage to be different. That is the root meaning of *kadosh* in Hebrew. It means something distinctive and set apart. "Be holy for I the Lord your God am holy" is one of the most counter-intuitive sentences in the whole of religious literature. How can we be like God? He is infinite; we are finite. He is eternal; we are mortal. He is vaster than the universe; we are a mere speck on its surface. Yet, says the Torah, in one respect we can be.

God is in, but not of, the world. So we are called on to be in, but not of, the world. We don't worship nature. We don't follow fashion. We don't behave like everyone else just because everyone else does. We don't conform. We dance to a different music. We don't live in the present. We remember our people's past and help build our people's future. Not by accident does the word *kadosh* also have the meaning of marriage, *kiddushin*, because to marry means to be faithful to one another, as God pledges Himself to be faithful to us and as we are to Him, even in the hard times.

To be holy means to bear witness to the presence of God in our, and our people's, lives. Israel – the Jewish people – is the people who in themselves give testimony to One beyond themselves. To be Jewish means to live in the conscious presence of the God we can't see but can sense as the force within ourselves urging us to be more courageous, just, and generous than ourselves. That's what Judaism's rituals are about: reminding us of the presence of the Divine.

Every individual on earth has an ethnicity. But only one people was ever asked collectively to be holy. That, to me, is what it is to be a Jew.

Emor

Holy Times

P*arashat Emor* contains a chapter dedicated to the festivals of the
Jewish year. There are five such passages in the Torah. Two, both in the
book of Exodus (Ex. 23:14–17; 34:18, 22–23), are very brief. They refer
only to the three pilgrimage festivals, Pesaḥ, Shavuot, and Sukkot. They
do not specify their dates, merely their rough position in the agricultural
year. Nor do they mention the specific commands related to the festivals.

This leaves three other festival accounts, the one in our *parasha*, a second one in Numbers 28–29, and the third in Deuteronomy 16.
What is striking is how different they are. This is not, as critics maintain,
because the Torah is a composite document but rather because it comes
at its subject-matter from multiple perspectives – a characteristic of the
Torah mindset as a whole.

The long section on the festivals in Numbers is wholly dedicated to the special additional sacrifices [the *musaf*] brought on
holy days including Shabbat and Rosh Ḥodesh. A memory of this is
preserved in the *Musaf* prayers for these days. These are holy times
from the perspective of the Tabernacle, the Temple, and later the
synagogue.

The account in Deuteronomy is about society. Moses at the end
of his life told the next generation where they had come from, where

they were going to, and the kind of society they were to construct. It was to be the opposite of Egypt. It would strive for justice, freedom, and human dignity.

One of Deuteronomy's most important themes is its insistence that worship be centralised "in the place that God will choose," which turned out to be Jerusalem. The unity of God was to be mirrored in the unity of the nation, something that could not be achieved if every tribe had its own temple, sanctuary, or shrine. That is why, when it comes to the festivals, Deuteronomy speaks only of Pesaḥ, Shavuot, and Sukkot, and not Rosh HaShana, or Yom Kippur, because only on those three was there a duty of *aliya leregel*, pilgrimage to the Temple.

Equally significant is Deuteronomy's focus – not found elsewhere – on social inclusion: "You, your sons and daughters, your male and female servants, the Levites within your gates, and the stranger, the orphan, and the widow living among you." Deuteronomy is less about individual spirituality than about the kind of society that honours the presence of God by honouring our fellow humans, especially those at the margins of society. The idea that we can serve God while being indifferent to, or dismissive of, our fellow human beings is utterly alien to the vision of Deuteronomy.

Which leaves the account in this *parasha*. It too is distinctive. Unlike the Exodus and Deuteronomy passages it includes Rosh HaShana and Yom Kippur. It also tells us about the specific mitzvot of the festivals, most notably Sukkot: it is the only place where the Torah mentions the *arba minim*, the "four kinds," and the command to live in a sukka.

It has, though, various structural oddities. The most striking one is the fact that it includes Shabbat in the list of the festivals. This would not be strange in itself. After all, Shabbat is one of the holy days. What is strange is the *way it speaks about* Shabbat:

> The Lord said to Moses: Speak to the Israelites and say to them: The appointed times [*mo'adei*] of the Lord, which you are to proclaim [*tikre'u*] as sacred assemblies [*mikra'ei kodesh*]. These are My appointed festivals [*mo'adai*]. Six days shall you work, but the seventh day is a Sabbath of Sabbaths, a day of sacred assembly

[*mikra kodesh*]. You are not to do any work; wherever you live, it is a Sabbath to the Lord. (23:1–3)

There is then a paragraph break, after which the whole passage seems to begin again:

These are the Lord's appointed times [*mo'adei*] festivals, the sacred assemblies [*mikra'ei kodesh*] you are to proclaim [*tikre'u*] at their appointed times [*bemo'adam*]. (v. 4)

This structure, with its two beginnings, puzzled the commentators. Even more was the fact that the Torah here seems to be calling Shabbat a *moed*, an appointed time, and a *mikra kodesh*, a sacred assembly, which it does nowhere else. As Rashi puts it: "What has Shabbat to do with the festivals?" The festivals are annual occurrences, Shabbat is a weekly one. The festivals depend on the calendar fixed by the *beit din*. That is the meaning of the phrase, "the sacred assemblies *you are to proclaim* at their appointed times." Shabbat, however, does not depend on any act by the *beit din* and is independent of both the solar and lunar calendar. Its holiness comes directly from God and from the dawn of creation. Bringing the two together under a single heading seems to make no sense. Shabbat is one thing, *mo'adim* and *mikra'ei kodesh* are something else. So what connects the two?

Rashi tells us it is to emphasise the holiness of the festivals. "Whoever desecrates the festivals, it is as if he had desecrated Shabbat, and whoever observes the festivals it is as if he had observed Shabbat." The point Rashi is making is that we can imagine someone saying that he respects Shabbat because it is God-given, but the festivals are of an altogether lesser sanctity, first because we are permitted certain kinds of work, such as cooking and carrying, and second because they depend on a human act of fixing the calendar. The inclusion of Shabbat among the festivals is to negate this kind of reasoning.

Nahmanides offers a very different explanation. Shabbat is stated before the festivals just as it is stated before Moses' instructions to the people to begin work on the construction of the Sanctuary, to tell us that just as the command to build the Sanctuary does not override Shabbat, so the command to celebrate the festivals does not override Shabbat. So, although we may cook and carry on festivals, we may not do so if a festival falls on Shabbat.

By far the most radical explanation was given by the Vilna Gaon. According to him, the words "Six days shall you work, but the seventh day is a Sabbath of Sabbaths," *do not apply to the days of the week but to the days of the year.* There are seven holy days specified in our *parasha*: the first and seventh day of Pesaḥ, one day of Shavuot, Rosh HaShana, Yom Kippur, the first day of Sukkot, and Shemini Atzeret. On six of them we are allowed to do some work, such as cooking and carrying, but on the seventh, Yom Kippur, we are not, because it is a "Sabbath of Sabbaths" (see verse 32). The Torah uses two different expressions for the prohibition of work on festivals in general and on the "seventh day." On the festivals what is forbidden is *melekhet avoda* ("burdensome or servile work"), whereas on the seventh day what is forbidden is *melakha*, "any work," even if not burdensome. So Yom Kippur is to the year what Shabbat is to the week.

The Vilna Gaon's reading allows us to see something else: that holy time is patterned on what I have called (in the introduction to the siddur)[1] *fractals*: the same pattern at different levels of magnitude. So the structure of the week – six days of work followed by a seventh that is holy – is mirrored in the structure of the year – six days of lesser holiness plus a seventh, Yom Kippur, of supreme holiness. As we will see in two chapters' time (Lev. 25), the same pattern appears on an even larger scale: six ordinary years followed by the year of *Shemitta*, "release."

Wherever the Torah wishes to emphasise the dimension of *holiness* (the word *kodesh* appears no less than twelve times in Leviticus 23), it makes systematic use of the number and concept of seven. So there are not only seven holy days in the annual calendar. There are also seven paragraphs in the chapter. The word "seven" or "seventh" occurs repeatedly (eighteen times) as does the word for the seventh day, *Shabbat*, in one or other of its forms (fifteen times). The word "harvest" appears seven times.

---

1. "Understanding Jewish Prayer," in *The Koren Shalem Siddur* (Jerusalem: Koren Publishers, 2017).

However, it seems to me that Leviticus 23 is telling another story as well – a deeply spiritual one. Recall our claim (made in the essay on *Parashat Ki Tissa*) that the Tabernacle was built because Moses argued that the people *needed God to be close*. They wanted to encounter Him not only at the top of the mountain, but also in the midst of the camp; not only as a terrifying power overturning empires and dividing the sea, but also as a constant presence in their lives. That was why God gave the Israelites the Sanctuary (Ex. 25–40) and its service (i.e., the book of Leviticus as a whole).

That is why the list of the festivals in Leviticus emphasises not the *social* dimension we find in Deuteronomy, or the *sacrificial* dimension we find in Numbers, but rather the *spiritual* dimension of encounter, closeness, *the meeting of the human and the Divine*. This explains why we find in this chapter, more than in any other, two key words. One is *moed*, the other is *mikra kodesh*, and both are deeper than they seem.

The word *moed* does not just mean "appointed time." We find the same word in the phrase *ohel moed* meaning "tent of meeting." If the *ohel moed* was the *place* where man and God met, then the *mo'adim* in our chapter are the *times* when we and God meet. This idea is given beautiful expression in the last line of the mystical song we sing on Shabbat, *Yedid Nefesh*, "Hurry, beloved, for the appointed time [*moed*] has come." *Moed* here means a tryst – an appointment made between lovers to meet at a certain time and place.

As for the phrase *mikra kodesh*, it comes from the same root as the word that gives the entire book its name: *vayikra*, meaning "to be summoned in love." A *mikra kodesh* is not just a holy day. It is a meeting to which we have been called in affection by One who holds us close.

Much of the book of Leviticus is about the holiness of place, the Sanctuary. Some of it is about the holiness of people, the *kohanim*, the priests, and Israel as a whole, as "a kingdom of priests." In chapter 23 the Torah turns to the holiness of time and the times of holiness.

We are spiritual beings but we are also physical beings. *We cannot be spiritual, close to God, all the time.* That is why there is secular time as well as holy time. But one day in seven, we stop working and enter the presence of the God of creation. On certain days of the year, the festivals, we celebrate the God of history. The holiness of Shabbat is determined by God alone because He alone created the universe. The holiness of the festivals is partially determined by us (i.e., by the fixing of the calendar), because history is a partnership between us and God. But in two respects they are the same. They are both times of meeting (*moed*), and they are both times when we feel ourselves called, summoned, invited as God's guests (*mikra kodesh*).

We can't always be spiritual. God has given us a material world with which to engage. But on the seventh day of the week, and (originally) seven days in the year, God gives us dedicated time in which we feel the closeness of the *Shekhina* and are bathed in the radiance of God's love.

Behar

Family Feeling

I argued in the essay on *Parashat Kedoshim* that Judaism is more than an ethnicity. It is a call to holiness. In one sense, however, there *is* an important ethnic dimension to Judaism.

It is best captured in the 1980s joke about an advertising campaign in New York. Throughout the city there were giant posters with the slogan, "You have a friend in the Chase Manhattan Bank." Underneath one, an Israeli had scribbled the words, "But in Bank Leumi you have *mishpoḥa*." Jews are, and are conscious of being, a single extended family.

This is particularly evident in this *parasha*. Repeatedly we read of social legislation couched in the language of family:

> When you buy or sell to your neighbour, let no one wrong *his brother*. (Lev. 25:14)

> If your brother becomes impoverished and sells some of his property, his near redeemer is to come to you and redeem what *his brother* sold. (v. 25)

> If *your brother* is impoverished and indebted to you, you must support him; he must live with you like a foreign resident. Do

not take interest or profit from him, but fear your God and let *your brother* live with you. (vv. 35–36)

If *your brother* becomes impoverished and is sold to you, do not work him like a slave. (v. 39)

"Your brother" in these verses is not meant literally. At times it means your relative, but mostly it means your fellow Jew. This is a distinctive way of thinking about society and our obligations to others. Jews are not just citizens of the same nation or adherents of the same faith. We are members of the same extended family. We are – biologically or electively – children of Abraham and Sarah. For the most part, we share the same history. On the festivals we relive the same memories. We were forged in the same crucible of suffering. We are more than friends. We are *mishpoḥa*, family.

The concept of family is absolutely fundamental to Judaism. Consider the book of Genesis, the Torah's starting point. It is not primarily about theology, doctrine, dogma. It is not a polemic against idolatry. It is about families: husbands and wives, parents and children, brothers and sisters.

At key moments in the Torah, God Himself defines His relationship with the Israelites in terms of family. He tells Moses to say to Pharaoh in His name: "My child, My firstborn, Israel" (Ex. 4:22). When Moses wants to explain to the Israelites why they have a duty to be holy, He says, "You are children of the Lord your God" (Deut. 14:1). If God is our parent, then we are all brothers and sisters. We are related by bonds that go to the very heart of who we are.

The prophets continued the metaphor. There is a lovely passage in Hosea in which the prophet describes God as a parent teaching a young child how to take its first faltering steps: "When Israel was a child, I loved him, and out of Egypt I called my son…. It was I who taught Ephraim to walk, taking them by the arms…. To them I was like one who lifts a little child to the cheek, and I bent down to feed them" (Hos. 11:1–4).

The same image is continued in rabbinic Judaism. In one of the most famous phrases of prayer, R. Akiva used the words *Avinu Malkeinu*, "Our Father, our King." That is a precise and deliberate expression. God is indeed our sovereign, our lawgiver, and our judge, but before He is any of these things, He is our parent and we are His children. That is why we believe divine compassion will always override strict justice.

This concept of Jews as an extended family is powerfully expressed in Maimonides' laws of charity:

> The entire Jewish people and all those who attach themselves to them are like brothers, as it states: "You are children of the Lord your God" [Deut. 14:1]. And if a brother will not show mercy to a brother, who will show mercy to them? To whom do the poor of Israel lift up their eyes? To the gentiles who hate them and pursue them? Their eyes are turned to their brethren alone.[1]

This sense of kinship, fraternity, and the family bond is at the heart of the idea of *kol Yisrael arevim zeh bazeh*, "All Jews are responsible for one another." Or as R. Shimon bar Yoḥai put it, "When one Jew is injured, all Jews feel the pain."[2]

Why is Judaism built on this model of the family? Partly to tell us that God did not choose an elite of the righteous or a sect of the likeminded. He chose a family – Abraham and Sarah's descendants – extended through time. The family is the most powerful vehicle of continuity, and the kinds of changes Jews were expected to make to the world could not be achieved in a single generation. Hence the importance of the family as a place of education ("You shall teach these things repeatedly to your children" [Deut. 6:7]) and of handing the story on, especially on Pesaḥ through the Seder service.

Another reason is that family feeling is the most primal and powerful moral bond. The scientist J. B. S. Haldane famously said, when asked whether he would jump into a river and risk his life to save his drowning brother, "No, but I would do so to save two brothers or eight cousins." The point he was making was that we share 50 per cent of our genes with our siblings, and an eighth with our cousins. Taking a risk to save them is a way of ensuring that our genes are passed on to the next

---

1. Maimonides, *Mishneh Torah, Hilkhot Matnot Aniyim* 10:2.
2. *Mekhilta DeRabbi Shimon bar Yoḥai* on Exodus 19:6.

generation. This principle, known as "kin selection," is the most basic form of human altruism. It is where the moral sense is born.

That is a key insight, not only of biology but also of political theory. Edmund Burke (1729–1797) famously said, "To be attached to the subdivision, to love the little platoon we belong to in society, is the first principle (the germ as it were) of public affections. It is the first link in the series by which we proceed towards a love to our country, and to mankind."[3] Likewise Alexis de Tocqueville said, "As long as family feeling was kept alive, the opponent of oppression was never alone."[4]

Strong families are essential to free societies. Where families are strong, a sense of altruism exists that can be extended outward, from family to friends, to neighbours, to community, and from there to the nation as a whole.

It was the sense of family that kept Jews linked in a web of mutual obligation despite the fact that they were scattered across the world. Does it still exist? Sometimes the divisions in the Jewish world go so deep, and the insults hurled by one group against another are so brutal that one could almost be persuaded that it does not. In the 1950s Martin Buber expressed the belief that the Jewish people in the traditional sense no longer existed. *Knesset Yisrael*, the covenantal people as a single entity before God, was no more. The divisions between Jews, religious and secular, Orthodox and non-Orthodox, Zionist and non-Zionist, had, he thought, fragmented the people beyond hope of repair.

Yet that conclusion is premature for precisely the reason that makes family so elemental a bond. Argue with your friend and tomorrow he may no longer be your friend, but argue with your brother and tomorrow he is still your brother. The book of Genesis is full of sibling rivalries, but they do not all end the same way. The story of Cain and Abel ends with Abel dead. The story of Isaac and Ishmael ends with their standing together at Abraham's grave. The story of Esau and Jacob reaches a climax when, after a long separation, they meet, embrace, and go their separate ways. The story of Joseph and his brothers begins with

---

3. Edmund Burke, *Reflections on the French Revolution* (The Harvard Classics, 1909–14).
4. Alexis de Tocqueville, "Principal Causes Which Tend to Maintain the Democratic Republic in the United States."

animosity but ends with forgiveness and reconciliation. Even the most dysfunctional families can eventually come together.

The Jewish people remains a family, often divided, always argumentative, but bound in a common bond of fate nonetheless. As our *parasha* reminds us, that person who has fallen is our brother or sister, and ours must be the hand that helps them rise again.

Beḥukkotai

A Sense of Direction

Smartphones can do amazing things – few more amazing than Waze, the Israeli-designed satellite navigation system acquired by Google in 2013. But there is one thing even Waze cannot do. It can tell you how to get there, but it cannot tell you where to go. That is something you must decide.

The most important decision we can make in life is to choose where we want eventually to be. Without a sense of destiny and destination, our lives will be directionless. If we don't know where we want to go, we will never get there, no matter how fast we travel. Yet despite this, there are people who spend months planning a holiday, but not even a day planning a life. They simply let it happen.

That is what our *parasha* is about, applied to a nation, not an individual. God, through Moses, set out the stark choice:

> If you follow My statutes and carefully obey My commands, I will send you rain in its season and the ground will yield its crops and the trees their fruit.... I will grant peace in the land, and you will lie down and no one will make you afraid. (Lev. 26:3–6)

If, on the other hand, "You do not listen to Me, and do not keep all these commands" (v. 14), then disaster will follow. The curses set out here at length are among the most frightening of all biblical texts – a portrait of national catastrophe, bleak and devastating.

The entire passage, both the blessings and the curses, can be read supernaturally or naturally. Read the first way, Israel's fate, at least in biblical times, was a direct result of its faithfulness or lack of it to the Torah. God was constantly intervening miraculously in history to reward the good and punish the bad. Every drought and famine, every bad harvest or military defeat, was the result of sin. Every peaceful and productive year was the result of obedience to God. That is how Israel's prophets understood history.

But there is also a more naturalistic reading, which says that divine providence works through us, internally rather than externally. If you are the Israelites in the Land of Israel, you will always be surrounded by empires and enemies bigger and stronger than you are. You will always be vulnerable to the hazards of rainfall and drought because Israel, unlike the Nile Delta or the Tigris-Euphrates valley, has no natural, reliable, predictable supply of water. You will always, therefore, find yourself looking up to the heavens. Even quite secular Jews often understand this – most famously David Ben Gurion when he said, "In Israel, in order to be a realist you have to believe in miracles."

According to this reading, the way of life set out in the Torah is unique in ways that are natural rather than supernatural. It is indeed the word of God, but not God as a perpetual strategic intervener in history, but rather, God as guide as to how to live in such a way as to be blessed. The Torah is a set of instructions for life issued by the Designer of life. That is what the Sages meant when they said that at the beginning of time, "God looked into the Torah and created the world." Living according to the Torah means, in this view, aligning yourself with the forces that make for human flourishing, especially if you are a tiny people surrounded by enemies.

What was unique about the society envisaged by the Torah is that every individual mattered. Justice was to be paramount. The rich could not buy special treatment and the poor were not left destitute. When it came to communal celebrations, everyone – especially the orphan, the widow, the stranger – was to be included.

Everyone had at least some share in the harvest of grain and fruit. Employers were to treat employees with fairness and sensitivity. Even though there were still slaves, one day in seven they would enjoy the same freedom as their owners. This meant that everyone had a stake in society. Therefore they would defend it with their lives. The Israelites were not an army conscripted by a ruler for the purpose of his own self-aggrandisement. That is why they were capable of defeating armies and nations many times their size.

Above all, they were to have a sense of destiny and destination. That is the meaning of the keyword that runs like a refrain through the curses: *keri*, a word that appears seven times in our *parasha* and nowhere else in Tanakh. "If you walk with Me with *keri*…then I will walk with you with *keri*" (Lev. 26:23–24).

There are many interpretations of this word. Targum Onkelos reads it as "hard-heartedly," Saadia Gaon as "rebelliously," Rashi as "treating as a casual concern." Others understand it as "harshly," or "with hostility." Maimonides, however (partially echoed by Rashi, Rashbam, Ibn Ezra, Ḥizkuni, and others), understands it as related to the word *mikreh*, meaning "chance." Hence the meaning of the passage according to Maimonides is: "If you believe that what happens to you is simply a matter of chance, then, says God, I will leave you to chance."

On this reading, the book of Leviticus ends as it began, with the fateful choice between *mikra* (with an *alef*) and *mikreh* (with a *heh*): between seeing life as a call, a summons, a vocation, a destiny,[1] and seeing it as an accident, a random happening with no ultimate meaning whatsoever.

So it is in the life of nations and individuals. If you see what happens to you as mere chance, your fate will be governed by mere chance. That is what the Sages meant when they said, "Wherever [the Torah] says, 'And it came to pass,' it is always a prelude to tragedy" (Megilla 10b). If you simply let things come to pass, you will find yourself exposed to the vagaries of fortune and the whims of others. But if you believe you are here for a purpose, your life will take on the directedness of that

---

1. See above, *Parashat Vayikra*, "The Pursuit of Meaning."

purpose. Your energies will be focused. A sense of mission will give you strength. You will do remarkable things.

That was the special insight Jews brought to the world. They did not believe – as people did in ancient times and as atheists do today – that the universe is governed by mere chance. Was it mere chance that a random fluctuation in the quantum field produced the Big Bang that brought the universe into being? Or that the universe just happened to be regulated by precisely the six mathematical constants necessary for it to give rise to stars and planets and the chemical elements essential for the emergence of life? Was it mere chance that life did in fact emerge from inanimate matter? Or that among the hundred million life forms that have existed on earth, just one, Homo sapiens, was capable of asking the question "Why?"

There is nothing self-contradictory about such a view. It is compatible with all the science we now know, perhaps with all the science we will ever know. That is the universe as *keri*. Many people think this way. They always did. In this view, there is no "Why," neither for nations, nor for individuals. Life just happens. We are here by accident.

Jews believe otherwise. No one said it better than the Catholic historian Paul Johnson:

> No people has ever insisted more firmly than the Jews that history has a purpose and humanity a destiny. At a very early stage in their collective existence they believed they had detected a divine scheme for the human race, of which their own society was to be a pilot. They worked out their role in immense detail. They clung to it with heroic persistence in the face of savage suffering. Many of them believe it still. Others transmuted it into Promethean endeavours to raise our condition by purely human means. The Jewish vision became the prototype for many similar grand designs for humanity, both divine and man-made. The Jews therefore stand right at the centre of the perennial attempt to give human life the dignity of a purpose.[2]

2. Paul Johnson, "Prologue" to *A History of the Jews* (London: Weidenfeld and Nicolson, 1987).

The people who change the world are those who believe that life has a purpose, a direction, a destiny. They know where they want to go and what they want to achieve. In the case of Judaism that purpose is clear: to show what it is to create a small clearing in the desert of humanity where freedom and order coexist, where justice prevails, the weak are cared for and those in need are given help, where we have the humility to attribute our successes to God and our failures to ourselves, where we cherish life as the gift of God and do all we can to make it holy. In other words: precisely the opposite of the violence and brutality that is today being perpetrated by some religious extremists in the name of God.

To achieve this, though, we have to have a sense of collective purpose. That is the choice that Moses, speaking in the name of God, set before the Israelites. *Mikra* or *mikreh*? Does life just happen? Or is it a call from God to create moments of moral and spiritual beauty that redeem our humanity from the ruthless pursuit of power? "To give human life the dignity of a purpose." That is what Jews are called on to show the world.

Numbers
במדבר

Bemidbar

The Sound of Silence

P*arashat Bemidbar* is usually read on the Shabbat before Shavuot.
So the Sages connected the two. Shavuot is the time of the giving of
the Torah. *Bemidbar* means, "In the desert." What then is the connection between the desert and the Torah, the wilderness and God's word?

The Sages gave several interpretations. According to the *Mekhilta*, the Torah was given publicly, openly, and in a place no one owns
because had it been given in the Land of Israel, Jews would have said
to the nations of the world, "You have no share in it." Instead, whoever
wants to come and accept it, let them come and accept it.[1]

Another explanation: Had the Torah been given in Israel the
nations of the world would have had an excuse for not accepting it. This
follows the rabbinic tradition that before God gave the Torah to the
Israelites He offered it to all the other nations and each found a reason
to decline.[2]

Yet another: Just as the wilderness is free – it costs nothing to
enter – so the Torah is free. It is God's gift to us.[3]

---

1. *Mekhilta, Yitro, Baḥodesh,* 1.
2. Ibid., 5.
3. Ibid.

But there is another, more spiritual reason. The desert is a place of silence. There is nothing visual to distract you, and there is no ambient noise to muffle sound. To be sure, when the Israelites received the Torah, there was thunder and lightning and the sound of a shofar. The earth felt as if it were shaking at its foundations. But in a later age, when the prophet Elijah stood at the same mountain after his confrontation with the prophets of Baal, he encountered God not in the whirlwind, or the fire, or the earthquake, but in the *kol demama daka*, the still, small voice, literally "the sound of a slender silence" (I Kings 19:9–12). I define this as *the sound you can only hear if you are listening*. In the silence of the *midbar*, the desert, you can hear the *Medaber*, the Speaker, and the *medubar*, that which is spoken. To hear the voice of God you need a listening silence in the soul.

Many years ago British television produced a documentary series, *The Long Search*, on the world's great religions.[4] When it came to Judaism, the presenter Ronald Eyre seemed surprised by its blooming, buzzing confusion, especially the loud, argumentative voices in the *beit midrash*, the house of study. Remarking on this to Elie Wiesel, he asked, "Is there such a thing as a *silence* in Judaism?" Wiesel replied: "Judaism is full of silences...but *we don't talk about them*."

Judaism is a very verbal culture, a religion of holy words. Through words, God created the universe: "And God said, Let there be...and there was." According to the Targum, it is our ability to speak that makes us human. It translates the phrase "and man became a living soul" (Gen. 2:7) as "and man became a *speaking* soul." Words create. Words communicate. Our relationships are shaped, for good or bad, by language. Much of Judaism is about the power of words to make or break worlds.

So silence in Tanakh often has a negative connotation. "Aaron was silent," says the Torah, after the death of his two sons Nadav and Avihu (Lev. 10:3). "The dead do not praise You," says Psalm 115, "nor do those who go down to the silence [of the grave]." When Job's friends came to comfort him after the loss of his children and other afflictions, "they sat down with him on the ground for seven days and seven nights,

---

4. BBC television, first shown 1977.

yet no one spoke a word to him, for they saw that his pain was very great" (Job 2:13).

But not all silence is sad. Psalms tells us that "to You, silence is praise" (Ps. 65:2). If we are truly in awe at the greatness of God, the vastness of the universe, and the almost infinite extent of time, our deepest emotions will indeed lie too deep for words. We will experience silent communion.

The Sages valued silence. They called it "a fence to wisdom" (Mishna Avot 3:13). If words are worth a coin, silence is worth two (Megilla 18a). R. Shimon ben Gamliel said, "All my days I have grown up among the wise, and I have found nothing better than silence" (Mishna Avot 1:17).

The service of the priests in the Temple was accompanied by silence. The Levites sang in the courtyard, but the priests – unlike their counterparts in other ancient religions – neither sang nor spoke while offering the sacrifices. One scholar, Israel Knohl, has accordingly spoken of "the silence of the sanctuary." The Zohar (2a) speaks of silence as the medium in which both the Sanctuary above and the Sanctuary below are made.

There were Jews who cultivated silence as a spiritual discipline. Bratslav Hasidim meditate in the fields. There are Jews who practise *taanit dibbur*, a "fast of words." Our most profound prayer, the private saying of the *Amida*, is called *tefilla belaḥash*, the "silent prayer." It is based on the precedent of Hannah, praying for a child. "She spoke in her heart. Her lips moved but her voice was not heard" (I Sam. 1:13).

God hears our silent cry. In the agonising tale of how Sarah told Abraham to send Hagar and her son away, the Torah tells us that when their water ran out and the young Ishmael was at the point of dying, Hagar cried, yet God heard "the voice of the child" (Gen. 21:16–17). Earlier when the angels came to visit Abraham and told him that Sarah would have a child, Sarah laughed inwardly, that is, silently, yet she was heard by God (Gen. 18:12–13). God hears our thoughts even when they are not expressed in speech.

The silence that counts in Judaism is thus a listening silence – and listening is the supreme religious art. Listening means making space for others to speak and be heard. As I point out in my commentary to the siddur,[5] there is no English word that remotely equals the Hebrew verb SH-M-A in its wide range of senses: to listen, to hear, to pay attention, to understand, to internalise, and to respond in deed.

This was one of the key elements in the Sinai covenant, when the Israelites, having already said twice, "All that God says, we will do," then said, "All that God says, we will do and we will hear [*venishma*]" (Ex. 24:7). It is the *nishma* – listening, hearing, heeding, responding – that is the key religious act.

Thus Judaism is not only a religion of doing and speaking; it is also a religion of listening. Faith is *the ability to hear the music beneath the noise.* There is the silent music of the spheres, about which Psalm 19 speaks:

> The heavens declare the glory of God
> The skies proclaim the work of His hands.
> Day to day they pour forth speech,
> Night to night they communicate knowledge.
> There is no speech, there are no words,
> Their voice is not heard.
> Yet their music carries throughout the earth.

There is the voice of history that was heard by the prophets, and there is the commanding voice of Sinai, that continues to speak to us across the abyss of time. I sometimes think that people in the modern age have found the concept of "Torah from heaven" problematic, not because of some new archaeological discovery, but because we have lost the habit of listening to the sound of transcendence, a voice beyond the merely human.

It is fascinating that despite his often-fractured relationship with Judaism, Sigmund Freud created in psychoanalysis a deeply Jewish form of healing. He himself called it the "speaking cure," but it is in fact a *listening* cure. Almost all effective forms of psychotherapy involve deep listening.

Is there enough listening in the Jewish world today? Do we, in marriage, really listen to our spouses? Do we as parents truly listen to our children? Do we, as leaders, hear the unspoken fears of those we

---

5. *Koren Shalem Siddur.*

seek to lead? Do we internalise the sense of hurt of the people who feel excluded from the community? Can we really claim to be listening to the voice of God if we fail to listen to the voices of our fellow humans?

In his poem "In memory of W B Yeats," W H Auden wrote:

> In the deserts of the heart
> Let the healing fountain start.

From time to time we need to step back from the noise and hubbub of the social world and create in our hearts the stillness of the desert where, within the silence, we can hear the *kol demama daka*, the still, small voice of God, telling us we are loved, we are heard, we are embraced by God's everlasting arms, we are not alone.[6]

---

6. For more on the theme of listening, see *Parashat Bereshit*, "The Art of Listening," and *Parashat Ekev*, "The Spirituality of Listening."

Naso

The Blessing of Love

At 176 verses, *Naso* is the longest of the *parashot*. Yet one of its most moving passages, and the one that has had the greatest impact over the course of history, is very short indeed and is known by almost every Jew, namely the priestly blessings:

> The Lord said to Moses:
>
> Tell Aaron and his sons, "Thus shall you bless the Israelites. Say to them:
>
> May the Lord bless you and protect you;
> May the Lord make His face shine on you and be gracious to you;
> May the Lord turn His face toward you and give you peace."
>
> Let them set My name on the Israelites, and I will bless them. (Num. 6:23–27)

This is among the oldest of all prayer texts. It was used by the priests in the Temple. It is said today by the *kohanim* in the reader's repetition of the *Amida*, in Israel every day, in most of the Diaspora only on festivals.

It is used by parents as they bless their children on Friday night. It is often said to the bride and groom under the *ḥuppa*. It is the simplest and most beautiful of all blessings.

It also appears in the oldest of all biblical texts that have physically survived till today. In 1979 the archaeologist Gabriel Barkay was examining ancient burial caves at Ketef Hinnom, outside the walls of Jerusalem in the area now occupied by the Menachem Begin Heritage Center. A thirteen-year-old boy who was assisting Barkay discovered that beneath the floor of one of the caves was a hidden chamber. There the group discovered almost one thousand ancient artefacts including two tiny silver scrolls no more than an inch long.

They were so fragile that it took three years to work out a way of unrolling them without causing them to disintegrate. Eventually the scrolls turned out to be *kemayot*, amulets, containing, among other texts, the priestly blessings. Scientifically dated to the sixth century BCE, the age of Jeremiah and the last days of the First Temple, they are four centuries older than the most ancient of biblical texts known hitherto, the Dead Sea Scrolls. Today the amulets can be seen in the Israel Museum, testimony to the ancient connection of Jews to the land and the continuity of Jewish faith itself.

What gives the priestly blessings their power is their simplicity and beauty. They have a strong rhythmic structure. The lines contain three, five, and seven words respectively. In each, the second word is "the Lord." In all three verses the first part refers to an activity on the part of God – "bless," "make His face shine," and "turn His face toward." The second part describes the effect of the blessing on us, giving us protection, grace, and peace.

They also travel inward, as it were. The first verse, "May the Lord bless you and protect you," refers, as the commentators note, to *material* blessings: sustenance, physical health, and so on. The second, "May the Lord make His face shine on you and be gracious to you," refers to moral blessing. *Ḥen*, grace, is what we show to other people and they to us. It is interpersonal. Here we are asking God to give some of His grace to us and others so that we can live together without the strife and envy that can so easily poison relationships.

The third is the most inward of all. There is a lovely story about a crowd of people who have gathered on a hill by the sea to watch a great ship pass by. A young child is waving vigorously. One of the men in the crowd asks him why. He says, "I am waving so the captain of the ship can see me and wave back." "But," said the man, "the ship is far away, and there is a crowd of us here. What makes you think that the captain can see you?" "Because," said the boy, "the captain of the ship is my father. He will be looking for me among the crowd."

That is roughly what we mean when we say, "May the Lord turn His face toward you." There are seven billion people now living on this earth. What makes any of us more than a face in the crowd, a wave in the ocean, a grain of sand on the sea shore? The fact that we are God's children. He is our parent. He turns His face toward us. He cares.

The God of Abraham is not a mere force of nature, or even all the forces of nature combined. A tsunami does not pause to ask who its victims will be. There is nothing personal about an earthquake or a tornado. The word *Elokim* means something like "the force of forces, cause of causes, the totality of all scientifically discoverable laws." It refers to those aspects of God that are impersonal. It also refers to God in His attribute of justice, since justice is essentially impersonal.

But the name we call *Hashem* – the name used in the priestly blessings, and in almost all the priestly texts – is God as He relates to us as individuals, each with our unique configuration of hopes and fears, gifts and possibilities. *Hashem* is the aspect of God that allows us to use the word "You." He is the God who speaks to us and who listens when we speak to Him. How this happens, we do not know, but *that* it happens is central to Jewish faith.

That we call God *Hashem* is the transcendental confirmation of our significance in the scheme of things. We matter as individuals because God cares for us as a parent for a child. That, incidentally, is one reason why the priestly blessings are all in the singular, to emphasise that God blesses us not only collectively but also individually. One life, said the Sages, is like a universe.[1]

Hence the meaning of the last of the priestly blessings. The knowledge that God turns His face toward us – that we are not just an indiscernible face in a crowd, but that God relates to us in our uniqueness

---

1. See Mishna Sanhedrin 4:5.

and singularity – is the most profound and ultimate source of peace. Competition, strife, lawlessness, and violence come from the psychological need to prove that *we matter*. We do things to prove that I am more powerful, or richer, or more successful than you. I can make you fear. I can bend you to my will. I can turn you into my victim, my subject, my slave. All of these things testify not to faith, but to a profound failure of faith.

Faith means that I believe that God cares about me. I am here because He wanted me to be. The soul He gave me is pure. Even though I am like the child on the hill watching the ship pass by, I know that God is looking for me, waving to me as I wave to Him. That is the most profound inner source of peace. We do not need to prove ourselves in order to receive a blessing from God. All we need to know is that His face is turned toward us. When we are at peace with ourselves, we can begin to make peace with the world.

So the blessings become longer and deeper: from the external blessing of material goods to the interpersonal blessing of grace between ourselves and others, to the most inward of them all, the peace of mind that comes when we feel that God sees us, hears us, holds us in His everlasting arms.

One further detail of the priestly blessings is unique, namely the blessing that the Sages instituted to be said by the *kohanim* over the mitzva: "Blessed are You ... who has made us holy with the holiness of Aaron and has commanded us to bless His people Israel *with love*."

It is the last word, *be'ahava*, that is unusual. It appears in no other blessing over the performance of a command. It seems to make no sense. Ideally, we should fulfill *all* the commands with love. But an absence of love does not invalidate any other command. In any case, the blessing over the performance of a command is a way of showing that we are acting intentionally. There was an argument between the Sages as to whether mitzvot in general require intention (*kavana*) or not.[2] But whether they do or not, making a blessing beforehand shows that we do have the intention to fulfil the command. But intention is one thing, emotion is another. Surely what matters is that the *kohanim* recite the

---

2. See Rosh HaShana 28a.

blessing and God will do the rest. What difference does it make whether they do so in love or not?

The commentators wrestle with this question. Some say that the fact that the *kohanim* are facing the people when they bless means that they are like the cherubim in the Tabernacle, whose faces "were turned to one another" as a sign of love. Others change the word order. They say that the blessing really means, "who has made us holy with the holiness of Aaron and *with love* has commanded us to bless His people Israel." "Love" here refers to *God's* love for Israel, not that of the *kohanim*.

However, it seems to me that the explanation is this: The Torah explicitly says that though the *kohanim* say the words, it is God who sends the blessing. "Let them put My name on the Israelites, and I will bless them." Normally when we fulfil a mitzva, *we* are doing something. But *when the kohanim bless the people, they are not doing anything in and of themselves. Instead they are acting as channels through which God's blessing flows into the world and into our lives.* Only love does this. Love means that we are focused not on ourselves but on another. Love is selflessness. And only selflessness allows us to be a channel through which flows a force greater than ourselves, the love that as Dante said, "moves the sun and the other stars,"[3] the love that brings new life into the world.

To bless, we must love, and to be blessed is to know that we are loved by the One vaster than the universe who nonetheless turns His face toward us as a parent to a beloved child. To know that is to find true spiritual peace.

---

3. Dante Alighieri, *Divina Commedia*, Paradiso 33.

Behaalotekha

From Despair to Hope

T here have been times when one passage in this *parasha* was for me little less than life-saving. No leadership position is easy. Leading Jews is harder still. And spiritual leadership can be hardest of them all. Leaders have a public face that is usually calm, upbeat, optimistic, and relaxed. But behind the façade we can all experience storms of emotion as we realise how deep are the divisions between people, how intractable are the problems we face, and how thin the ice on which we stand. Perhaps we all experience such moments at some point in our lives, when we know where we are and where we want to be, but simply cannot see a route from here to there. That is the prelude to despair.

Whenever I felt that way, I would turn to the searing moment in our *parasha* when Moses reached his lowest ebb. The precipitating cause was seemingly slight. The people were engaged in their favourite activity: complaining about the food. With self-deceptive nostalgia, they spoke about the fish they ate in Egypt, and the cucumbers, melons, leeks, onions, and garlic. Gone is their memory of slavery. All they can recall is the cuisine. At this, understandably, God was very angry (Num. 11:10). But Moses was more than angry. He suffered a complete emotional breakdown. He said this to God:

Why have You brought this evil on Your servant? Why have I failed to find favour in Your eyes, that You have placed the burden of this whole people on me? Did I conceive this whole people? Did I give birth to it, that You should say to me, Carry it in your lap as a nurse carries a baby? ... Where can I find meat to give to this whole people when they cry to me saying, Give us meat to eat? I cannot carry this whole people on my own. It is too heavy for me. If this is what You are doing to me, then, if I have found favour in Your eyes, kill me now, and let me not look upon this my evil. (Num. 11:11–15)

This for me is the benchmark of despair. Whenever I felt unable to carry on, I would read this passage and think, "If I haven't yet reached this point, I'm OK." Somehow the knowledge that the greatest Jewish leader of all time had experienced this depth of darkness was empowering. It said that the feeling of failure does not necessarily mean that you have failed. All it means is that you have not yet succeeded. Still less does it mean that *you are* a failure. To the contrary, failure comes to those who take risks; and the willingness to take risks is absolutely necessary if you seek, in however small a way, to change the world for the better.

What is striking about Tanakh is the way it documents these dark nights of the soul in the lives of some of the greatest heroes of the spirit. Moses was not the only prophet to pray to die. Three others did so: Elijah (I Kings 19:4), Jeremiah (Jer. 20:7–18), and Jonah (Jonah 4:3).[1] The Psalms, especially those attributed to King David, are shot through with moments of despair: "My God, my God, why have You forsaken me?" (Ps. 22:2); "From the depths I cry to You" (Ps. 130:1); "I am a helpless man abandoned among the dead.... You have laid me in the lowest pit, in the dark, in the depths" (Ps. 88:5–7).

What Tanakh is telling us in these stories is profoundly liberating. Judaism is not a recipe for blandness or bliss. It is not a guarantee that you

---

1. So of course did Job, but Job was not a prophet, nor according to many commentators was he even Jewish. The book of Job is about another subject altogether, namely: Why do bad things happen to good people? That is a question about God, not about humanity.

will be spared heartache and pain. It is not what the Stoics sought, *apatheia*, a life undisturbed by passion. Nor is it a path to *nirvana*, stilling the fires of feeling by extinguishing the self. These things have a spiritual beauty of their own, and their counterparts can be found in the more mystical strands of Judaism. But they are not the world of the heroes and heroines of Tanakh.

Why so? Because Judaism is a faith for those who seek to change the world. That is unusual in the history of faith. Most religions are about accepting the world the way it is. *Judaism is a protest against the world that is in the name of the world that ought to be.* To be a Jew is to seek to make a difference, to change lives for the better, to heal some of the scars of our fractured world. But *people don't like change.* That's why Moses, David, Elijah, and Jeremiah found life so hard.

We can say precisely what brought Moses to despair. He had faced a similar challenge before. Back in the book of Exodus the people had made the same complaint:

> If only we had died by the hand of the Lord in the land of Egypt, when we sat by the fleshpots and ate bread to the full, for you have brought us out into this desert to starve this whole assembly to death. (Ex. 16:3)

Moses, on that occasion, experienced no crisis. The people were hungry and needed food. That was a legitimate request.

Since then, though, they had experienced the twin peaks of the revelation at Mount Sinai and the construction of the Tabernacle. They had come closer to God than any nation had ever done before. Nor were they starving. Their complaint was not that they had no food. They had the manna. Their complaint was that it was boring: "Now we have lost our appetite (literally, "our soul is dried up"); we never see anything but this manna!" (Num. 11:6). They had reached the spiritual heights but they remained the same recalcitrant, ungrateful, small-minded people they had been before.[2]

---

2. Note that the text attributes the complaint to the *asafsuf*, the rabble, the riffraff, which some commentators take to mean the "mixed multitude" who joined the Israelites on the exodus.

That was what made Moses feel that his entire mission had failed and would continue to fail. His mission was to help the Israelites create a society that would be the opposite of Egypt, that would liberate instead of oppress; dignify, not enslave. But the people had not changed. Worse, they had taken refuge in the most absurd nostalgia for the Egypt they had left: memories of fish, cucumbers, garlic, and the rest. Moses had discovered it was easier to take the Israelites out of Egypt than to take Egypt out of the Israelites. If the people had not changed by now, it was a reasonable assumption that they never would. Moses was staring at his own defeat. There was no point in carrying on.

God then comforted him. First, He told him to gather seventy elders with whom to share the burdens of leadership, then He told him not to worry about the food. The people would soon have meat in plenty. It came in the form of a huge avalanche of quails.

What is most striking about this story is that thereafter Moses appears to be a changed man. Told by Joshua that there might be a challenge to his leadership, he replies: "Are you jealous on my behalf? Would that all the Lord's people were prophets, that the Lord would put His spirit on them" (Num. 11:29). In the next chapter, when his own brother and sister begin to criticise him, he reacts with total calm. When God punishes Miriam, Moses prays on her behalf. It is specifically at this point in the long biblical account of Moses' life that the Torah says, "The man Moses was very humble, more so than any other man on earth" (Num. 12:3).

The Torah is giving us a remarkable account of the psychodynamics of emotional crisis. The first thing it is telling us is that it is important, in the midst of despair, not to be alone. God performs the role of comforter. It is He who lifts Moses from the pit of despair. He speaks directly to Moses' concerns. He tells him he will not have to lead alone in the future. There will be others to help him. Then He tells him not to be anxious about the people's complaint. They would soon have so much meat that it would make them ill, and they would not complain about the food again.

The essential principle here is what the Sages meant when they said, "A prisoner cannot release himself from prison" (Berakhot 5b). It needs someone else to lift you out of depression. That is why Judaism is so insistent on not leaving people alone at times of maximum vulnerability. Hence the principles of visiting the sick, comforting mourners, including the lonely ("the stranger, the orphan, and the widow") in festive celebrations, and offering hospitality – an act said to be "greater than receiving the *Shekhina*" (Shabbat 127a). Precisely because depression isolates you from others, remaining alone intensifies the despair. What the seventy elders actually did to help Moses is unclear. But simply *being there with him* was part of the cure.

The other thing it is telling us is that surviving despair is a character-transforming experience. It is when your self-esteem is ground to dust that you suddenly realise that *life is not about you*. It is about others, and ideals, and a sense of mission or vocation. What matters is the cause, not the person. That is what true humility is about. As the wise saying goes, popularly attributed to C. S. Lewis: *Humility is not about thinking less of yourself. It is about thinking of yourself less.*

When you have arrived at this point, even if you have done so through the most bruising experiences, you become stronger than you ever believed possible. You have learned not to put your self-image on the line. You have learned not to think in terms of self-image at all. That is what R. Yoḥanan meant when he said, "Greatness is humility."[3] Greatness is a life turned outward, so that other people's suffering matters to you more than your own. The mark of greatness is the combination of strength and gentleness that is among the most healing forces in human life.

Moses believed he was a failure. That is worth remembering every time we think we are failures. His journey from despair to self-effacing strength is one of the great psychological narratives in the Torah, a timeless tutorial in hope.

---

3. *Pesikta Zutrata, Ekev.*

Shelaḥ

Two Kinds of Fear

One of the most powerful addresses I ever heard was given by the Lubavitcher Rebbe, Rabbi Menachem Mendel Schneerson, on this *parasha*, the story of the spies. For me, it was nothing less than life-changing.

He asked the obvious questions. How could ten of the spies have come back with a demoralising, defeatist report? How could they say, we cannot win, the people are stronger than us, their cities are well fortified, they are giants and we are grasshoppers?

They had seen with their own eyes how God had sent a series of plagues that brought Egypt, the strongest and longest-lived of all the empires of the ancient world, to its knees. They had seen the Egyptian army with its cutting-edge military technology, the horse-drawn chariot, drown in the Reed Sea while the Israelites passed through it on dry land. Egypt was far stronger than the Canaanites, Perrizites, Jebusites, and other minor kingdoms that they would have to confront in conquering the land. Nor was this an ancient memory. It had happened not much more than a year before.

What is more, they already knew that, far from being giants confronting grasshoppers, the people of the land were terrified of the

Israelites. They had said so themselves in the course of singing the Song at the Sea:

> The peoples have heard; they tremble;
> Pangs have seized the inhabitants of Philistia.
> Now are the chiefs of Edom dismayed;
> Trembling seizes the leaders of Moab;
> All the inhabitants of Canaan have melted away.
> Terror and dread fall upon them;
> Because of the greatness of Your arm, they are still as a stone.
> (Ex. 15:14–16)

The people of the land were afraid of the Israelites. Why then were the spies afraid of them?

What is more, continued the Rebbe, the spies were not people plucked at random from among the population. The Torah states that they were "all of them men who were heads of the people of Israel" (Num. 13:3). They were leaders. They were not people given lightly to fear.

The questions are straightforward, but the answer the Rebbe gave was utterly unexpected. *The spies were not afraid of failure,* he said. *They were afraid of success.*

What was their situation now? They were eating manna from heaven. They were drinking water from a miraculous well. They were surrounded by Clouds of Glory. They were camped around the Sanctuary. They were in continuous contact with the *Shekhina*. Never had a people lived so close to God.

What would be their situation if they entered the land? They would have to fight battles, maintain an army, create an economy, farm the land, worry about whether there would be enough rain to produce a crop, and all the other thousand distractions that come from living in the world. What would happen to their closeness to God? They would be preoccupied with mundane and material pursuits. Here they could spend their entire lives learning Torah, lit by the radiance of the Divine. There they would be no more than one more nation in a world of nations, with the same kind of economic, social, and political problems that every nation has to deal with.

The spies were not afraid of failure. They were afraid of success. Their mistake was the mistake of very holy men. They wanted to spend their lives in the closest possible proximity to God. What they did not understand was that God seeks, in the hasidic phrase, "a dwelling in the lower worlds." One of the great differences between Judaism and other religions is that while others seek to lift people to heaven, Judaism seeks to bring heaven down to earth.

Much of Torah is about things not conventionally seen as religious at all: labour relations, agriculture, welfare provisions, loans and debts, land ownership, and so on. It is not difficult to have an intense religious experience in the desert, or in a monastic retreat, or in an ashram. Most religions have holy places and holy people who live far removed from the stresses and strains of everyday life. There was one such Jewish sect in Qumran, known to us through the Dead Sea Scrolls, and there were certainly others. About this there is nothing unusual at all.

But that is not the Jewish project, the Jewish mission. God wanted the Israelites to create a model society where human beings were not treated as slaves, where rulers were not worshipped as demigods, where human dignity was respected, where law was impartially administered to rich and poor alike, where no one was destitute, no one was abandoned to isolation, no one was above the law, and no realm of life was a morality-free zone. That requires a society, and a society needs a land. It requires an economy, an army, fields and flocks, labour, and enterprise. All these, in Judaism, become ways of bringing the *Shekhina* into the shared spaces of our collective life.

The spies feared success, not failure. It was the mistake of deeply religious men. But it was a mistake.

That is the spiritual challenge of the greatest event in two thousand years of Jewish history: the return of Jews to the Land and State of Israel. Perhaps never before and never since has there been a political movement accompanied by so many dreams as Zionism. For some it was the fulfilment of prophetic visions, for others the secular achievement of people who had decided to take history into their own hands. Some saw it as a Tolstoy-like reconnection with land and soil, others a Nietzschean assertion of will and power. Some saw it as a refuge from European antisemitism, others as the first flowering of messianic redemption. Every Zionist thinker had his or her version of utopia, and to a remarkable degree they all came to pass.

But Israel always was something simpler and more basic. Jews have known virtually every fate and circumstance between tragedy and triumph in the almost four thousand years of their history, and they have lived in almost every land on earth. But in all that time there was only one place where they could do what they were called on to do from the dawn of their history: to build their own society in accord with their highest ideals, a society that would be different from their neighbours and become a role model of how a society, an economy, an educational system, and the administration of welfare could become vehicles for bringing the Divine Presence down to earth.

It is not difficult to find God in the wilderness, if you do not eat from the labour of your hands and if you rely on God to fight your battles for you. Ten of the spies, according to the Rebbe, sought to live that way forever. But that, suggested the Rebbe, is not what God wants from us. He wants us to engage with the world. He wants us to heal the sick, feed the hungry, fight injustice with all the power of law, and combat ignorance with universal education. He wants us to show what it is to love the neighbour and the stranger, and say, with R. Akiva, "Beloved is humanity because we are each created in God's image" (Mishna Avot 3:14).

Jewish spirituality lives in the midst of life itself, the life of society and its institutions. To create it we have to battle with two kinds of fear: fear of failure and fear of success. Fear of failure is common; fear of success is rarer but no less debilitating. Both come from the reluctance to take risks. Faith is the courage to take risks. It is not certainty; it is the ability to live with uncertainty. It is the ability to hear God saying to us as He said to Abraham, "Walk on ahead of Me" (Gen. 17:1).

The Rebbe lived what he taught. He sent emissaries out to virtually every place on earth where there were Jews. In so doing, he transformed Jewish life. He knew he was asking his followers to take risks, by going to places where the whole environment would be challenging in many ways, but he had faith in them and in God and in the Jewish mission whose place is in the public square where we share our faith with others and do so in deeply practical ways.

It is challenging to leave the desert and go out into the world with all its trials and temptations, but that is where God wants us to be, bringing His spirit to the way we run an economy, a welfare system, a judiciary, a health service, and an army, healing some of the wounds of the world and bringing, to places often shrouded in darkness, fragments of divine light.

Koraḥ

Hierarchy and Politics:
The Never-Ending Story

I t was a classic struggle for power. The only thing that made it different from the usual dramas of royal courts, parliamentary meetings, or corridors of power was that it took place in Burgers' Zoo in Arnhem, Holland, and the key characters were male chimpanzees.

Frans de Waal's study, *Chimpanzee Politics*,[1] has rightly become a classic. In it he describes how the alpha male, Yeroen, having been the dominant force for some time, found himself increasingly challenged by a young pretender, Luit. Luit could not depose Yeroen on his own, so he formed an alliance with another young contender, Nikkie. Eventually Luit succeeded and Yeroen was deposed.

Luit was good at his job. He was skilled at peacekeeping within the group. He stood up for the underdog and as a result was widely respected. The females recognised his leadership qualities and were always ready to groom him and let him play with their children. Yeroen had nothing to gain by opposing him. He was already too old to become alpha male again. Nonetheless, Yeroen decided to join forces with the

---

1. Frans de Waal, *Chimpanzee Politics* (London: Cape, 1982).

young Nikkie. One night they caught Luit unawares and killed him. The deposed alpha male had his revenge.

Reading the story I thought of the story of Hillel in Mishna Avot (2:6): "He saw a skull floating upon the water, and said: Because you drowned others, you were drowned; and those who drowned you, will themselves be drowned." In fact, so humanlike were power struggles among the chimpanzees that in 1995, Newt Gingrich, Republican Speaker of the House of Representatives, included de Waal's work among the twenty-five books he recommended young congressional Republicans to read.[2]

Korah was a graduate of the same Machiavellian school of politics. He understood the three ground rules. First you have to be a populist. Play on people's discontents and make it seem as if you are on their side against the current leader. "You have gone too far!" he said to Moses and Aaron. "The whole community is holy, every one of them, and the Lord is with them. Why then do you set yourselves above the Lord's assembly?" (Num. 16:3).

Second, assemble allies. Korah himself was a Levite. His grievance was that Moses had appointed his brother Aaron as high priest. Evidently he felt that as Moses' cousin – son of Yitzhar, the brother of Moses' and Aaron's father Amram – the position should have gone to him. He thought it unfair that both leadership roles should have gone to a single family within the clan.

Korah could hardly expect much support from within his own tribe. The other Levites had nothing to gain by deposing Aaron. Instead he found allies among two other disaffected groups: the Reubenites, Dathan and Abiram, and "250 Israelites who were men of rank within the community, representatives at the assembly, and famous" (v. 2). The Reubenites were aggrieved that as descendants of Jacob's firstborn, they had no special leadership roles. According to Ibn Ezra, the 250 "men of rank" were upset that, after the sin of the golden calf, leadership had passed from the firstborn within each tribe to the single tribe of Levi.

The revolt was bound eventually to fail since their grievances were different and could not all be satisfied. But that has never stopped

---

2. This essay was written in the days following the Brexit vote in Britain, when a struggle was taking place over the leadership of both main political parties. I leave it to the reader to draw any comparisons, either with primate politics or the story of Korah.

unholy alliances. People with a grudge are more intent on deposing the current leader than on any constructive plan of action of their own. "Hate defeats rationality," said the Sages.[3] Injured pride, the feeling that honour should have gone to you, not him, has led to destructive and self-destructive action for as long as humans have existed on earth.

Third, choose the moment when the person you seek to depose is vulnerable. Nahmanides notes that the Korah revolt took place immediately after the episode of the spies and the ensuing verdict that the people would not enter the land until the next generation. So long as the Israelites, whatever their complaints, felt that they were moving toward their destination, there was no realistic chance of rousing the people in revolt. Only when they realised that they would not live to cross the Jordan was rebellion possible. The people seemingly had nothing to lose.

The comparison between human and chimpanzee politics is not meant lightly. Judaism has long understood that Homo sapiens is a mix of what the Zohar calls *nefesh habehamit* and *nefesh haElokit*, the animal soul and the Godly soul. We are not disembodied minds. We have physical desires and these are encoded in our genes. Scientists speak today about three systems: the "reptile" brain that produces the most primal fight-or-flight responses; the "monkey" brain that is social, emotional, and sensitive to hierarchy; and the human brain, the prefrontal cortex, that is slow, reflective, and capable of thinking through consequences of alternative courses of action. This confirms what Jews and others, Plato and Aristotle among them, have long known. It is in the tension and interplay between these systems that the drama of human freedom is played out.

In his most recent book, Frans de Waal notes that "among chimpanzees, hierarchy permeates everything." Among the females this is taken for granted and does not lead to conflict. But among males, "power is always up for grabs." It "has to be fought for and jealously guarded against contenders." Male chimpanzees are "schmoozing and scheming Machiavellians."[4] The question is: Are we?

---

3. Bereishit Rabba 55:8.
4. Frans de Waal, *Are We Smart Enough to Know How Smart Animals Are?* (New York: Norton, 2016), 168.

This is not a minor question. It may even be the most important of all if humanity is to have a future. Anthropologists agree that the earliest humans, the hunter-gatherers, were generally egalitarian. Everyone had his or her part to play in the group. Their main tasks were to stay alive, find food, and avoid predators. There was no such thing as accumulated wealth. It was only with the development of agriculture, cities, and trade that hierarchy came to dominate human societies. There was usually an absolute leader, a governing (literate) class, and the masses, used as labour in monumental building schemes and as troops for the imperial army. Judaism enters the world as a protest against this kind of structure.

We see this in the opening chapter of the Torah in which God creates the human person in His image and likeness, meaning that we are all equally fragments of the Divine. Why, asked the Sages, was man created singly? "So that no one could say, My ancestors were greater than yours" (Mishna Sanhedrin 4:5). Something of this egalitarianism can be heard in Moses' remark to Joshua, "Would that all the Lord's people were prophets, that He would rest His spirit on them" (Num. 11:29).

However, like many of the Torah's ideals – among them vegetarianism, the abolition of slavery, and the institution of monogamy – egalitarianism could not happen overnight. It would take centuries, millennia, and in many respects has not yet been fully achieved.

There were two hierarchical structures in biblical Israel. There were kings and there were priests, among them the high priest. Both were introduced after a crisis: monarchy after the failure of the rule of the "judges," the Levitical and Aaronide priesthood after the sin of the golden calf. Both led, inevitably, to tension and division.

Biblical Israel survived as a united kingdom[5] for only three generations of kings and then split in two. The priesthood became a major source of division in the late Second Temple period, leading to sectarian divisions between Sadducees, Boethusians, and the rest. The story of Korah explains why. Where there is hierarchy, there will be competition as to who is the alpha male.

---

5. Following the Brexit vote, the question is being asked in Britain as to whether the United Kingdom will remain a united kingdom.

Is hierarchy an inevitable feature of all advanced civilisations? Maimonides seems to say yes. For him, monarchy was a positive institution, not a mere concession. Abrabanel seems to say no. There are passages in his writing that suggest he was a utopian anarchist who believed that in an ideal world no one would rule over anyone. We would each acknowledge only the sovereignty of God.

Putting together the story of Korah and Frans de Waal's chimpanzee version of *House of Cards*,[6] the conclusion seems to follow that where there is hierarchy, there will be struggles to be alpha male. The result is what Thomas Hobbes called "a perpetual and restless desire of power after power, that ceaseth only in death."[7]

That is why the rabbis focused their attention not on the hierarchical crowns of kingship or priesthood but on the non-hierarchical crown of Torah, which is open to all who seek it. Here competition leads not to conflict but to an increase of wisdom,[8] and where Heaven itself, seeing Sages disagree, says, "These and those are the words of the living God."[9]

The Korah story repeats itself in every generation. The antidote is daily immersion in the alternative world of Torah study that seeks truth not power, and values all equally as voices in a sacred conversation.

---

6. Michael Dobbs, *House of Cards* (New York: Harper Collins, 1989).
7. Thomas Hobbes, *Leviathan* (1651), pt. 1, ch. 11.
8. Bava Batra 21a.
9. Eruvin 13b; Gittin 6b.

Ḥukkat

Healing the Trauma
of Loss

It took me two years to recover from the death of my father, of
blessed memory. To this day, almost twenty years later, I am not sure
why. He did not die suddenly or young. He was well into his eighties. In
his last years he had to undergo five operations, each of which sapped
his strength a little more. Besides which, as a rabbi, I had to officiate at
funerals and comfort the bereaved. I knew what grief looked like.

The Sages were critical of one who mourns too much too long.[1]
They said that God Himself says of such a person, "Are you more com-
passionate than I am?" Maimonides rules:

> A person should not become excessively broken-hearted because
> of a person's death, as it says, "Do not weep for the dead nor
> bemoan him" (Jer. 22:10). This means, do not weep excessively.
> For death is the way of the world, and one who grieves exces-
> sively at the way of the world is a fool."[2]

---

1. Moed Katan 27b.
2. Maimonides, *Mishneh Torah, Hilkhot Avel* 13:11.

With rare exceptions, the outer limit of grief in Jewish law is a year, not more.

Yet knowing these things did not help. We are not always masters of our emotions. Nor does comforting others prepare you for your own experience of loss. Jewish law regulates outward conduct not inward feeling, and when it speaks of feelings, like the commands to love and not to hate, halakha generally translates this into behavioural terms, assuming, in the language of the *Sefer HaḤinukh,* that "the heart follows the deed."[3]

I felt an existential black hole, an emptiness at the core of my being. It deadened my sensations, leaving me unable to sleep or focus, as if life was happening at a great distance, and as if I was a spectator watching a film out of focus with the sound turned off. The mood eventually passed, but while it lasted I made some of the worst mistakes of my life.

I mention these things because they are the connecting thread of *Parashat Ḥukkat.* The most striking episode is the moment when the people complain about the lack of water. Moses does something wrong, and though God sends water from a rock, He also sentences Moses to an almost unbearable punishment: "Because you did not have sufficient faith in Me to sanctify Me before the Israelites, therefore you shall not bring this assembly into the land I have given you" (Num. 20:12).

The commentators debate exactly what he did wrong. Was it that he lost his temper with the people ("Listen now, you rebels" [v. 10])? That he hit the rock instead of speaking to it? That he made it seem as if it was not God, but he and Aaron who were responsible for the water ("Shall we bring water out of this rock for you?" [ibid.])?

What is more puzzling still is why he lost control at that moment. He had faced the same problem before, but he had never lost his temper before. In Exodus 15 the Israelites at Mara complained that the water was undrinkable because it was bitter. In Exodus 17 at Massa-and-Meriva they complained that there was no water. God then told Moses to take his staff and *hit* the rock, and water flowed from it. So when in our *parasha* God tells Moses, "Take the staff... and *speak* to the rock" (v. 8), it was surely a forgivable mistake to assume that God meant him also to hit

---

3. *Sefer HaḤinukh,* command 16.

it. That is what He had said last time. Moses was following precedent. And if God did not mean him to hit the rock, why did He command him to take his staff?

What is even harder to understand is the order of events. *God had already told Moses exactly what to do.* Gather the people. Speak to the rock, and water will flow. This was *before* Moses made his ill-tempered speech, beginning, "Listen now, you rebels." It is understandable to lose your composure when you are faced with a problem that seems insoluble. This had happened to Moses earlier when the people complained about the lack of meat. But it makes no sense at all to do so when God has already told you, "Speak to the rock.... It will pour forth its water, and you will bring water out of the rock for them, and so you will give the community and their livestock water to drink." Moses had received the solution. Why then was he so agitated about the problem?

Only after I lost my father did I understand the passage. What had happened immediately before? The first verse of the chapter states: "The people stopped at Kadesh. There, Miriam died and was buried." Only then does it state that the people had no water. An ancient tradition explains that the people had hitherto been blessed by a miraculous source of water in the merit of Miriam. When she died, the water ceased.

However, it seems to me that the deeper connection lies not between the death of Miriam and the lack of water, but between her death and Moses' loss of emotional equilibrium. Miriam was his elder sister. She had watched over his fate when, as a baby, he had been placed in a basket and floated down the Nile. She had had the courage and enterprise to speak to Pharaoh's daughter and suggest that he be nursed by a Hebrew, thus reuniting Moses with his mother and ensuring that he grew up knowing who he was and to which people he belonged. He owed his sense of identity to her. Without Miriam, he could never have become the human face of God to the Israelites, law-giver, liberator, and prophet. Losing her, he not only lost his sister. He lost the human foundation of his life.

Bereaved, you lose control of your emotions. You find yourself angry when the situation calls for calm. You hit when you should speak, and you speak when you should be silent. Even when God has told you what to do, you are only half-listening. You hear the words but they do not fully enter your mind. Maimonides asks the question, how was it that Jacob, a prophet, did not know that his son Joseph was still alive. He answers, because he was in a state of grief, and the *Shekhina* does not enter us when we are in a state of grief.[4] Moses at the rock was not so much a prophet as a man who had just lost his sister. He was inconsolable and not in control. He was the greatest of the prophets. But he was also human, rarely more so than here.

Our parasha is about mortality. That is the point. God is eternal, we are ephemeral. As we say in the *UNetaneh Tokef* prayer on Rosh HaShana and Yom Kippur, we are "a fragment of pottery, a blade of grass, a flower that fades, a shadow, a cloud, a breath of wind." We are dust and to dust we return, but God is life forever.

At one level, the story of Moses at the rock is about sin and punishment: *"Because you did not have sufficient faith in Me to sanctify Me … therefore you shall not bring this assembly into the land I have given you."* We may not be sure what the sin exactly was, or why it merited so severe a punishment, but at least we know the ball-park, the territory to which the story belongs.

Nonetheless it seems to me that – here as in so many other places in the Torah – there is a story beneath the story, and it is a different one altogether. *Ḥukkat* is about death, loss, and bereavement. Miriam dies. Aaron and Moses are told they will not live to enter the Promised Land. Aaron dies, and the people mourn for him for thirty days. Together they constituted the greatest leadership team the Jewish people has ever known, Moses the supreme prophet, Aaron the first high priest, and Miriam perhaps the greatest of them all.[5] What the *parasha* is telling us is that for each of us there is a Jordan we will not cross, a promised land we will not enter. "It is not for you to complete the task" (Mishna Avot 2:16). Even the greatest are mortal.

That is why the *parasha* begins with the ritual of the red heifer, whose ashes, mixed with the ash of cedar wood, hyssop, and scarlet wool, and dissolved in "living water," are sprinkled over one who has been in contact with the dead so that they may enter the Sanctuary.

---

4. Maimonides, *Shemona Perakim* 7, based on Pesaḥim 117a.
5. There are many midrashim on this theme about Miriam's faith, courage, and foresight.

This is one of the most fundamental principles of Judaism. *Death defiles.* For most religions throughout history, life-after-death has proved more real than life itself. That is where the gods live, thought the Egyptians. That is where our ancestors are alive, believed the Greeks and Romans and many primitive tribes. That is where you find justice, thought many Christians. That is where you find paradise, thought many Muslims.

Life after death and the resurrection of the dead are fundamental, non-negotiable principles of Jewish faith, but Tanakh is conspicuously quiet about them. It is focused on finding God in this life, on this planet, notwithstanding our mortality. "The dead do not praise God," says the Psalm (115:17). God is to be found in life itself with all its hazards and dangers, bereavements and grief. We may be no more than "dust and ashes" (Gen. 18:27), as Abraham said, but life itself is a never-ending stream, "living water," and it is this that the rite of the red heifer symbolises.

With great subtlety the Torah mixes law and narrative together – the law before the narrative because God provides the cure before the disease. Miriam dies. Moses and Aaron are overwhelmed with grief. Moses, for a moment, loses control, and he and Aaron are reminded that they too are mortal and will die before entering the land. Yet this is, as Maimonides said, "the way of the world." We are embodied souls. We are flesh and blood. We grow old. We lose those we love. Outwardly we struggle to maintain our composure but inwardly we weep. Yet life goes on, and what we began, others will continue.

Those we loved and lost live on in us, as we will live on in those we love. For love is as strong as death,[6] and the good we do never dies.[7]

---

6. Song of Songs 8:6.
7. See Proverbs 10:2, 11:4.

Balak

What Makes God Laugh

T here is an old saying that what makes God laugh is seeing our plans for the future.[1] However, if Tanakh is our guide, what makes God laugh is human delusions of grandeur. From the vantage point of heaven, the ultimate absurdity is when humans start thinking of themselves as godlike.

There are several pointed examples in the Torah. One whose full import has only recently become clear occurs in the story of the Tower of Babel. Men gather together in the plain of Shinar and decide to build a city and a tower "that will reach to heaven" (Gen. 11:4). As it happens, we have archaeological confirmation of this fact. Several Mesopotamian ziggurats, including the temple of Marduk in Babylon, have been found with inscriptions saying that they reach heaven.[2]

The idea was that tall buildings – man-made mountains – allowed humans to climb to the dwelling place of the gods and thus communicate

---

1. The John Lennon version is: "Life is what happens while you are making other plans."
2. The Tower of Babel is referred to in the Enuma Elish as "Esagila," which means "the house of the lifting up of the head." Nabopolassar and Nebuchadnezzar both repaired this building, inscriptions to which say that they "raised high the head" of the tower "to rival the heavens." Nahum Sarna, *Understanding Genesis* (New York: Schocken Books, 1970), 73.

with them. The Mesopotamian city states were among the first places of civilisation, itself one of the turning points in the history of human life on earth. Before the birth of agriculture, the ancients lived in fear of nature: of predators, of other tribes and bands, and of the vicissitudes of heat and cold, drought and flood. Their fate depended on matters beyond their control.

Only with the spread of domesticated animals and agriculture did people gather in towns, then cities, then empires. A tipping point occurred in the balance of power between nature and culture. For the first time humans were not confined to adapting to their environment. They could adapt their environment to suit them. At this point they – especially the rulers – began to see themselves as gods, demigods, or people with the power to influence the gods.

The most conspicuous symbol of this was buildings on a monumental scale: the ziggurats of Babylon and other Mesopotamian cities, and the pyramids of Egypt. Built on the flat land of the Tigris-Euphrates valley and the Nile delta, they towered over their surroundings. The great pyramid of Giza, built even before the birth of Abraham, was so monumental that it remained the tallest man-made structure on earth for four thousand years.

The fact that these were artificial mountains built by human hands suggested to their builders that humans had acquired godlike powers. They had constructed a stairway to heaven. Hence the significance of the phrase in the Torah's account of the tower, "And the Lord *came down to see* the city and the tower, which the children of man had built" (Gen. 11:5). This is God laughing. On earth, humans thought they had reached the sky, but to God the building was so infinitesimal, so microscopic, that He had to come down even to see it. Only with the invention of flight do we now know how small the tallest building looks when you are looking down from a mere 30,000 feet.

To end their hubris God simply "confused their language" (v. 7). They no longer understood one another. The entire project was turned into French farce. We can visualise the scene. A foreman calls for a brick and is handed a hammer. He tells a worker to go right, and he turns left. The project foundered in a welter of incomprehension. Men thought they could climb to heaven, but in the end they could not even understand what the person next to them was saying. The unfinished tower became a symbol of the inevitable failure of vaunting ambition. The builders achieved what they sought but not in the way they intended. They wanted to "make a name for themselves" (v. 4) and they succeeded, but instead of becoming a byword for man's ability to reach the sky, Babel became babble, an emblem of confusion. Hubris became nemesis.

The second example was Egypt during the early plagues. Moses and Aaron turned the water of the Nile into blood, and filled Egypt with frogs. We then read that the Egyptian magicians did likewise to show that they had the same power. So concerned were they to show that they could do what the Hebrews could do, that they entirely failed to realise that they were making things worse, not better. The real skill would have been to turn blood back into water, and make frogs not appear but disappear.

We hear the divine laughter especially in the third plague: lice. For the first time, the magicians tried and failed to replicate the effect. Defeated, they turned to Pharaoh and said, "It is the finger of God." The humour comes when we remember that for the Egyptians the symbol of power was monumental architecture: pyramids, temples, palaces, and statues on a massive scale. God showed them His power by way of the tiniest of insects, painful yet almost invisible to the eye. Again hubris became nemesis. When people think they are big, God shows them they are small, and vice versa. It is those who think themselves small – supremely so Moses, the humblest of men – who are truly great.

This explains the otherwise curious episode of Balaam's talking donkey. This is not a fanciful tale, nor simply a miracle. It arose because of the way the people of Moab and Midian thought of Balaam – and perhaps, by extension, the way he thought of himself. Balak the Moabite king, together with the leaders of the Midianites, sent a delegation to Balaam asking him to curse the Israelites: "Come now, curse this people for me, since they are too mighty for me…for I know that whom you bless is blessed, and whom you curse is cursed" (Num. 22:6).

This is a pagan understanding of the holy man: the shaman, the magus, the wonder-worker, the person with access to supernatural powers. The Torah's view is precisely the opposite. It is God who blesses and curses, not human beings. "I will bless those who bless you and those who curse you I will curse," God said to Abraham (Gen. 12:3). "They shall place My name on the children of Israel and I will bless them," He said about the priests (Num. 6:27). The idea that you can hire a holy man to curse someone essentially presupposes that God can be bribed. The narrative is admittedly obscure. God tells Balaam not to go. Balak sends a second delegation with a more tempting offer. This time God tells Balaam to go with them but to say only what He instructs him to say. The next morning Balaam sets out to go with the Moabites, but the text now states that God was "angry" with him for going (22:22). That is when the episode of the donkey takes place.

The donkey sees an angel barring the way. It turns aside into a field but Balaam hits it and forces it back to the path. The angel is still barring the way and the donkey veers into a wall, crushing Balaam's foot. Balaam hits it again, but finally it lies down and refuses to move. That is when the donkey begins to speak. Balaam then looks up and sees the angel, who had been hitherto invisible to him.

Why did God first tell Balaam *not* to go, then that he *should* go, and then was angry when he went? Evidently God could read his mind and knew that Balaam really did want to curse the Israelites. We know this because later, after the attempt to curse the Israelites failed, Balaam succeeded in causing them harm, advising the Midianites to get their women to seduce the Israelite men, thus provoking the anger of God (31:16). Balaam was no friend of the Israelites.

But the story of the talking donkey is another instance of divine laughter. Here was a man reputed to be a maestro of supernatural forces. People thought he had the power to bless or curse whomever he chose. God, the Torah tells us, is not like that at all. He had two messages, one for the Moabites and Midianites, another for Balaam himself.

He showed the Moabites and Midianites that Israel is not cursed but blessed. The more you attempt to curse them, the more they will be blessed and you yourself will be cursed. That is as true today as it was then. There are movements throughout the world which curse the state and people of Israel. The greater the malice of Israel's enemies, the stronger Israel becomes and the more disasters its enemies bring upon their own people.

God had a different message for Balaam himself, and it was very blunt. If you think you can control God, then, says God, I will show you that I can turn a donkey into a prophet and a prophet into a donkey. Your animal will see angels to which you yourself are blind. Balaam was forced to admit:

> How can I curse those whom God has not cursed?
> How can I denounce those whom the Lord has not denounced?
> (23:8)

Hubris always eventually becomes nemesis. In a world in which rulers engaged in endless projects of self-aggrandisement, Israel alone produced a literature in which they attributed their successes to God and their failures to themselves. Far from making them weak, this made them extraordinarily strong.

So it is with us as individuals. I had a beloved friend, no longer alive, about whom it was said that "he took God so seriously that he didn't need to take himself seriously at all." Pagan prophets like Balaam had not yet learned the lesson we must all one day learn: that what matters is not that God does what we want, but that we do what He wants. God laughs at those who think they have godlike powers. The opposite is true. The smaller we see ourselves, the greater we become.

Pinḥas

Moses' Disappointment

Hidden beneath the surface of *Parashat Pinḥas* the Sages uncovered a story of great poignancy. Moses, having seen his sister and brother die, knew that his own time on earth was coming to a close. He prayed to God to appoint a successor:

> May the Lord, God of the spirits of all mankind, appoint a man over this community to go out and come in before them, one who will lead them out and bring them in, so the Lord's people will not be like sheep without a shepherd. (Num. 27:16–17)

There is, though, an obvious question. Why does this episode appear here? It should surely have been positioned seven chapters earlier, either at the point at which God told Moses and Aaron that they would die without entering the land, or shortly thereafter when we read of the death of Aaron.

The Sages sensed two clues to the story beneath the story. The first is that it appears immediately after the episode in which the daughters of Tzelophehad sought and were granted their father's share in the land. It was this that triggered Moses' request. A midrash explains:

What was Moses' reason for making this request after declaring the order of inheritance? Just this, that when the daughters of Tzelophehad inherited from their father, Moses reasoned: The time is right for me to make my own request. If daughters inherit, it is surely right that my sons should inherit my glory. (Numbers Rabba 21:14)

The second clue lies in God's words to Moses immediately before he made the request for the appointment of a successor:

Then the Lord said to Moses, "Go up this mountain of Abarim and see the land I have given the Israelites. After you have seen it, you too will be gathered to your people, *as your brother Aaron was*." (Num. 27:12–13)

The italicised words are seemingly redundant. God was telling Moses he would soon die. Why did He need to add, "as your brother Aaron"? On this the midrash says: This teaches us that Moses wanted to die the way Aaron did. The *Ktav Sofer* explains: Aaron had the privilege of knowing that his children would follow in his footsteps. Elazar, his son, was appointed as high priest in his lifetime. To this day *kohanim* are direct descendants of Aaron. Moses likewise longed to see one of his sons, Gershom or Eliezer, take his place as leader of the people. It was not to be. That is the story beneath the story.

It had an aftermath. In the book of Judges we read of a man named Micah who established an idolatrous cult in the territory of Ephraim and hired a Levite to officiate in the shrine. Some men from the tribe of Dan, moving north to find more suitable land for themselves, came upon Micah's house, and seized both the idolatrous artefacts and the Levite, whom they persuaded to become their priest, saying, "Come with us, and be our father and priest. Isn't it better that you serve a tribe and clan in Israel as priest rather than just one man's household?" (Judges 18:19).

Only at the end of the story (v. 30) are we told the name of the idolatrous priest: Jonathan son of Gershom son of Moses. In our texts the letter *nun* has been inserted into the last of these names, so that it can be read as Manasseh rather than Moses. However, the letter, unusually, is written above the line, as a superscription. The Talmud says that the *nun* was added to avoid besmirching the name of Moses himself, by disclosing that his grandson had become an idolatrous priest.

How are we to explain Moses' apparent failure with his own children and grandchildren? One suggestion made by the Sages was that it had to do with the fact that for years he lived in Midian with his father-in-law Jethro who was at the time an idolatrous priest. Something of the Midianite influence re-appeared in Jonathan three generations later.

Alternatively there are hints here and there that Moses himself was so preoccupied with leading the people that he simply did not have time to attend to the spiritual needs of his children. For instance, when Jethro came to visit his son-in-law after the division of the Red Sea, he brought with him Moses' wife Zipporah and their two sons. They had not been with him until then.

The rabbis went further in speculating about the reason that Moses' own sister and brother, Miriam and Aaron, spoke negatively about him. What they were referring to, said the Sages, is the fact that Moses had physically separated from his wife. He had done so because the nature of his role was such that he had to be in a state of purity the whole time because at any moment he might have to speak or be spoken to by God. They were, in short, complaining that he was neglecting his own family.

A third explanation has to do with the nature of leadership itself. Bureaucratic authority – authority in virtue of office – can be passed down from parent to child. Monarchy is like that. So is aristocracy. So are some forms of religious leadership, like the priesthood. But charismatic authority – in virtue of personal qualities – is never automatically handed on across the generations. Moses was a prophet, and prophecy depends almost entirely on personal qualities. That, incidentally, is why, though kingship and priesthood in Judaism were male prerogatives, prophecy was not. There were prophetesses as well as prophets. In this respect Moses was not unusual. Few charismatic leaders have children who are also charismatic leaders.

A fourth explanation offered by the Sages was quite different. On principle, God did not want the crown of Torah to pass from parent to child in dynastic succession. Kingship and priesthood did. But the crown of Torah, they said, belongs to anyone who chooses to take hold of it and bear its responsibilities. "Moses commanded us the Torah as an inheritance of the congregation of Jacob" (Deut. 33:4), meaning that it belongs to all of us, not just an elite. The Talmud elaborates:

> Be careful [not to neglect] the children of the poor, because from them Torah goes forth.... Why is it not usual for scholars to give birth to sons who are scholars?
>
> R. Joseph said: So that it should not be said that the Torah is their inheritance.
>
> R. Shisha son of R. Idi said: So that they should not be arrogant toward the community.
>
> Mar Zutra said: Because they act highhandedly against the community.
>
> R. Ashi said: Because they call people asses.
>
> Rabina said: Because they do not first utter a blessing over the Torah. (Nedarim 81a)

In other words, the "crown of Torah" was deliberately not hereditary because it might become the prerogative of the rich. Or because children of great scholars might take their inheritance for granted. Or because it could lead to arrogance and contempt for others. Or because learning itself might become a mere intellectual pursuit rather than a spiritual exercise ("they do not first utter a blessing over the Torah").

However, there is a fifth factor worthy of consideration. Some of the greatest figures in Jewish history did not succeed with all their children. Abraham fathered Ishmael. Isaac and Rebecca gave birth to Esau. All twelve of Jacob's children stayed within the fold, but three of them – Reuben, Shimon, and Levi – disappointed their father. Of Shimon and Levi he said, "Let my soul not enter their plot; let my spirit not unite with their meeting" (Gen. 49:6). On the face of it, he was dissociating himself from them.[1] Nonetheless, the three great leaders

---

1. Note however that Rashi interprets the curse as limited specifically to Zimri, descendant of Shimon, and Koraḥ, descendant of Levi.

of the Israelites throughout the exodus – Moses, Aaron, and Miriam – were all children of Levi.

Solomon gave birth to Rehoboam, whose disastrous leadership divided the kingdom. Hezekiah, one of Judah's greatest kings, was the father of Manasseh, one of the worst. *Not all parents succeed with all their children all the time.* How could it be otherwise? We each possess freedom. We are each, to some extent, who we chose to become. Neither genes nor upbringing can guarantee that we become the person our parents want us to be. Nor is it right that parents should over-impose their will on children who have reached the age of maturity.

Often this is for the best. Abraham did not become an idolater like his father Terah. Manasseh, the archetypal evil king, was grandfather to Josiah, one of the best. These are important facts. Judaism places parenthood, education, and the home at the heart of its values. One of our first duties is to ensure that our children know about and come to love our religious heritage. But sometimes we fail. Children may go their own way, which is not ours. *If this happens to us we should not be paralysed with guilt.* Not everyone succeeded with all their children, not even Abraham, or Moses, or David, or Solomon. Not even God Himself. "I have raised children and brought them up but they have rebelled against Me" (Is. 1:2).

Two things rescued the story of Moses and his children from tragedy. The book of Chronicles (I Chr. 23:16, 24:20) refers to Gershom's son not as Jonathan but as Shevual or Shuvael, which the rabbis translated as "return to God." In other words, Jonathan eventually repented of his idolatry and became again a faithful Jew. However far a child has drifted, he or she may, in the course of time, come back.

The other is hinted at in the genealogy in Numbers 3. It begins with the words, "These are the children of Aaron and Moses," but goes on to list only Aaron's children. On this the rabbis say that because Moses taught Aaron's children they were regarded as his own. In general, "disciples" are called "children."[2]

We may not all have children. Even if we do, we may, despite our best endeavours, find them at least temporarily following a different

---

2. See Rashi on Numbers 3:1.

path. But we can all leave something behind us that will live on. Some do so by following Moses' example: teaching, facilitating, or encouraging the next generation. Some do so in line with the rabbinic statement that "the real offspring of the righteous are good deeds."[3]

When our children follow our path we should be grateful. When they go beyond us, we should give special thanks to God. And when they choose another way, we must be patient, knowing that the greatest Jew of all time had the same experience with one of his grandchildren. And we must never give up hope. Moses' grandson returned. In almost the last words of the last of the prophets, Malachi foresaw a time when God "will turn the hearts of the fathers to their children, and the hearts of the children to their fathers" (Mal. 3:24). The estranged will be reunited in faith and love.

---

3. Rashi on Genesis 6:9.

Matot

Keeping Our Word

Parashat *Matot* opens with an account of the laws of vows and oaths. What is it doing here near the end of the book of Numbers, as the Israelites approach the destination of their journey to the Promised Land?

Vows and oaths are obligations created by words. They are commitments to do something or refrain from doing something. A vow, *neder*, affects the status of an object. I may vow not to eat something. That something is now, for me, forbidden food. An oath, *shevua*, affects the person not the object. What is now forbidden is not the food but the act of eating it. Both acts bind: that is the primary meaning of the word *issar*.

Such is the sanctity of such undertakings that there are demanding rules that have to be met if they are to be annulled. You cannot do it yourself: the *parasha* sets out some of the ground rules, the rest of which were supplied by the oral tradition. So seriously does Judaism treat verbal undertakings that one act of annulment, *Kol Nidrei*, takes place at the start of the holiest day of the year, Yom Kippur.

The superficial reason for the law of vows appearing here is that the previous section of the Torah dealt with communal sacrifices. Individuals also brought sacrifices, sometimes because they were bound to do so but at other times because they voluntarily chose to do so. Hence the laws of voluntary undertakings.

But there is a deeper reason. The Israelites were nearing the land. They were about to construct a society unlike any other. It was to be a free society based on a covenant between the people and God. The rule of law was to be secured not by the use of force but by people honouring their moral commitments, their voluntary undertaking to God that what He commanded, they would do.

A covenantal society is one in which words are holy, sacrosanct. This is the principle at the heart of Judaism as a code of collective freedom, a constitution of liberty.

This needs explanation. Any society needs laws. Without that, it descends into anarchy. There are three reasons why people obey laws. The first is that they will be punished if they don't. This is a society based on power. The second is that it is to their advantage to do so. This is a society based on self-interest.

Both have shortcomings. Power corrupts. So, at times, does the pursuit of self-interest. When power is corrupted, there is a loss of freedom. When self-interest prevails, there is a loss of social cohesion. When people care about themselves but not others, the successful thrive while others suffer. Justice and compassion give way to greed and exploitation.

The Torah sets forth a third way, in which people obey the law because they have voluntarily undertaken to do so. This is a society based not on power or the pursuit of self-interest but on freely embraced moral obligation. The Torah is the story of how the Israelites came to this unique and radical idea: the politics of covenant.

Ironically it was one of the great critics of Judaism, Friedrich Nietzsche, who had the insight to see that the capacity to bind ourselves by words is the basis of both morality and human freedom. This is what he says in his book *On the Genealogy of Morality*:

> To breed an animal with the prerogative to promise – is that not precisely the paradoxical task which nature has set herself with regard to humankind? Is it not the real problem of humankind?

Homo sapiens is distinguished from other animals by its use of language. That is well known. What Nietzsche saw, however, is that we use language in many different ways. We use it to describe, communicate, categorise, and explain. Language in this sense is a kind of picture of reality, a translation of what is into a set of signs, symbols, and images.

But we can also use language in a quite different way – not to describe what is, but to commit ourselves to some form of behaviour in the future.

So for instance when a groom says to his bride under the *ḥuppa*, "Behold you are betrothed to me," he is not describing a marriage. He is getting married. He is undertaking a set of obligations to the woman he has chosen as his wife. Philosophers nowadays call this a performative utterance.

Nietzsche saw how fundamental this is to the human condition:

> In order to have that degree of control over the future, man must first learn to distinguish between what happens by accident and what by design … and before he can do this, man himself will really have to become reliable, regular, necessary, even in his own self-image, so that he, as someone making a promise is, is answerable for his own future!

When we bind ourselves by words we are using language not to describe but to create – to create an orderly future out of the chaos of human instincts and desires. What makes humans unique is not just the use of language. Other animals use forms of language. Dolphins do. So do primates. Even bees perform complex dances that convey information to other bees.

What is unique to humans is that we use language to bind our own future behaviour so that we can form with other human beings bonds of mutuality and trust. One such bond is the promise. Another is marriage. A third – unique to Judaism – is society understood as a covenant, a set of mutually binding promises between the Jewish people and God.

It is this use of language, not to describe something already in existence but to create something that didn't exist before, that links us to God. God used words to bring the natural universe into being: "And

God said ... and there was." We use words to bring a social universe into being. What the Torah is telling us is that words create because words are holy; that is to say, they bind. When words bind, they generate trust. Trust is to society what predictability is to nature: the basis of order as opposed to chaos.

Social institutions in a free society depend on trust, and trust means that we keep our word. We do what we say we are going to do. If we make a vow, an oath, a promise, a verbal undertaking, then we hold ourselves bound by it. This means that we will actually fulfil our commitment unless we can establish that, due to circumstances unforeseeable at the time, we are simply unable to do so.

If trust breaks down, social relationships break down, and then society depends on law enforcement agencies or some other use of force. When force is widely used, society is no longer free. The only way free human beings can form collaborative and co-operative relationships without recourse to force is by the use of verbal undertakings honoured by those who make them.

Freedom needs trust; trust needs people to keep their word; and keeping your word means treating words as holy, vows and oaths as sacrosanct. Only under very special and precisely formulated circumstances can you be released from your undertakings. That is why, as the Israelites approached the holy land where they were to create a free society, they had to be reminded of the sacred character of vows and oaths.

The temptation to break your word when it is to your advantage to do so can sometimes be overwhelming. That is why belief in God – a God who oversees all we think, say, and do, and who holds us accountable to our commitments – is so fundamental. Although it sounds strange to us now, the father of toleration and liberalism, John Locke (England, seventeenth century), held that citizenship should not be extended to atheists because, not believing in God, they could not be trusted to honour their word.

So the appearance of laws about vows and oaths at the end of the book of Numbers, as the Israelites are approaching the holy land, is no accident, and the moral is still relevant today. A free society depends on trust. Trust depends on keeping your word. That is how humans imitate God by using language to create.

Words create moral obligations, and moral obligations, under-taken responsibly and honoured faithfully, create the possibility of a free society.

So – always do what you say you are going to do. If we fail to keep our word, eventually we will lose our freedom.

Masei

The Complexity of Human Rights

The book of Numbers comes to a close that is very strange indeed. Earlier in *Parashat Pinḥas* we read of how the five daughters of Tzelophehad came to Moses with a claim based on justice and human rights.[1] Their father had died without sons. Inheritance – in this case, of a share in the land – passes through the male line, but here there was no male line. Surely their father was entitled to his share, and they were his only heirs. By rights that share should come to them: "Why should our father's name be disadvantaged in his family merely because he did not have a son? Give us a portion of land along with our father's brothers" (Num. 27:4).

Moses had received no instruction about such an eventuality, so he asked God directly. God ruled in favour of the women. "The daughters of Tzelophehad are right. You shall give them possession of

---

1. The word "rights" is, of course, an anachronism here. The concept was not born until the seventeenth century. Nonetheless it is not absurd to suggest that this is what is implied in the daughters' claim, "Why should our father's name be disadvantaged?" (Num. 27:4).

an inheritance among their father's brothers and transfer the inheritance of their father to them" (v. 7). He gave Moses further instructions about the disposition of inheritance, and the narrative then passes on to other matters.

Only now, right at the end of the book, does the Torah report on an event that arose directly from that case. Leaders of Tzelophehad's tribe, Manasseh, son of Joseph, came and made the following complaint. If the land were to pass to Tzelophehad's daughters and they married men from another tribe, the land would eventually pass to their husbands, and thus to their husband's tribes. Thus land that had initially been granted to the tribe of Manasseh might be lost to it in perpetuity.

Again, Moses took the case to God, who offered a simple solution. The daughters of Tzelophehad were entitled to the land, but so too was the tribe. Therefore, if they wish to take possession of the land, they must marry men from within their own tribe. That way both claims could be honoured. The daughters did not lose their right to the land but they did lose some freedom in choosing a marriage partner.

The two passages are intimately related. They use the same terminology. Both Tzelophehad's daughters and the leaders of the clan "draw near." They use the same verb to describe their potential loss: *yigara*, "disadvantaged, diminished." God replies in both cases with the same locution, "*kein... dovrot/dovrim*," rightly do they speak.[2] Why then are the two episodes separated in the text? Why does the book of Numbers end on this seemingly anticlimactic note? And does it have any relevance today?

Numbers is a book is about individuals. It begins with a census, whose purpose is less to tell us the actual number of Israelites than to "lift" their "heads" (4:2, 22), the unusual locution the Torah uses to convey the idea that when God orders a census it is to tell the people that they each count. The book also focuses on the psychology of individuals. We read of Moses' despair, of Aaron and Miriam's criticism of him,

---

2. These two passages may well be the source of the story of the rabbi who hears both sides of a marital dispute, and says to both husband and wife, "You are right." The rabbi's disciple asks, "How can they both be right?" to which the rabbi replies, "You too are right."

of the spies who lacked the courage to come back with a positive report, and of the malcontents, led by Korah, who challenged Moses' leadership. We read of Joshua and Caleb, Eldad and Medad, Dathan and Abiram, Zimri and Phinehas, Balak and Balaam, and others. This emphasis on individuals reaches a climax in Moses' prayer to "God of the spirits of all flesh" (24:16) to appoint a successor – understood by the Sages and Rashi to mean, appoint a leader who will deal with each individual as an individual, who will relate to people in their uniqueness and singularity.

That is the context of the claim of Tzelophehad's daughters. They were claiming their rights as individuals. Justly so. As many of the commentators pointed out, the behaviour of the women throughout the wilderness years was exemplary, while that of the men was the opposite. The men, not the women, gave gold for the golden calf. The spies were men. A famous comment by the *Kli Yakar* (Rabbi Shlomo Ephraim Luntschitz, 1550–1619) suggests that had Moses sent women instead, they would have come back with a positive report.[3] Recognising the justice of their cause, God affirmed their rights as individuals.

But society is not built on individuals alone. As the book of Judges points out, individualism is another name for chaos: "In those days there was no king in Israel, everyone did what was right in their own eyes" (Judges 17:6, 21:25). Hence the insistence, throughout Numbers, on the central role of the tribes as the organising principle of Jewish life. The Israelites were numbered tribe by tribe. The Torah sets out their precise encampment around the *Mishkan* and the order in which they were to journey. In *Parashat Naso*, at inordinate length, the Torah repeats the gifts of each tribe at the inauguration of the *Mishkan*, despite the fact that they each gave exactly the same. The tribes were not accidental to the structure of Israel as a society. Like the United States of America, whose basic political structure is that of a federation of (originally thirteen, now fifty) states, so Israel was (until the appointment of a king) a federation of tribes.

The existence of something like tribes is fundamental to a free society.[4] The modern State of Israel is built on a vast panoply of

---

3. *Kli Yakar* on Numbers 13:2.
4. See, most recently, Sebastian Junger, *Tribe: On Homecoming and Belonging* (Fourth Estate, 2016).

ethnicities – Ashkenazic, Sephardic, Jews from Eastern, Central, and Western Europe, Spain and Portugal, Arab lands, Russia, Ethiopia, America, South Africa, Australia, and other places, some hasidic, some yeshivaish, others "modern," others "traditional," yet others secular and cultural. We each have a series of identities, based partly on family background, partly on occupation, partly on locality and community. These "mediating structures," larger than the individual but smaller than the state, are where we develop our complex, vivid, face-to-face interactions and identities. They are the domain of family, friends, neighbours, and colleagues, and they make up what is collectively known as civil society. A strong civil society is essential to freedom.[5]

That is why, alongside individual rights, a society must make space for group identities. The classic instance of the opposite came in the wake of the French Revolution. In the course of the debate in the French Revolutionary Assembly in 1789, the Count of Clermont-Tonnerre made his famous declaration, "To the Jews as individuals, everything. To the Jews as a nation, nothing." If they insisted on defining themselves as a nation, that is, as a distinct subgroup within the republic, said the Count, "we shall be compelled to expel them."

Initially, this sounded reasonable. Jews were being offered civil rights in the new secular nation state. However, it was anything but. It meant that Jews would have to give up their identity as Jews in the public domain. Nothing – not religious or ethnic identity – should stand between the individual and the state. It was no accident that a century later, France became one of the epicentres of European antisemitism, beginning with Édouard Drumont's vicious *La France Juive*, 1886, and culminating in the Dreyfus trial. Hearing the Parisian crowd shout "*Mort aux Juifs*," Theodor Herzl realised that Jews had still not been accepted as citizens of Europe, despite all the protestations to the contrary. Jews found themselves regarded as a tribe in a Europe that claimed to have abolished tribes. European emancipation recognised individual rights but not collective ones.

---

5. This is the argument made most powerfully by Edmund Burke and Alexis de Tocqueville.

The primatologist Frans de Waal, whose work among the bonobos we mentioned above on *Parashat Korah*, makes the point powerfully. Almost the whole of modern Western culture, he says, was built on the idea of autonomous, choosing individuals. But that is not who we are. We are people with strong attachments to family, friends, neighbours, allies, co-religionists, and people of the same ethnicity. He continues:

> A morality exclusively concerned with individual rights tends to ignore the ties, needs and interdependencies that have marked our existence from the very beginning. It is a cold morality that puts space between people, assigning each person to his or her own little corner of the universe. How this caricature of a society arose in the minds of eminent thinkers is a mystery.[6]

That is precisely the point the Torah is making when it divides the story of the daughters of Tzelophehad into two. The first part, in *Parashat Pinhas*, is about individual rights, the rights of Tzelophehad's daughters to a share in the land. The second, at the end of the book, is about group rights, in this case the right of the tribe of Manasseh to its territory. The Torah affirms both, because both are necessary to a free society.

Many of the most seemingly intractable issues in contemporary Jewish life have appeared because Jews, especially in the West, are used to a culture in which individual rights are held to override all others. We should be free to live as we choose, worship as we choose, and identify as we choose. But a culture based solely on individual rights will undermine families, communities, traditions, loyalties, and shared codes of reverence and restraint.

Despite its enormous emphasis on the value of the individual, Judaism also insists on the value of those institutions that preserve and protect our identities as members of groups that make them up. We have rights as individuals but identities only as members of tribes. Honouring both is delicate, difficult, and necessary. The book of Numbers ends by showing us how.

---

6. Frans de Waal, *Good Natured* (Harvard University Press, 1996), 167.

Deuteronomy
דברים

Devarim

To 120: Growing Old, Staying Young

On March 27, 2012, to celebrate the diamond jubilee of the Queen, an ancient ceremony took place at Buckingham Palace. A number of institutions presented Loyal Addresses to the Queen, thanking her for her service to the nation. Among them was the Board of Deputies of British Jews. Its then president, Vivian Wineman, included in his speech the traditional Jewish blessing on such occasions. He wished her well "until a hundred and twenty."

The Queen was amused and looked quizzically at Prince Philip. Neither of them had heard the expression before. Later the Prince asked what it meant, and we explained. A hundred and twenty is stated as the outer limit of a normal human lifetime in Genesis 6:3. The number is especially associated with Moses, about whom the Torah says, "Moses was 120 years old when he died, yet his eyes were undimmed and his strength undiminished" (Deut. 34:7). Together with Abraham, a man of very different personality and circumstance, Moses is a model of how to age well. With the growth of human longevity, this has become a significant and challenging issue for many of us. How do you grow old yet stay young?

237

The most sustained research into this topic is the Grant Study, begun in 1938, which has tracked the lives of 268 Harvard students for almost eighty years, seeking to understand what characteristics – from personality type to intelligence, health, habits, and relationships – contribute to human flourishing. For more than thirty years, the project was directed by George Vaillant, whose books *Aging Well* and *Triumphs of Experience* have explored this fascinating territory.[1]

Among the many dimensions of successful aging, Vaillant identifies two that are particularly relevant in the case of Moses. The first is what he calls *generativity*,[2] namely taking care of the next generation. He quotes John Kotre who defines it as "to invest one's substance in forms of life and work that will outlive the self."[3] In middle or later life, when we have established a career, a reputation, and a set of relationships, we can either stagnate or decide to give back to others: to community, society, and the next generation. Generativity is often marked by undertaking new projects, often voluntary ones, or by learning new skills. Its marks are openness and care.

The other relevant dimension is what Vaillant calls *keeper of the meaning*. By this he means the wisdom that comes with age, something that is often more valued by traditional societies than modern or postmodern ones. The "elders" mentioned in Tanakh are people valued for their experience. "Ask your father and he will tell you, your elders, and they will explain to you," says the Torah (Deut. 32:7). "Is not wisdom found among the aged? Does not long life bring understanding?" says the book of Job (12:12).

Being a keeper of the meaning means handing on the values of the past to the future. Age brings the reflection and detachment that allows us to stand back and not be swept along by the mood of the moment, or passing fashion, or the madness of the crowd. We need that wisdom, especially in an age as fast-paced as ours where huge success can come

---

1. George Vaillant, *Aging Well* (Boston: Little, Brown, 2003); *Triumphs of Experience* (Cambridge, Massachusetts: Harvard University Press, 2012).
2. The concept of generativity is drawn from the work of Erik Erikson, who saw it – and its opposite, stagnation – as one of one of the eight developmental stages of life.
3. John Kotre, *Outliving the Self: Generativity and the Interpretation of Lives* (Baltimore: Johns Hopkins University Press, 1984), 10.

to people still quite young. Examine the careers of recent iconic figures like Bill Gates, Larry Page, Sergey Brin, and Mark Zuckerberg, and you will discover that at a certain point they turned to older mentors who helped steer them through the white-water rapids of their success. *Aseh lekha rav*, "Acquire for yourself a teacher" (Mishna Avot 1:6, 16) remains essential advice.

What is striking about the book of Deuteronomy, set entirely in the last month of Moses' life, is how it shows the aged but still passionate and driven leader, turning to the twin tasks of generativity and keeper of the meaning.

It would have been easy for him to retire into an inner world of reminiscence, recalling the achievements of an extraordinary life, chosen by God to be the person who led an entire people from slavery to freedom and to the brink of the Promised Land. Alternatively he could have brooded on his failures; above all, the fact that he would never physically enter the land to which he had spent forty years leading the nation. There are people – we have all surely met them – who are haunted by the sense that they have not won the recognition they deserved or achieved the success of which they dreamed when they were young.

Moses did neither of those things. Instead in his last days he turned his attention to the next generation and embarked on a new role. No longer Moses the liberator and lawgiver, he took on the task for which he has become known to tradition: *Moshe Rabbenu*, "Moses our teacher." It was, in some ways, his greatest achievement.

He told the young Israelites who they were, where they had come from, and what their destiny was. He gave them laws, and did so in a new way. No longer was the emphasis on the divine encounter, as it had been in Exodus, or on sacrifices as it was in Leviticus, but rather on the laws in their social context. He spoke about justice, care for the poor, consideration for employees, and love for the stranger. He set out the fundamentals of Jewish faith in a more systematic way than in any other book of Tanakh. He told them of God's love for their ancestors, and urged them to reciprocate that love with all their heart, soul, and might. He renewed the covenant, reminding the people of the blessings they would enjoy if they kept faith with God, and the curses that would befall them if they did not. He taught them the great song in *Haazinu*, and gave the tribes his death-bed blessing.

He showed them the meaning of *generativity*, leaving behind a legacy that would outlive him, and what it is to be a *keeper of meaning*, summoning all his wisdom to reflect on past and future, giving the young the gift of his long experience. By way of personal example, he showed them what it is to grow old while staying young.

At the very end of the book, we read that at the age of 120, Moses' "eye was undimmed and his natural energy was unabated" (Deut. 34:7). I used to think that these were simply two descriptions until I realised that the first was the explanation of the second. Moses' energy was unabated *because* his eye was undimmed, meaning that he never lost the idealism of his youth, his passion for justice, and for the responsibilities of freedom.

It is all too easy to abandon your ideals when you see how hard it is to change even the smallest part of the world, but when you do, you become cynical, disillusioned, disheartened. That is a kind of spiritual death. The people who don't, who never give up, who "do not go gentle into that good night,"[4] who still see a world of possibilities around them and encourage and empower those who come after them, keep their spiritual energy intact.

There are people who do their best work young. Felix Mendelssohn wrote the *Octet* at the age of 16, and the *Overture to a Midsummer Night's Dream* a year later, the greatest pieces of music ever written by one so young. Orson Welles had already achieved greatness in theatre and radio when he made *Citizen Kane*, one of the most transformative films in the history of cinema, at the age of 26.

But there were many others who kept getting better the older they became. Mozart and Beethoven were both child prodigies, yet they wrote their greatest music in the last years of their life. Claude Monet painted his shimmering landscapes of water lilies in his garden in Giverny in his 80s. Verdi wrote *Falstaff* at the age of 85. Benjamin Franklin invented the bifocal lens at age 78. The architect Frank Lloyd Wright completed designs for the Guggenheim Museum at 92. Michelangelo, Titian, Matisse, and Picasso all remained creative into their ninth

---

4. The first line of Dylan Thomas' poem of that title.

decade. Judith Kerr who came to Britain when Hitler came to power in 1933 and wrote the children's classic *The Tiger Who Came to Tea*, recently won her first literary award at the age of 93. David Galenson in his *Old Masters and Young Geniuses* argues that those who are conceptual innovators do their best work young, while experimental innovators, who learn by trial and error, get better with age.[5]

There is something moving about seeing Moses, at almost 120, looking forward as well as back, sharing his wisdom with the young, teaching us that while the body may age, the spirit can stay young *ad me'a ve'esrim*, until 120, if we keep our ideals, give back to the community, and share our wisdom with those who will come after us, inspiring them to continue what we could not complete.

---

5. David Galenson, *Old Masters and Young Geniuses* (Princeton: Princeton University Press, 2007).

Va'ethanan

The Power of Why

In a much-watched TED talk Simon Sinek asked the question: How do great leaders inspire action?[1] What made people like Martin Luther King and Steve Jobs stand out from their contemporaries who may have been no less gifted, no less qualified? His answer: Most people talk about *what*. Some people talk about *how*. Great leaders, though, start with *why*. This is what makes them transformative.[2]

Sinek's lecture was about business and political leadership. The most powerful examples, though, are directly or indirectly religious. Indeed I argued in *The Great Partnership*[3] what makes Abrahamic monotheism different is that it believes there *is* an answer to the question, why. Neither the universe nor human life is meaningless, an accident, a mere happenstance. As Freud, Einstein, and Wittgenstein all said, religious faith is faith in the meaningfulness of life.

---

1. https://www.youtube.com/watch?v=u4ZoJKF_VuA.
2. For a more detailed account, see the book based on the talk: Simon Sinek, *Start with Why: How Great Leaders Inspire Everyone to Take Action* (New York: Portfolio, 2009).
3. Jonathan Sacks, *The Great Partnership: Science, Religion, and the Search for Meaning* (New York: Schocken Books, 2012).

Rarely is this shown in a more powerful light than in *Va'ethanan*. There is much in Judaism about *what*: what is permitted, what forbidden, what is sacred, what is secular. There is much, too, about *how*: how to learn, how to pray, how to grow in our relationship with God and with other people. There is relatively little about *why*.

In *Va'ethanan* Moses says some of the most inspiring words ever uttered about the why of Jewish existence. That is what made him the great transformational leader he was, and it has consequences for us, here, now.

To have a sense of how strange Moses' words were, we must recall several facts. The Israelites were still in the desert. They had not yet entered the land. They had no military advantages over the nations they would have to fight. Ten of the twelve spies had argued, almost forty years before, that the mission was impossible. In a world of empires, nations, and fortified cities, the Israelites must have seemed to the untutored eye defenceless, unproven, one more horde among the many who swept across Asia and Africa in ancient times. Other than their religious practices, few contemporary observers would have seen anything about them to set them apart from the Jebusites and Perizzites, Midianites and Moabites, and the other petty powers that populated that corner of the Middle East.

Yet in this *parasha* Moses communicated an unshakeable certainty that what had happened to them would eventually change and inspire the world. Listen to his language:

> Ask now about the former days, long before your time, from the day God created human beings on the earth; ask from one end of the heavens to the other. Has anything so great as this ever happened, or has anything like it ever been heard of? Has any other people heard the voice of God speaking out of fire, as you have, and lived? Has any god ever tried to take for himself one nation out of another nation by miracles, signs, and wonders, by war, by a mighty hand and an outstretched arm, or by great and awesome deeds, like all the things the Lord your God did for you in Egypt before your eyes? (Deut. 4:32–34)

Moses was convinced that Jewish history was, and would remain, unique. In an age of empires, a small, defenceless group had been liberated from the greatest empire of all by a power not their own, by God Himself. That was Moses' first point: the singularity of Jewish history as a narrative of redemption.

His second was the uniqueness of revelation:

> What other nation is so great as to have their gods near them the way the Lord our God is near us whenever we pray to Him? And what other nation is so great as to have such righteous decrees and laws as this body of laws I am setting before you today? (4:7–8)

Other nations had gods to whom they prayed and offered sacrifices. They too attributed their military successes to their deities. But no other nation saw God as their sovereign, legislator, and law-giver. Elsewhere law represented the decree of the king or, in more recent centuries, the will of the people. In Israel, uniquely, even when there was a king, he had no legislative power. Only in Israel was God seen not just as a power but as the architect of society, the orchestrator of its music of justice and mercy, liberty and dignity.

The question is why. Toward the end of the chapter Moses gives one answer: "Because He loved your ancestors and chose their descendants after them" (Deut. 4:37). God loved Abraham, not least because Abraham loved God. And God loved Abraham's children because they were his children and He had promised the patriarch that He would bless and protect them.

Earlier though Moses had given a different kind of answer, not incompatible with the second, but different:

> See, I have taught you decrees and laws as the Lord my God commanded me…. Observe them carefully, for *this is your wisdom and understanding in the eyes of the nations,* who will hear about all these decrees and say, "Surely this great nation is a wise and understanding people." (4:5–6)

Why did Moses, or God, care whether or not other nations saw Israel's laws as wise and understanding? Judaism was and is a love story between God and a particular people, often tempestuous, sometimes serene, frequently joyous, but close, intimate, even inward-looking. What has the rest of the world to do with it?

But the rest of the world does have something to do with it. Judaism was never meant for Jews alone. In his first words to Abraham, God already said, "I will bless those who bless you, and those who curse you, I will curse; through you all the families of the earth will be blessed" (Gen. 12:3). Jews were to be a source of blessing to the world.

God is the God of all humanity. In Genesis He spoke to Adam, Eve, Cain, Noah, and made a covenant with all humankind before He made one with Abraham. In Egypt, whether in Potiphar's house, or prison, or Pharaoh's palace, Joseph continually talked about God. He wanted the Egyptians to know that nothing he did, he did himself. He was merely an agent of the God of Israel. There is nothing here to suggest that God is indifferent to the nations of the world.

Later in the days of Moses, God said that He would perform signs and wonders so that "the *Egyptians* will know that I am the Lord" (Ex. 7:5). He called Jeremiah to be "a prophet to the nations." He sent Jonah to the Assyrians in Nineveh. He had Amos deliver oracles to the other nations before He sent him an oracle about Israel. In perhaps the most astonishing prophecy in Tanakh, He sent Isaiah the message that a time will come when God will bless Israel's enemies: "The Lord Almighty will bless them, saying, 'Blessed be Egypt My people, Assyria My handiwork, and Israel My inheritance'" (Is. 19:26).

God is concerned with all humanity. Therefore what we do as Jews makes a difference to humanity, not just in a mystical sense, but as exemplars of what it means to love and be loved by God. Other nations would look at Jews and sense that some larger power was at work in their history. As the late Milton Himmelfarb put it:

> Each Jew knows how thoroughly ordinary he is; yet taken together, we seem caught up in things great and inexplicable....

The number of Jews in the world is smaller than a small statistical error in the Chinese census. Yet we remain bigger than our numbers. Big things seem to happen around us and to us.[4]

We were not called on to convert the world. We were called on to inspire the world. As the prophet Zechariah put it, a time will come when "ten people from all languages and nations will take firm hold of one Jew by the hem of his robe and say, 'Let us go with you, because we have heard that God is with you'" (Zech. 8:23). Our vocation is to be God's ambassadors to the world, giving testimony through the way we live that it is possible for a small people to survive and thrive under the most adverse conditions, to construct a society of law-governed liberty for which we all bear collective responsibility, and to "act justly, love mercy, and walk humbly" (Micah 6:8) with our God. *Va'ethanan* is the mission statement of the Jewish people.

And others were and still are inspired by it. The conclusion I have drawn from a lifetime lived in the public square is that *non-Jews respect Jews who respect Judaism.* They find it hard to understand why Jews, in countries where there is genuine religious liberty, abandon their faith or define their identity in purely ethnic terms.

Speaking personally, I believe that the world in its current state of turbulence needs the Jewish message, which is that God calls on us to be *true to our faith and a blessing to others regardless of their faith.* Imagine a world in which everyone believed this. It would be a world transformed.

We are not just another ethnic minority. We are the people who predicated freedom on teaching our children to love, not hate. Ours is the faith that consecrated marriage and the family, and spoke of responsibilities long before it spoke of rights. Ours is the vision that sees alleviation of poverty as a religious task because, as Maimonides said, you cannot think exalted spiritual thoughts if you are starving or sick or homeless and alone.[5] We do these things not because we are conservative or liberal, Republicans or Democrats, but because we believe that is what God wants of us.

---

4. Milton Himmelfarb and Gertrude Himmelfarb, *Jews and Gentiles* (New York: Encounter, 2007), 141.
5. Maimonides, *The Guide for the Perplexed*, III:27.

Much is written these days about the *what* and *how* of Judaism, but all too little about the *why*. Moses, in the last month of his life, taught the why. That is how the greatest of leaders inspired action from his day to ours.

If you want to change the world, start with why.

Ekev

The Spirituality of Listening

I t is one of the most important words in Judaism, and also one of the least understood. Its two most famous occurrences are in the previous *parasha* and this one: "*Hear* O Israel, the Lord our God, the Lord is one" (Deut. 6:4), and "It shall come to pass if you *surely listen* to My commandments which I am commanding you today, to love the Lord your God and to serve Him with all your heart and all your soul" (11:13) – the openings of the first and second paragraphs of the *Shema*. It also appears in the first line of the *parasha*: "It shall come to pass, if you *listen* to these laws" (7:12)

The word, of course, is *shema*. I have argued above[1] that it is fundamentally untranslatable into English since it means so many things: to hear, to listen, to pay attention, to understand, to internalise, to respond, to obey. It is one of the motif-words of the book of Deuteronomy, where it appears no less than ninety-two times – more than in any other book of the Torah. Time and again in the last month of his life Moses told the people, *Shema*: listen, heed, pay attention. Hear what I am saying. Hear

---

1. See *Mishpatim*: "Doing and Hearing."

what God is saying. Listen to what He wants from us. If you would only listen... *Judaism is a religion of listening.* This is one of its most original contributions to civilisation.

The twin foundations on which Western culture was built were ancient Greece and ancient Israel. They could not have been more different. Greece was a profoundly visual culture. Its greatest achievements had to do with the eye, with seeing. It produced some of the greatest art, sculpture, and architecture the world has ever seen. Its most characteristic group events – theatrical performances and the Olympic Games – were spectacles: performances that were watched. Plato thought of knowledge as a kind of depth vision, seeing beneath the surface to the true form of things.

This idea – that knowing is seeing – remains the dominant metaphor in the West even today. We speak of *insight, foresight,* and *hindsight.* We offer an *observation.* We adopt a *perspective.* We *illustrate.* We *illuminate.* We *shed light* on an issue. When we understand something, we say, *"I see."*[2]

Judaism offered a radical alternative. It is faith in a God we cannot see, a God who cannot be represented visually. The very act of making a graven image – a visual symbol – is a form of idolatry. As Moses reminded the people in *Parashat Va'ethanan* when the Israelites had a direct encounter with God at Mount Sinai, "You heard the sound of words, but saw no image; there was only a voice" (Deut. 4:12). God communicates in sounds, not sights. He speaks. He commands. He calls. That is why the supreme religious act is *Shema.* When God speaks, we listen. When He commands, we try to obey.

Rabbi David Cohen (1887–1972), known as the Nazirite, a disciple of Rav Kook and the father of Rabbi Shear-Yashuv Cohen, chief rabbi of Haifa, pointed out that in the Babylonian Talmud all the metaphors of understanding are based not on seeing but on hearing. *Ta shema,* "come and hear." *Ka mashma lan,* "It teaches us this." *Shema mina,* "Infer from this." *Lo shemiya lei,* "He did not agree." A traditional teaching is called

---

2. See George Lakoff and Mark Johnson, *Metaphors We Live By* (Chicago: University of Chicago Press, 1980).

shamaita, "that which was heard." And so on.[3] All of these are variations on the word *shema.*[4]

This may seem like a small difference, but it is in fact a huge one. For the Greeks, the ideal form of knowledge involved detachment. There is the one who sees, the subject, and there is that which is seen, the object, and they belong to two different realms. A person who looks at a painting, or a sculpture, or a play in a theatre, or the Olympic Games, is not himself part of the art, or the drama, or the athletic competition. He or she is a spectator, not a participant.

Speaking and listening are not forms of detachment. They are forms of engagement. They create a relationship. The Hebrew word for knowledge, *daat,* implies involvement, closeness, intimacy. "And Adam *knew* Eve his wife and she conceived and gave birth" (Gen. 4:1). That is knowing in the Hebrew sense, not the Greek. We can enter into a relationship with God, even though He is infinite and we are finite, because we are linked by words. In revelation, God speaks to us. In prayer, we speak to God. If you want to understand any relationship, between husband and wife, or parent and child, or employer and employee, pay close attention to how they speak and listen to one another. Ignore everything else.

The Greeks taught us the forms of knowledge that come from observing and inferring, namely science and philosophy. The first scientists and the first philosophers came from Greece from the sixth to the fourth centuries BCE.

But not everything can be understood by seeing and appearances alone. There is a powerful story about this told in the first book of Samuel. Saul, Israel's first king, *looked* the part. He was tall. "From his shoulders and upward he was higher than any of the people" (I Sam. 9:2, 10:23). He was the *image* of a king. But morally, temperamentally, he was not a leader at all; he was a follower.

---

3. This appears in the opening pages of his work, *Kol Nevua.*
4. To be sure, the Zohar uses a visual term, *ta ḥazi,* "Come and see." There is a broad kinship between Jewish mysticism and Platonic or neo-Platonic thought. For both, knowing is a form of depth-seeing.

God then told Samuel to anoint another king in his place, and told him it would be one of the children of Yishai. Samuel went to Yishai and was struck by the appearance of one of his sons, Eliav. He thought he must be the one God meant. But God said to him, "Do not be impressed by his appearance or his height, for I have rejected him. God does not see as people do. *People look at the outward appearance, but the Lord looks at the heart*" (I Sam. 16:7).

Jews and Judaism taught that we cannot see God, but we can hear Him and He hears us. It is through the word – speaking and listening – that we can have an intimate relationship with God as our parent, our partner, our sovereign, the One who loves us and whom we love. We cannot demonstrate God scientifically. We cannot prove God logically. These are Greek, not Jewish, modes of thought. I believe that from a Jewish perspective, trying to prove the existence of God logically or scientifically is a mistaken enterprise.[5] God is not an object but a subject. The Jewish mode is to relate to God in intimacy and love, as well as awe and reverence.

One fascinating modern example came from a Jew who, for much of his life, was estranged from Judaism, namely Sigmund Freud. He called psychoanalysis the "speaking cure," but it is better described as the "listening cure."[6] It is based on the fact that active listening is in itself therapeutic. It was only after the spread of psychoanalysis, especially in America, that the phrase "I hear you" came into the English language as a way of communicating empathy.[7]

There is something profoundly spiritual about listening. It is the most effective form of conflict resolution I know. Many things can create conflict, but what sustains it is the feeling on the part of at least

---

5. To be sure, many of the great medieval Jewish philosophers did just that. They did so under the influence of neo-Platonic and neo-Aristotelian thought, itself mediated by the great philosophers of Islam. The exception was Judah Halevi in *The Kuzari*.
6. See Adam Philips, *Equals* (London: Faber and Faber, 2002), xii. See also Salman Akhtar, *Listening to Others: Developmental and Clinical Aspects of Empathy and Attunement* (Lanham: Jason Aronson, 2007).
7. Note that there is a difference between empathy and sympathy. Saying "I hear you" is a way of indicating – sincerely or otherwise – that I take note of your feelings, not that I necessarily agree with them or you.

one of the parties that they have not been heard. They have not been listened to. We have not "heard their pain." There has been a failure of empathy. That is why the use of force – or for that matter, boycotts – to resolve conflict is so profoundly self-defeating. It may suppress it for a while, but it will return, often more intense than before. Job, who has suffered unjustly, is unmoved by the arguments of his comforters. It is not that he insists on being right: what he wants is to be heard. Not by accident does justice presuppose the rule of *audi alteram partem*, "Hear the other side."

Listening lies at the very heart of relationship. It means that we are open to the other, that we respect him or her, that their perceptions and feelings matter to us. We give them permission to be honest, even if this means making ourselves vulnerable in so doing. A good parent listens to their child. A good employer listens to his or her workers. A good company listens to its customers or clients. A good leader listens to those he or she leads. Listening does not mean agreeing, but it does mean caring. Listening is the climate in which love and respect grow.

In Judaism we believe that our relationship with God is an ongoing tutorial in our relationships with other people. How can we expect God to listen to us if we fail to listen to our spouse, our children, or those affected by our work? And how can we expect to encounter God if we have not learned to listen. On Mount Horeb, God taught Elijah that He was not in the whirlwind, the earthquake, or the fire, but in the *kol demama daka*, the "still, small voice" (I Kings 19:12) that I define as *a voice you can only hear if you are listening*.

Crowds are moved by great speakers, but lives are changed by great listeners. Whether between us and God, or us and other people, listening is the prelude to love.[8]

---

8. For more on the theme of listening, see above, *Parashat Bereshit*, "The Art of Listening," and *Parashat Bemidbar*, "The Sound of Silence."

Re'eh

The Deep Power of Joy

On October 14, 1663, the famous diarist Samuel Pepys paid a visit to the Spanish and Portuguese Synagogue in Creechurch Lane in the city of London. Jews had been exiled from England in 1290 but in 1656, following an intercession by Rabbi Menasseh ben Israel of Amsterdam, Oliver Cromwell concluded that there was in fact no legal barrier to Jews living there. So for the first time since the thirteenth century Jews were able to worship openly.

The first synagogue, the one Pepys visited, was simply a private house belonging to a successful Portuguese Jewish merchant, Antonio Fernandez Carvajal, that had been extended to house the congregation. Pepys had been in the synagogue once before, at the memorial service for Carvajal who died in 1659. That occasion had been sombre and decorous. What he saw on his second visit was something else altogether, a scene of celebration that left him scandalised. This is what he wrote in his diary:

> ... after dinner my wife and I, by Mr. Rawlinson's conduct, to the Jewish Synagogue: where the men and boys in their vayles (i.e., *tallitot*), and the women behind a lattice out of sight; and some things stand up, which I believe is their Law, in a press (i.e., the *Aron*) to which all coming in do bow; and at the putting on

their vayles do say something, to which others that hear him do cry Amen, and the party do kiss his vayle. Their service all in a singing way, and in Hebrew. And anon their Laws that they take out of the press are carried by several men, four or five several burthens in all, and they do relieve one another; and whether it is that every one desires to have the carrying of it, I cannot tell, thus they carried it round about the room while such a service is singing…. But, Lord! to see the disorder, laughing, sporting, and no attention, but confusion in all their service, more like brutes than people knowing the true God, would make a man forswear ever seeing them more and indeed I never did see so much, or could have imagined there had been any religion in the whole world so absurdly performed as this.

Poor Pepys. No one told him that the day he chose to come to the synagogue was Simḥat Torah, nor had he ever seen in a house of worship anything like the exuberant joy of the day when we dance with the Torah scroll as if the world was a wedding and the book a bride, with the same abandon as King David when he brought the holy ark into Jerusalem.

Joy is not the first word that naturally comes to mind when we think of the severity of Judaism as a moral code or the tear-stained pages of Jewish history. As Jews we have degrees in misery, postgraduate qualifications in guilt, and gold-medal performances in wailing and lamentation. Someone once summed up the Jewish festivals in three sentences: "They tried to kill us. We survived. Let's eat." Yet in truth what shines through so many of the psalms is pure, radiant joy. And joy is one of the keywords of the book of Deuteronomy. The root s-m-ḥ appears once each in Genesis, Exodus, Leviticus, and Numbers, but twelve times in Deuteronomy, seven of them in our *parasha*.

What Moses says again and again is that joy is what we should feel in the Land of Israel, the land given to us by God, the place to which the whole of Jewish life since the days of Abraham and Sarah has been a journey. The vast universe with its myriad galaxies and stars is God's work of art, but within it planet earth, and within that the Land of Israel, and the sacred city of Jerusalem, is where He is closest, where His presence lingers in the air, where the sky is the blue of heaven and the stones are a golden throne. There, said Moses, in "the place the Lord your God will choose…to place His Name there for His dwelling" (Deut. 12:5), you will celebrate the love between a small and otherwise insignificant people and the God who, taking them as His own, lifted them to greatness. It will be there, said Moses, that the entire tangled narrative of Jewish history will become lucid, where a whole people – "you, your sons and daughters, your male and female servants, and the Levites from your towns, who have no hereditary portion with you" – will sing together, worship together, and celebrate the festivals together, knowing that history is not about empire or conquest, nor society about hierarchy and power; that commoner and king, Israelite and priest, are all equal in the sight of God, all voices in His holy choir, all dancers in the circle at whose centre is the radiance of the Divine. This is what the covenant is about: the transformation of the human condition through what Wordsworth called "the deep power of joy."[1]

Happiness (in Greek *eudaemonia*), Aristotle said, is the ultimate purpose of human existence. We desire many things, but usually as a means to something else. Only one thing is always desirable in itself, and never for the sake of something else, namely happiness.[2]

There is such a sentiment in Judaism. The biblical word for happiness, *ashrei*, is the first word of the book of Psalms and a key word of our daily prayers. But far more often, Tanakh speaks about *simḥa*, joy – and they are different things. Happiness is something you can feel alone, but joy, in Tanakh, is something you share with others. For the first year of marriage, rules Deuteronomy (24:5), a husband must "stay at home and bring joy to the wife he has married." Bringing first-fruits to the Temple, "You and the Levite and the stranger living among you shall rejoice in all the good things the Lord your God has given to you and your household" (26:11). In one of the most extraordinary lines in the Torah, Moses says that curses will befall the nation not because they served idols or abandoned God but *"because you did not serve the Lord your God with joy and*

1. William Wordsworth, "Lines Composed a Few Miles above Tintern Abbey, on Revisiting the Banks of the Wye during a Tour, July 13, 1798."
2. Aristotle, *Nicomachean Ethics*, 1097a 30–34.

gladness out of the abundance of all things" (28:47). A failure to rejoice is the first sign of decadence and decay.

There are other differences. Happiness is about a lifetime, but joy lives in the moment. Happiness tends to be a cool emotion, but joy makes you want to dance and sing. It's hard to feel happy in the midst of uncertainty. But you can still feel joy. King David in the Psalms spoke of danger, fear, dejection, sometimes even despair, but his songs usually end in the major key:

> For His anger lasts only a moment,
> but His favour lasts a lifetime;
> weeping may stay for the night,
> but rejoicing comes in the morning…
>
> You turned my wailing into dancing;
> You removed my sackcloth and clothed me with joy,
> that my heart may sing Your praises and not be silent.
> Lord my God, I will praise You forever. (Ps. 30:6–13)

In Judaism joy is the supreme religious emotion. Here we are, in a world filled with beauty. Every breath we breathe is the spirit of God within us. Around us is the love that moves the sun and all the stars. We are here because someone wanted us to be. The soul that celebrates, sings.

And yes, life is full of grief and disappointments, problems and pains, but beneath it all is the wonder that we are here, in a universe filled with beauty, among people each of whom carries within them a trace of the face of God. Robert Louis Stevenson rightly said: "Find out where joy resides and give it a voice far beyond singing. For to miss the joy is to miss all."[3]

In Judaism, faith is not a rival to science, an attempt to explain the universe. It's a sense of wonder, born in a feeling of gratitude. Judaism is about taking life in both hands and making a blessing over it. It is as if God had said to us: I made all this for you. This is My gift. Enjoy it and

---

3. Robert Louis Stevenson, "The Lantern-Bearers," in *The Lantern-Bearers and Other Essays* (New York: Cooper Square Press, 1999).

help others to enjoy it also. Wherever you can, heal some of the pain that people inflict on one another, or the thousand natural shocks that flesh is heir to. Because pain, sadness, fear, anger, envy, resentment are things that cloud your vision and separate you from others and from Me.

Kierkegaard once wrote: "It takes moral courage to grieve. It takes religious courage to rejoice."[4] I believe that with all my heart. So I am moved by the way Jews, who know what it is to walk through the valley of the shadow of death, still see joy as the supreme religious emotion. Every day we begin our morning prayers with a litany of thanks, that we are here, with a world to live in, family and friends to love and be loved by, about to start a day full of possibilities, in which, by acts of loving kindness, we allow God's presence to flow through us into the lives of others. Joy helps heal some of the wounds of our injured, troubled world.

---

4. Søren Kierkegaard, *Journals and Papers*, 2179.

Shofetim

The Greatness of Humility

At a dinner to celebrate the work of a communal leader, the guest speaker paid tribute to the leader's many qualities: his dedication, hard work, and foresight. As he sat down the leader leaned over and said, "You forgot to mention one thing." "What was that?" asked the speaker. The leader replied, "My humility."

Quite so. Great leaders have many qualities, but humility is usually not one of them. With rare exceptions they tend to be ambitious, with a high measure of self-regard. They expect to be obeyed, honoured, respected, even feared. They may wear their superiority effortlessly – Eleanor Roosevelt called this "wearing an invisible crown" – but there is a difference between this and humility.

This makes one provision in our *parasha* unexpected and powerful. The Torah is speaking about a king. Knowing, as Lord Acton put it, that "power tends to corrupt and absolute power corrupts absolutely,"[1] it specifies three temptations to which a king in ancient times was exposed. A king, it says, should not accumulate many horses, or wives,

---

1. Transcript of Letter to Bishop Mandell Creighton, April 5, 1887, published in *Historical Essays and Studies*, edited by J. N. Figgis and R. V. Laurence (London: Macmillan, 1907).

or wealth – the three traps into which, centuries later, King Solomon eventually fell. Then it adds:

> When [the king] is established on his royal throne, he is to write for himself on a scroll a copy of this Torah…. It is to be with him, and he is to read it all the days of his life so that he may learn to be in awe of the Lord his God and follow carefully all the words of this law and these decrees and *not feel superior to his brethren* or turn from the law to the right or to the left. Then he and his descendants will reign a long time in the midst of Israel. (Deut. 17:18–20)

If a king, whom all are bound to honour, is commanded to be humble – "*not feel superior to his brethren*" how much more so the rest of us. Moses, the greatest leader the Jewish people ever had, was "very humble, more so than anyone on the face of the earth" (Num. 12:3). Was it that he was great because he was humble, or humble because he was great? Either way, as R. Yoḥanan said of God Himself, "Wherever you find His greatness there you find His humility."[2]

This is one of the genuine revolutions Judaism brought about in the history of spirituality. The idea that a king in the ancient world should be humble would have seemed farcical. We can still today see, in the ruins and relics of Mesopotamia and Egypt, an almost endless series of vanity projects created by rulers in honour of themselves. Ramses II had four statues of himself and two of Queen Nefertiti placed on the front of the Temple at Abu Simbel. At 33 feet high, they are almost twice the height of Lincoln's statue in Washington.

Aristotle would not have understood the idea that humility is a virtue. For him the *megalopsychos*, the great-souled man, was an aristocrat, conscious of his superiority to the mass of humankind. Humility, along with obedience, servitude, and self-abasement, was for the lower orders, those who had been born not to rule but to be ruled. The idea that a king should be humble was a radically new idea introduced by Judaism and later adopted by Christianity.

---

2. *Pesikta Zutrata, Ekev.*

This is a clear example of how spirituality makes a difference to the way we act, feel, and think. *Believing that there is a God in whose presence we stand means that we are not the centre of our world.* God is. "I am dust and ashes," said Abraham, the father of faith. "Who am I?" said Moses, the greatest of the prophets. This did not render them servile or sycophantic. It was precisely at the moment Abraham called himself dust and ashes that he challenged God on the justice of His proposed punishment of Sodom and the cities of the plain. It was Moses, the humblest of men, who urged God to forgive the people, and if not, "blot me out of the book You have written" (Ex. 32:32). These were among the boldest spirits humanity has ever produced.

There is a fundamental difference between two words in Hebrew: *anava*, "humility," and *shiflut*, "self-abasement." So different are they that Maimonides defined humility as the middle path between *shiflut* and pride.[3] Humility is not low self-regard. That is *shiflut*. Humility means that you are secure enough not to need to be reassured by others. It means that you don't feel you have to prove yourself by showing that you are cleverer, smarter, more gifted or successful than others. You are secure because you live in God's love. He has faith in you even if you do not. You do not need to compare yourself to others. You have your task, they have theirs, and that leads you to co-operate, not compete.

This means that you can see other people and value them for what they are. They are not just a series of mirrors at which you look only to see your own reflection. Secure in yourself you can value others. Confident in your identity you can value the people not like you. Humility is the self turned outward. It is the understanding that "it's not about you."

Already in 1979, the late Christopher Lasch published a book entitled *The Culture of Narcissism*, subtitled, *American life in an age of diminished expectations*. It was a prophetic work. In it he argued that the breakdown of family, community, and faith had left us fundamentally insecure, deprived of the traditional supports of identity and worth. He did not live to see the age of the selfie, the Facebook profile, designer labels worn on the outside, and the many other forms of "advertisements

---

3. Maimonides, *Shemona Perakim* 4; Commentary to Avot, 4:4. In *Hilkhot Teshuva* 9:1, he defines *shiflut* as the opposite of *malkhut*, sovereignty.

for myself," but he would not have been surprised. Narcissism, he argued, is a form of insecurity, needing constant reassurance and regular injections of self-esteem. It is, quite simply, not the best way to live.

I sometimes think that narcissism and the loss of religious faith go hand in hand. When we lose faith in God, what is left at the centre of consciousness is the self. It is no coincidence that the greatest of modern atheists, Nietzsche, was the man who saw humility as a vice, not a virtue. He described it as the revenge of the weak against the strong. Nor is it accidental that one of his last works was entitled, "Why I Am So Clever."[4] Shortly after writing it he descended into the madness that enveloped him for the last eleven years of his life.

You do not have to be religious to understand the importance of humility. In 2014, the *Harvard Business Review* published the results of a survey that showed that "the best leaders are humble leaders."[5] They learn from criticism. They are confident enough to empower others and praise their contributions. They take personal risks for the sake of the greater good. They inspire loyalty and strong team spirit. And what applies to leaders applies to each of us as marriage partners, parents, fellow-workers, members of communities, and friends.

One of the most humble people I ever met was the late Lubavitcher Rebbe, Rabbi Menachem Mendel Schneerson. There was nothing self-abasing about him. He carried himself with quiet dignity. He was self-confident and had an almost regal bearing. But when you were alone with him, he made you feel you were the most important person in the room. It was an extraordinary gift. It was "royalty without a crown." It was, in the words of Spencer W. Kimball, "greatness in plain clothes." It taught me that humility is not thinking you are small. It is thinking that other people have greatness within them.

Ezra Taft Benson said that "pride is concerned with *who* is right; humility is concerned with *what* is right." To serve God in love, said Maimonides, is to do what is truly right because it is truly right and for

---

4. Part of the work published as *Ecce Homo*.
5. Jeanine Prime and Elizabeth Salib, "The Best Leaders Are Humble Leaders," *Harvard Business Review*, May 12, 2014.

no other reason.[6] Love is selfless. Forgiveness is selfless. So is altruism. When we place the self at the centre of our universe, we eventually turn everyone and everything into a means to our ends. That diminishes them, which diminishes us. Humility means living by the light of that which is greater than me. When God is at the centre of our lives, we open ourselves up to the glory of creation and the beauty of other people. The smaller the self, the wider the radius of our world.

---

6. Maimonides, *Hilkhot Teshuva* 10:2.

Ki Tetzeh

The Limits of Love

I n a *parasha* laden with laws, one in particular is full of fascination. Here it is:

> If a man has two wives, one loved, the other unloved [*senua*, literally "hated"], and both the loved and the unloved bear him sons, but the firstborn is the son of the unloved wife, then when he wills his property to his sons, he must not give the rights of the firstborn to the son of the beloved wife in preference to his actual firstborn, the son of the unloved wife. He must recognise [the legal rights of] the firstborn of his unloved wife so as to give him a double share of all he has, for he is the first of his father's strength. The birthright is legally his. (Deut. 21:15–17)

The law makes eminent sense. In biblical Israel the firstborn was entitled to a double share in his father's inheritance.[1] What the law tells us is that this is not at the father's discretion. He cannot choose to transfer

---

1. This is already implicit in the story of Jacob, Reuben, and Joseph (see below). The Sages also inferred it from the episode of the daughters of Tzelophehad; see Numbers 27:7; Bava Batra 118b.

this privilege from one son to another, in particular he cannot do this by favouring the son of the wife he loves most if, in fact, the firstborn came from another wife.

The opening three laws – a captive woman taken in the course of war, the above law about the rights of the firstborn, and the "stubborn and rebellious son" – are all about dysfunctions within the family. The Sages said that they were given in this order to hint that someone who takes a captive woman will suffer from strife at home, and the result will be a delinquent son.[2] In Judaism marriage is seen as the foundation of society. Disorder there leads to disorder elsewhere. So far, so clear.

What is extraordinary about it is that it seems to be in the sharpest possible conflict with a major narrative in the Torah, namely Jacob and his two wives, Leah and Rachel. Indeed the Torah, by its use of language, makes unmistakable verbal linkages between the two passages. One is the pair of opposites, *ahuva/senua*, "loved" and "unloved/hated." This is precisely the way the Torah describes Rachel and Leah.

Recall the context. Fleeing from his home to his uncle Laban, Jacob fell in love at first sight with Rachel and worked seven years for her hand in marriage. On the night of the wedding, however, Laban substituted his elder daughter Leah. When Jacob complained, "Why have you deceived me?" Laban replied, with intentional irony, "It is not done in our place to give the younger before the elder" (Gen. 29:25–26).[3] Jacob then agreed to work another seven years for Rachel. The second wedding took place a mere week after the first. We then read:

> And [Jacob] went in also to Rachel, and he loved also Rachel more than Leah…. God saw that Leah was unloved [*senua*] and He opened her womb, but Rachel remained barren. (29:30–31)

Leah called her firstborn Reuben, but her hurt at being less loved remained, and we read this at the birth of her second son:

---

2. Sanhedrin 107a.
3. A reference to Jacob buying Esau's birthright and taking his blessing.

> She became pregnant again and had a son. "God has heard that I was unloved [*senua*]," she said, "and He also gave me this son." She named the child Simeon. (v. 33)

The word *senua* appears only six times in the Torah, twice in the passage above about Leah, four times in our *parasha* in connection with the law of the rights of the firstborn.

There is an even stronger connection. The unusual phrase "first of [his father's] strength" appears only twice in the Torah, here ("for he is the first of his father's strength") and in relation to Reuben, Leah's firstborn: "Reuben, you are my firstborn, my might and the first of my strength, first in rank and first in power" (Gen. 49:3).

Because of these substantive and linguistic parallels, the attentive reader cannot but hear in the law in our *parasha* a retrospective commentary on Jacob's conduct vis-a-vis his own sons. Yet that conduct seems to have been precisely the opposite of what is legislated here. Jacob *did* transfer the right of the firstborn from Reuben, his actual firstborn, son of the less-loved Leah, to Joseph, the firstborn of his beloved Rachel. This is what he told Joseph:

> Now, the two sons who were born to you in Egypt before I came here shall be considered as mine. Ephraim and Manasseh shall be just like Reuben and Simeon to me. (Gen. 48:5)

Reuben should have received a double portion, but instead this went to Joseph. Jacob recognised each of Joseph's two sons as entitled to a full portion in the inheritance. So Ephraim and Manasseh each became a tribe in its own right. In other words, we seem to have a clear contradiction between Deuteronomy and Genesis.

How are we to resolve this? It may be that, despite the rabbinic principle that the patriarchs observed the whole Torah before it was given, this is only an approximation. Not every law was precisely the same before and after the covenant at Sinai. For instance, Nahmanides notes that the story of Judah and Tamar seems to describe a slightly different form of levirate marriage from the one set out in Deuteronomy.[4]

---

4. See Nahmanides on Genesis 38:8.

In any case, this is not the only apparent contradiction between Genesis and later law. There are others, not least the very fact that Jacob married two sisters, something categorically forbidden in Leviticus 18:18. Nahmanides' solution – an elegant one, flowing from his radical view about the connection between Jewish law and the Land of Israel – is that the patriarchs observed the Torah only while they were living in Israel itself.[5] Jacob married Leah and Rachel outside Israel, in the house of Laban in Haran (situated in today's Turkey).

Abrabanel gives a quite different explanation. The reason Jacob transferred the double portion from Reuben to Joseph was that God told him to do so. The law in Deuteronomy is therefore stated to make clear that the case of Joseph was an exception, not a precedent.

Ovadia Sforno suggests that the Deuteronomy prohibition applies only when the transfer of the firstborn's rights happens because the father favours one wife over another. It does not apply when the firstborn has been guilty of a sin that would warrant forfeiting his legal privilege. That is what Jacob meant when, on his deathbed, he said to Reuben: "Unstable as water, you will no longer be first, for you went up onto your father's bed, onto my couch and defiled it" (Gen. 49:4). This is stated explicitly in the book of Chronicles which says that "Reuben … was the firstborn, but when he defiled his father's marriage bed, his rights as firstborn were given to the sons of Joseph son of Israel" (I Chr. 5:1).

It is not impossible, though, that there is a different kind of explanation altogether. What makes the Torah unique is that it is a book about both *law* (the primary meaning of "Torah") and *history*. Elsewhere these are quite different genres. There is law, an answer to the question, "What may we or may we not do?" And there is history, an answer to the question, "What happened?" There is no obvious relationship between these two at all.

Not so in Judaism. In many cases, especially in *mishpat*, civil law, there is a connection between law and history, between what happened and what we should or should not do.[6] Much of biblical law, for example, emerges

---

5. Nahmanides on Genesis 26:5.
6. This is the subject of a famous essay by Robert Cover, "Nomos and Narrative," *Harvard Law Review* 1983–1984, available at http://digitalcommons.law.yale.edu/cgi/viewcontent.cgi?article=3690&context=fss_papers. Cover's view was that "no set

directly from the Israelites' experience of slavery in Egypt, as if to say: This is what our ancestors suffered in Egypt, therefore do not do likewise. Don't oppress your workers. Don't turn an Israelite into a lifelong slave. Don't leave your servants or employees without a weekly day of rest. And so on.

Not all biblical law is like this, but some is. It represents truth learned through experience, justice as it takes shape through the lessons of history. The Torah takes the past as a guide to the future: often positive but sometimes also negative. Genesis tells us, among other things, that Jacob's favouritism toward Rachel over Leah, and Rachel's firstborn, Joseph, over Leah's firstborn, Reuben, was a cause of lingering strife within the family. It almost led the brothers to kill Joseph, and it did lead to their selling him as a slave. According to Ibn Ezra, the resentment felt by the descendants of Reuben endured for several generations, and was the reason why Dathan and Abiram, both Reubenites, became key figures in the Korah rebellion.[7]

Jacob did what he did as an expression of love. His feeling for Rachel was overwhelming, as it was for Joseph, her elder son. Love is central to Judaism: not just love between husband and wife, parent and child, but also love for God, for neighbour and stranger. *But love is not enough.* There must also be justice and the impartial application of the law. People must feel that law is on the side of fairness. You cannot build a society on love alone. Love unites, but it also divides. It leaves the less-loved feeling abandoned, neglected, disregarded, "hated." It can leave in its wake strife, envy, and a vortex of violence and revenge.

That is what the Torah is telling us when it uses verbal association to link the law in our *parasha* with the story of Jacob and his sons in Genesis. It is teaching us that law is not arbitrary. It is rooted in the experience of history. Law is itself a *tikkun*, a way of putting right what went wrong in the past. We must learn to love; but we must also know the limits of love, and the importance of justice-as-fairness in families as in society.

---

of legal institutions or prescriptions exists apart from the narratives that locate it and give it meaning. For every constitution there is an epic, for each decalogue a scripture."

7. Ibn Ezra on Numbers 16:1.

Ki Tavo

We Are What We
Remember

O ne reason religion has survived in the modern world despite four centuries of secularisation is that it answers the three questions every reflective human being will ask at some time in his or her life: Who am I? Why am I here? How then shall I live?

These cannot be answered by the four great institutions of the modern West: science, technology, the market economy, and the liberal democratic state. Science tells us how, but not why. Technology gives us power, but cannot tell us how to use that power. The market gives us choices, but does not tell us which choices to make. The liberal democratic state as a matter of principle holds back from endorsing any particular way of life. The result is that contemporary culture sets before us an almost infinite range of possibilities, but does not tell us who we are, why we are here, and how we should live.

Yet these are fundamental questions. Moses' first question to God in their first encounter at the burning bush was "Who am I?" The plain sense of the verse is that it was a rhetorical question: Who am I to undertake the extraordinary task of leading an entire people to freedom? But beneath the plain sense was a genuine question of identity. Moses had been brought up by an Egyptian princess, the daughter of Pharaoh. When he rescued Jethro's daughters from the local Midianite shepherds, they went back and told their father, "An Egyptian man delivered us." Moses looked and spoke like an Egyptian.

He then married Zipporah, one of Jethro's daughters, and spent decades as a Midianite shepherd. The chronology is not entirely clear but since he was a relatively young man when he went to Midian and was eighty years old when he started leading the Israelites, he spent most of his adult life with his Midianite father-in-law, tending his sheep. So when he asked God, "Who am I?" (Ex. 3:11), beneath the surface there was a real question. Am I an Egyptian, a Midianite, or a Jew?

By upbringing he was an Egyptian, by experience he was a Midianite. Yet what proved decisive was his ancestry. He was a descendant of Abraham, the child of Amram and Yocheved. When he asked God his second question, "Who are You?" God first told him, "I will be what I will be" (ibid., v. 14). But then He gave him a second answer:

> Say to the Israelites, "The Lord, *the God of your fathers – the God of Abraham, the God of Isaac, and the God of Jacob* – has sent me to you." This is My name forever, the name you shall call Me from generation to generation. (v. 15)

Here too there is a double sense. On the surface God was telling Moses what to tell the Israelites when they asked, "Who sent you to us?" But at a deeper level the Torah is telling us about the nature of identity. The answer to the question, "Who am I?" is not simply a matter of where I was born, where I spent my childhood or my adult life, or of which country I am a citizen. Nor is it answered in terms of what I do for a living, or what my interests and passions are. These things are about *where* I am and *what* I am but not *who* I am.

God's answer – I am the God of your fathers – suggests some fundamental propositions. First, identity runs through genealogy. It is a matter of who my parents were, who their parents were, and so on. This is not always true. There are adopted children. There are children who make a conscious break from their parents. But for most of us, identity lies in uncovering the story of our ancestors, which, in the case of Jews, given the unparalleled dislocations of Jewish life, is almost always a tale of journeys, courage, suffering or escapes from suffering, and sheer endurance.

Second, the genealogy itself tells a story. Immediately after telling Moses to tell the people he had been sent by the God of Abraham, Isaac, and Jacob, God continued:

> Go, assemble the elders of Israel and say to them, "The Lord, the God of your fathers – the God of Abraham, Isaac, and Jacob – appeared to me and said: I have watched over you and have seen what has been done to you in Egypt. *And I have promised to bring you up* out of your misery in Egypt into the land of the Canaanites, Hittites, Amorites, Perizzites, Hivites, and Jebusites – a land flowing with milk and honey." (vv. 16–17)

It was not simply that God was the God of their ancestors. He was also the God who made certain promises: that He would bring them from slavery to freedom, from exile to the Promised Land. The Israelites were part of a narrative extended over time. They were part of an unfinished story, and God was about to write the next chapter.

What is more, when God told Moses that He was the God of the Israelites' ancestors, He added, "This is My eternal name, this is how I am to be recalled [*zikhri*] from generation to generation." God was saying here that He is *beyond* time – "This is My eternal name" – but when it comes to human understanding, He lives *within* time, "from generation to generation." The way He does this is through the handing on of memory: "This is how I am to be recalled." Identity is not just a matter of who my parents were. It is also a matter of *what they remembered and handed on to me*. Personal identity is shaped by individual memory. Group identity is formed by collective memory.[1]

All of this is by way of prelude to a remarkable law in *Parashat Ki Tavo*. It tells us that first-fruits were to be taken to "the place God

---

1. The classic works on group memory and identity are Maurice Halbwachs, *On Collective Memory* (Chicago: University of Chicago Press, 1992), and Jacques le Goff, *History and Memory* (New York: Columbia University Press, 1992).

chooses," i.e., Jerusalem. They were to be handed to the priest, and he who brought the offering was to make the following declaration:

> My father was a wandering Aramean, and he went down into Egypt with a few people and lived there and became a great, powerful, and populous nation. The Egyptians mistreated us and made us suffer, subjecting us to harsh labour. Then we cried out to the Lord, the God of our ancestors, and the Lord heard our voice and saw our suffering, our harsh labour, and our distress. The Lord then brought us out of Egypt with a strong hand and an outstretched arm, with great fearsomeness and with signs and wonders. He brought us to this place and gave us this land flowing with milk and honey. I am now bringing the first-fruits of the soil that You, Lord, have given me. (Deut. 26:5–10)

We know this passage because, at least since Second Temple times, it has been a central part of the Haggada, the story we tell at the Seder table. But note that it was originally to be said on bringing first-fruits, which was not on Pesaḥ. Usually it was done on Shavuot.

What makes this law remarkable is this: We would expect, when celebrating the soil and its produce, to speak of the God of nature. *But this text is not about nature. It is about history.* It is about a distant ancestor, a "wandering Aramean." It is the story of our ancestors. It is a narrative explaining why I am here, and why the people to whom I belong is what it is and where it is. There was nothing remotely like this in the ancient world, and there is nothing quite like it today. As Yosef Hayim Yerushalmi said in his classic book *Zakhor*,[2] *Jews were the first people to see God in history, the first to see an overarching meaning in history, and the first to make memory a religious duty.*

That is why Jewish identity has proven to be the most tenacious the world has ever known: the only identity ever sustained by a minority dispersed throughout the world for two thousand years, one that

---

2. Yosef Hayim Yerushalmi, *Zakhor: Jewish History and Jewish Memory* (Seattle: University of Washington Press, 1982). See also Lionel Kochan, *The Jew and His History* (London: Macmillan, 1977).

eventually led Jews back to the Land and State of Israel, turning Hebrew, the language of the Bible, into a living speech again after a lapse of many centuries in which it was used only for poetry and prayer. We are what we remember, and the first-fruits' declaration was a way of ensuring that Jews would never forget.

In the past few years, a spate of books has appeared in the United States asking whether the American story is still being told, still being taught to children, still framing a story that speaks to all its citizens, reminding successive generations of the battles that had to be fought for there to be, as Abrahm Lincoln expressed it, a "new birth of freedom," and the virtues needed for liberty to be sustained.[3] The sense of crisis in each of these works is palpable, and though the authors come from very different positions in the political spectrum, their thesis is roughly the same: if you forget the story, you will lose your identity. There is such a thing as a national equivalent of Alzheimer's. Who we are depends on what we remember, and in the case of the contemporary West, a failure of collective memory poses a real and present danger to the future of liberty.

Jews have told the story of who we are for longer and more devotedly than any other people on the face of the earth. That is what makes Jewish identity so rich and resonant. In an age in which computer and smartphone memories have grown so fast, from kilobytes to megabytes to gigabytes, while human memories have become so foreshortened, there is an important Jewish message to humanity as a whole. You can't delegate memory to machines. You have to renew it regularly and teach it to the next generation. Winston Churchill said: "The longer you can look back, the further you can see forward."[4] Or to put it slightly differently: Those who tell the story of their past have already begun to build their children's future.

---

3. Among the most important of these are Charles Murray, *Coming Apart* (New York: Crown, 2013); Robert Putnam, *Our Kids* (New York: Simon and Schuster, 2015); Os Guinness, *A Free People's Suicide* (Downer's Grove, Illinois: IVP, 2012); Eric Metaxas, *If You Can Keep It* (New York: Viking, 2016); and Yuval Levin, *The Fractured Republic* (New York: Basic Books, 2016).

4. Chris Wrigley, *Winston Churchill: A Biographical Companion* (Santa Barbara, Calif.: ABC-Clio, LLC, 2002), xxiv.

Nitzavim

Not in Heaven

When I was a student at university in the late 1960s, there was a well-known story about an American Jewish woman in her sixties travelling to north India to see a celebrated guru. Huge crowds were waiting to see the holy man, but she pushed through, saying that she needed to see him urgently. Eventually, she entered the tent and stood in the presence of the master himself. What she said has entered the realm of legend. She said, "Marvin, listen to your mother. Enough already. Come home."

Starting in the '60s, Jews made their way into many religions and cultures with one notable exception: their own. Yet Judaism has historically had its own mystics and meditators, its poets and philosophers, its holy men and women, its visionaries and prophets. It has often seemed as if the longing we have for spiritual enlightenment is in direct proportion to its distance, its foreignness, its unfamiliarity. We prefer the far to the near.

I used to think that this was unique to our strange age, but in fact, Moses already foresaw this possibility that in the future Jews would say that to find inspiration we have to ascend to heaven or cross the sea. It's anywhere but here. And so it was for much of Israel's history during the First and Second Temple periods. First came the era in which the people were tempted by the gods of the people around them: the Canaanite Baal, the Moabite Chemosh, or Marduk and Astarte in Babylon. Later, in Second Temple times, they were attracted to Hellenism. It is a strange phenomenon, best expressed in the memorable line of Groucho Marx: "I refuse to belong to a club that would accept me as a member."[1] Jews have long had a tendency to fall in love with people who don't love them and pursue almost any spiritual path so long as it is not their own.

When great minds leave Judaism, Judaism loses great minds. When those in search of spirituality go elsewhere, Jewish spirituality suffers. And this tends to happen in precisely the paradoxical way that Moses describes several times. It occurs in ages of affluence, not poverty; in eras of freedom, not slavery. When we seem to have little to thank God for, we thank God. When we have much to be grateful for, we forget.

The eras in which Jews worshipped idols or became Hellenised were Temple times when Jews lived in their land, enjoying either sovereignty or autonomy. The age in which, in Europe, they abandoned Judaism was the period of emancipation, from the late eighteenth to the early twentieth century when, for the first time, they enjoyed civil rights.

The surrounding culture in most of these cases was hostile to Jews and Judaism. Yet Jews tended toward adopting the culture that rejected them rather than embracing the one that was theirs by birth and inheritance, where they had the chance of feeling at home. The results were often tragic.

Becoming Baal worshippers did not lead to Israelites being welcomed by the Canaanites. Becoming Hellenised did not endear Jews to either the Greeks or the Romans. Abandoning Judaism in the nineteenth century did not end antisemitism; it inflamed it. Hence the power of Moses' insistence: to find truth, beauty, and spirituality, you don't have to climb to heaven or cross the sea. "The word is very near you; it is in your mouth and in your heart so you may obey it" (Deut. 30:14).

The result was that Jews enriched other cultures more than their own. Part of Mahler's Eighth Symphony is a Catholic mass. Irving Berlin, son of a *ḥazan*, wrote the famous song "I'm Dreaming of a White

---

1. Telegram to the Friars' Club of Beverly Hills to which he belonged, as recounted in *Groucho and Me* (Chicago: Bernard Geis Associates, 1959), 321.

Christmas." Felix Mendelssohn, grandson of one of the first "enlightened" Jews, Moses Mendelssohn, composed church music and rehabilitated Bach's long-neglected St. Matthew Passion. Simone Weil, one of the deepest Christian thinkers of the twentieth century, described by Albert Camus as "the only great spirit of our times," was born to Jewish parents. So was Edith Stein, celebrated by the Catholic Church as a saint and martyr, but murdered in Auschwitz because to the Nazis she was a Jew. And so on.

Was it the failure of Europe to accept the Jewishness of Jews and Judaism? Was it Judaism's failure to confront the challenge? The phenomenon is so complex it defies any simple explanation. But in the process, we lost great art, great intellect, great spirits and minds.

To some extent, the situation has changed both in Israel and the Diaspora. There has been much new Jewish music and a revival of Jewish mysticism. There have been important Jewish writers and thinkers. But we are still spiritually underachieving. The deepest roots of spirituality come from within: from within a culture, a tradition, a sensibility. They come from the syntax and semantics of the native language of the soul: "The word is very near you; it is in your mouth and in your heart so you may obey it."

The beauty of Jewish spirituality is precisely that in Judaism, God is close. You don't need to climb a mountain or enter an ashram to find the Divine Presence. It is there around the table at a Shabbat meal, in the light of the candles, and the simple holiness of the Kiddush wine, and the challot, in the praise of the *Eishet Ḥayil*, and the blessing of children, in the peace of mind that comes when you leave the world to look after itself for a day while you celebrate the good things that come not from working but resting, not from buying but enjoying, the gifts you have had all along but did not have time to appreciate.

In Judaism, God is close. He is there in the poetry of the Psalms. He is there listening in to our debates as we study a page of the Talmud or offer new interpretations of ancient texts. He is there in the joy of the festivals, the tears of Tisha B'Av, the echoes of the shofar of Rosh HaShana, and the contrition of Yom Kippur. He is there in the very air of the Land of Israel and the stones of Jerusalem, where the oldest of the old and the newest of the new mingle together like close friends.

God is near. Judaism needed no cathedrals, no monasteries, no abstruse theologies, no metaphysical ingenuities, beautiful though all these are; because for us God is the God of everyone and everywhere, who has time for each of us, and who meets us where we are, if we are willing to open our soul to Him.

I am a rabbi. For twenty-two years I was a chief rabbi. But in the end, I think it was we, the rabbis, who did not do enough to help people open their doors, their minds, and their feelings to the Presence beyond the universe, who created us in love that our ancestors knew so well and loved so much. We were afraid: of the intellectual challenges of an increasingly secular culture; of the social challenges of being in, yet not entirely of, the world; of the emotional challenge of finding Jews or Judaism or the State of Israel criticised and condemned. So we retreated behind a high wall, thinking that made us safe. High walls never make you safe; they only make you fearful.[2] The only thing that makes you safe is confronting the challenges without fear and inspiring others to do likewise.

What Moses meant in those extraordinary words, "It is not up in heaven … nor is it beyond the sea" (Deut. 30:12–13) was: "*Kinderlech*, your parents trembled when they heard the voice of God at Sinai. They were overwhelmed. They said: If we hear any more we will die. So God found ways in which you could meet Him without being overwhelmed. Yes, He is Creator, Sovereign, supreme power, first cause, mover of the planets and the stars. But He is also parent, partner, lover, friend. He is *Shekhina*, from *shakhen*, the neighbour next door.

"So thank Him every morning for the gift of life. Say the *Shema* twice daily for the gift of love. Join your voice to others in prayer so that His spirit may flow through you, giving you the strength and courage to change the world. When you can't see Him, it is because you are looking in the wrong direction. When He seems absent, He is there behind the door, but you have to open it.

"Don't treat Him like a stranger. He loves you. He believes in you. He wants your success. To find Him you don't have to climb to heaven or cross the sea. His is the voice you hear in the silence of the soul. His is the light you see when you open your eyes to wonder. His is the hand you touch in the pit of despair. His is the breath that gives you life."

---

2. See Rashi on Numbers 13:18.

Vayelekh

To Renew Our Days

T he moment had come. Moses was about to die. He had seen his sister Miriam and brother Aaron pre-decease him. He had prayed to God – not to live forever, not even to live longer, but simply, "Let me go over and see the good land beyond the Jordan" (Deut. 3:25). Let me complete the journey. Let me reach the destination. But God said no: "That is enough," the Lord said. "Do not speak to Me anymore about this matter" (v. 26). God, who had acceded to almost every other prayer Moses prayed, refused him this.[1]

What then did Moses do on these last days of his life? He issued two instructions, the last of the 613 commands, that were to have significant consequences for the future of Judaism and the Jewish people. The first is known as *hak'hel*, the command that the king summon the people to gather during Sukkot following the seventh, *Shemitta*, year:

---

1. There is an important lesson here: It is the prayers we pray for others and others pray for us that are answered; not always those we pray for ourselves That is why when we pray for the healing of the sick or the comfort of the mourners we do so specifically "in the midst of others" who are ill or bereaved. As Judah Halevi pointed out in *The Kuzari*, the interests of individuals may conflict with one another, which is why we pray communally, seeking the collective good.

> At the end of every seven years, in the year for cancelling debts, during the Festival of Tabernacles, when all Israel comes to appear before the Lord your God at the place He will choose, you shall read this law before them in their hearing. Assemble the people – men, women, and children, and the foreigners residing in your towns – so they can listen and learn to fear the Lord your God and follow carefully all the words of this law. Their children, who do not know this law, must hear it and learn to fear the Lord your God as long as you live in the land you are crossing the Jordan to possess. (Deut. 31:10–13)

There is no specific reference to this command in the later books of Tanakh, but there are accounts of very similar gatherings: covenant renewal ceremonies, in which the king or his equivalent assembled the nation, reading from the Torah or reminding the people of their history, and calling on them to reaffirm the terms of their destiny as a people in covenant with God.

That, in fact, is what Moses had been doing for the last month of his life. The book of Deuteronomy as a whole is a restatement of the covenant, almost forty years and one generation after the original covenant at Mount Sinai. There is another example in the last chapter of the book of Joshua (Josh. 24). Joshua had fulfilled his mandate as Moses' successor, bringing the people across the Jordan, leading them in their battles and settling the land.

Another occurred many centuries later in the reign of King Josiah. His grandfather, Manasseh, who reigned for fifty-five years, was one of the worst of Judah's kings, introducing various forms of idolatry, including child sacrifice. Josiah sought to return the nation to its faith, ordering among other things the cleansing and repair of the Temple. It was in the course of this restoration that a copy of the Torah was discovered,[2] sealed in a hiding place, to prevent it being destroyed during the many

---

2. This is Radak and Ralbag's understanding of the event. Abrabanel finds it difficult to believe that there were no other copies of the Torah preserved even during the idolatrous periods of the nation's history, and suggests that what was discovered sealed in the Temple was Moses' own Torah, written by his hand.

decades in which idolatry flourished and the Torah was almost forgotten. The king, deeply affected by this discovery, convened a *hak'hel*-type national assembly:

> Then the king called together all the elders of Judah and Jerusalem. He went up to the Temple of the Lord with the people of Judah, the inhabitants of Jerusalem, the priests and the prophets – all the people from the least to the greatest. He read in their hearing all the words of the Book of the Covenant, which had been found in the Temple of the Lord. The king stood by the pillar and renewed the covenant in the presence of the Lord – to follow the Lord and keep His commands, statutes, and decrees with all his heart and all his soul, thus confirming the words of the Covenant written in this book. Then all the people pledged themselves to the Covenant. (II Kings 23:1–3)

The most famous *hak'hel*-type ceremony was the national gathering convened by Ezra and Nehemiah after the second wave of returnees from Babylon (Neh. 8–10). Standing on a platform by one of the gates to the Temple, Ezra read the Torah to the assembly, having positioned Levites throughout the crowd so that they could explain to the people what was being said. The ceremony that began on Rosh HaShana, culminated after Sukkot when the people collectively "bound themselves with a curse and an oath to follow the Law of God, given through Moses the servant of God, and to obey carefully all the commands, regulations, and decrees of the Lord our Lord" (Neh. 10:29).

The other command – the last Moses gave the people – was contained in the words: "Now write down this song and teach it to the Israelites" (Deut. 31:19), understood by rabbinic tradition to be the command to write, or at least take part in writing, a *sefer Torah*. Why specifically these two commands, at this time?

Something profound was being transacted here. Recall that God had seemed brusque in His dismissal of Moses' request to be allowed to cross the Jordan. "That is enough.... Do not speak to Me anymore about this matter." Is this the Torah and this its reward? Is this how God repaid the greatest of the prophets? Surely not.

In these last two commands God was teaching Moses, and through him Jews throughout the ages, what immortality is – on earth, not just in heaven. We are mortal because we are physical, and no physical organism lives forever. We grow up, we grow old, we grow frail, we die. But we are not only physical. We are also spiritual. In these last two commands, we are taught what it is to be part of a spirit that has not died in four thousand years, and will not die so long as there is a sun, moon, and stars.[3]

God showed Moses, and through him us, how to become part of a civilisation that never grows old. It stays young because it repeatedly renews itself. The last two commands of the Torah are about renewal, first collective, then individual.

Hak'hel, the covenant renewal ceremony every seven years, ensured that the nation would regularly rededicate itself to its mission. I have often argued that there is one place in the world where this covenant renewal ceremony still takes place: the United States of America.

The concept of covenant played a decisive role in European politics in the sixteenth and seventeenth century, especially in Calvin's Geneva and in Scotland, Holland, and England. Its longest-lasting impact, though, was on America, where it was taken by the early Puritan settlers and remains part of its political culture even today. Almost every Presidential Inaugural Address – every four years since 1789 – has been, explicitly or implicitly, a covenant renewal ceremony, a contemporary form of *hak'hel*. In 1987, speaking at the bicentennial celebration of the American Constitution, President Ronald Reagan described the constitution as a kind of "covenant we've made not only with ourselves but with all of mankind…. It's a human covenant; yes, and beyond that, a covenant with the Supreme Being to whom our founding fathers did constantly appeal for assistance." America's duty, he said, is "to constantly renew their covenant with humanity…to complete the work begun 200 years ago, that grand noble work that is America's particular calling – the triumph of human freedom, the triumph of human freedom under God."[4]

---

3. See Jeremiah 31.
4. *Public Papers of the Presidents of the United States, Ronald Reagan, 1987*, 1040–43.

If *hak'hel* is national renewal, the command that we should each take part in the writing of a new *sefer Torah* is personal renewal. It was Moses' way of saying to all future generations: It is not enough for you to say, I received the Torah from my parents (or grandparents or great-grandparents). You have to take it and make it new in every generation.

One of the most striking features of Jewish life is that from Israel to Palo Alto, Jews are among the world's most enthusiastic users of information technology and have contributed disproportionately to its development (Google, Facebook, Waze). But we still write the Torah exactly as it was done thousands of years ago – by hand, with a quill, on a parchment scroll. This is not a paradox; it is a profound truth. People who carry their past with them, can build the future without fear.

Renewal is one of the hardest of human undertakings. Some years ago I sat with the man who was about to become prime minister of Britain. In the course of our conversation he said, "What I most pray for is that when we get there (he meant, 10 Downing Street), I never forget why I wanted to get there." I suspect he had in mind the famous words of Harold Macmillan, British prime minister between 1957 and 1963, who, when asked what he most feared in politics, replied, "Events, dear boy, events."

Things happen. We are blown by passing winds, caught up in problems not of our making, and we drift. When that happens, whether to individuals, institutions, or nations, we grow old. We forget who we are and why. Eventually we are overtaken by people (or organisations, or cultures) that are younger, hungrier, or more driven than us.

The only way to stay young, hungry, and driven is through periodic renewal, reminding ourselves of where we came from, where we are going, and why. To what ideals are we committed? What journey are we called on to continue? Of what story are we a part?

How precisely timed, therefore, and how beautiful, that at the very moment when the greatest of prophets faced his own mortality, God should give him, and us, the secret of immortality – not just in heaven but down here on earth. For when we keep to the terms of the covenant, and making it new again in our lives, we live on in those who come after us, whether through our children or our disciples, or those we have helped or influenced. We "renew our days as of old" (Lam. 5:21). Moses died, but what he taught and what he sought lives on.

Haazinu

The Arc of the Moral Universe

In majestic language, Moses breaks into song, investing his final testament to the Israelites with all the power and passion at his command. He begins dramatically but gently, calling heaven and earth to witness what he is about to say, sounding ironically very much like "The quality of mercy is not strained," Portia's speech in *The Merchant of Venice.*

> Listen, you heavens, and I will speak;
> hear, you earth, the words of my mouth.
> Let my teaching fall like rain
> and my words descend like dew,
> like showers on new grass,
> like abundant rain on tender plants. (Deut. 32:1–2)

But this is a mere prelude to the core message Moses wants to convey. It is the idea known as *tzidduk hadin,* vindicating God's justice. The way Moses puts it is this:

He is the Rock, His works are perfect,
and all His ways are just.
A faithful God who does no wrong,
upright and just is He. (v. 4)

This is a doctrine fundamental to Judaism and its understanding of evil and suffering in the world – a difficult but necessary doctrine. God is just. Why then do bad things happen?

Is He corrupt? No – the defect is in His children,
a crooked and perverse generation. (v. 5)

God requites good with good, evil with evil. When bad things happen to us it is because we have been guilty of doing bad things ourselves. The fault lies not in our stars but in ourselves.

Moving into the prophetic mode, Moses foresees what he has already predicted, even before they have crossed the Jordan and entered the land. Throughout the book of Deuteronomy he has been warning of the danger that in their land, once the hardships of the desert and the struggles of battle have been forgotten, the people will become comfortable and complacent. They will attribute their achievements to themselves, and they will drift from their faith. When this happens they will bring disaster on themselves:

Jeshurun grew fat and kicked –
you became fat, thick, gross –
They abandoned the God who made them
and scorned the Rock their Saviour…
You deserted the Rock, who fathered you;
And you forgot the God who gave you birth. (vv. 15–18)

This, the first use of the word Yeshurun in the Torah – from the root *yashar*, upright – is deliberately ironic. Israel once knew what it was to be upright, but it will be led astray by a combination of affluence, security, and assimilation to the ways of its neighbours. It will betray the terms of the covenant, and when that happens it will find that God is no longer with it. It will discover that history is a ravening wolf. Separated from the source of its strength, it will be overpowered by its enemies. All that the nation once enjoyed will be lost. It is a stark and terrifying message. Yet Moses is here bringing the Torah to a close with a theme that has been there from the beginning. God, creator of the universe, made a world that is fundamentally good: the word that echoes seven times in the first chapter of Genesis. It is humans, granted free will as God's image and likeness, who introduce evil into the world, and then suffer its consequences. Hence Moses' insistence that when trouble and tragedy appear, we should search for the cause within ourselves, and not blame God. God is upright and just. The defect is in us, His children.

This is perhaps the most difficult idea in the whole of Judaism. It is open to the simplest of objections, one that has sounded in almost every generation. If God is just, why do bad things happen to good people? This is the question asked not by skeptics, doubters, but by the very heroes of faith. We hear it in Abraham's plea, "Shall the Judge of all the earth not do justice?" (Gen. 18:25). We hear it in Moses' challenge, "Why have You done evil to this people?" (Ex. 5:22). It sounds again in Jeremiah: "Lord, You are always right when I dispute with You. Yet I must plead my case before You: Why are the wicked so prosperous? Why are evil people so happy?" (Jer. 12:1).

It is an argument that never ceased. It continued through the rabbinic literature. It was heard again in the *kinot*, the laments, prompted by the persecution of Jews in the Middle Ages. It sounds in the literature produced in the wake of the Spanish expulsion, and echoes still when we recall the Holocaust.

The Talmud says that of all the questions Moses asked God, this was the one to which God did not give an answer.[1] The simplest, deepest interpretation is given in Psalm 92, "The song of the Sabbath day." Though "the wicked spring up like grass," they will eventually be destroyed. The righteous, by contrast, "flourish like a palm tree and grow tall like a cedar in Lebanon." Evil wins in the short term but never in the long. The wicked are like grass, the righteous like a tree. Grass grows overnight but it takes years for a tree to reach its full height. In

---

1. Berakhot 7a.

the long run, tyrannies are defeated. Empires decline and fall. Goodness and rightness win the final battle. As Martin Luther King said in the spirit of the Psalm: "The arc of the moral universe is long, but it bends toward justice."

It is a difficult belief, this commitment to seeing justice in history under the sovereignty of God. Yet consider the alternatives. They are three. The first is to say that there is no meaning in history whatsoever. *Homo hominis lupus est,* "Man is wolf to man." As Thucydides said in the name of the Athenians: "The strong do as they want, the weak suffer what they must."[2] History is a Darwinian struggle to survive, and justice is no more than the name given to the will of the stronger party.

The second, about which I write in my book *Not in God's Name,*[3] is dualism, the idea that evil comes not from God but from an independent force. Satan, the Devil, the Antichrist, Lucifer, the Prince of Darkness, and the many other names given to the force that is not God but is opposed to Him and those who worship Him. This idea, which has surfaced in sectarian forms in each of the Abrahamic monotheisms, as well as in modern, secular totalitarianisms, is one of the most dangerous in all of history. It divides humanity into the unshakeably good and the irredeemably evil, giving rise to a long history of bloodshed and barbarism of the kind we see being enacted today in many parts of the world in the name of holy war against the greater and lesser Satan. This is dualism, not monotheism, and the Sages, who called it *shtei rashuyot,* "two powers or domains,"[4] were right to reject it utterly.

The third, debated extensively in the rabbinic literature, is to say that justice ultimately exists in the world to come, in life after death. Yet though this is an essential element of Judaism, it is striking how relatively little Judaism had recourse to it, recognising that the central thrust of Tanakh is on this world, and life before death. For it is here that we must work for justice, fairness, compassion, decency, the alleviation of

---

2. Thucydides, "The Melian Dialogue," in *History of the Peloponnesian War* (Book 5, chapters 84–116).
3. Jonathan Sacks, *Not in God's Name: Confronting Religious Violence* (New York: Schocken Books, 2017).
4. Berakhot 33b.

poverty, and the perfection, as far as lies within our power, of society and our individual lives. Tanakh almost never takes this option. God does not say to Jeremiah or Job that the answer to their question exists in heaven and they will see it as soon as they end their stay on earth. The passion for justice so characteristic of Judaism would dissipate entirely were this the only answer.

Difficult though Jewish faith is, it has had the effect through history of leading us to say: If bad things have happened, let us blame no one but ourselves, and let us labour to make them better. It was this that led Jews, time and again, to emerge from tragedy, shaken, scarred, limping like Jacob after his encounter with the angel, yet resolved to begin again, to rededicate ourselves to our mission and faith, to ascribe our achievements to God, and our defeats to ourselves.

Out of such humility, a momentous strength is born.

EDITOR'S NOTE

Haazinu is the last essay written by Rabbi Sacks, of
blessed memory, in his Spirituality series. We are
greatly saddened that he did not have the opportunity
to complete the essay on *Vezot Haberakha*, but are
comforted by the knowledge that his teachings will live
on for generations.

The Covenant & Conversation Series:

Maggid Books
The best of contemporary Jewish thought from
Koren Publishers Jerusalem Ltd.